KU-526-248

Introduction

How we can be healthy and how we can become healthy – by our own resources: that is what this book is all about, and what we hope to help you achieve. We are trying to make available to you a form of knowledge that will accompany you throughout your life and smooth your path to direct, personal experience of the factors that strengthen or weaken you physically, mentally and emotionally – without the need for any detours via the advice of experts and authorities.

To retain or regain your health, throughout an entire lifetime, with all its ups and downs, is in fact neither difficult nor complicated; nor does it need to be expensive or laborious. For a long time large areas of modern science, in particular orthodox medicine and psychology – closely interwoven with politics, religion, economics, industry and advertising – have effectively conspired to convince us to the contrary and make us believe that only the specialist with his secret knowledge and secret language is able to heal or to point the way to a healthy and meaningful life. They pursue this goal in part consciously, in part unconsciously, and for a variety of motives: in order that their throne remains untouched, their largely superfluous products (goods or ideologies) remain marketable, and above all we, the consumers and recipients of their 'favours', remain more easily amenable, subordinate and dependent.

We are pleased that so many people today wish to strike out in another direction. We want to help along this slow process of rethinking in every possible way. In so doing we shall have recourse to things that have always worked: to the basic materials and cornerstones of a healthy, dynamic and worthwhile life. We want to bring back to life all that is natural, plain and simple, without indiscriminately throwing overboard the genuine blessings which the modern age has brought us. In any case the future is not going to leave us any other choice in the matter – so why not take the first steps willingly and joyfully?

Nothing that awaits you in the following pages is new. It is age-old knowledge, tried and tested over thousands of years and found to be valid, effective and healing – natural laws and rhythms which in the space of a few decades we have needlessly forgotten or learnt to ignore: the influence of lunar rhythms and the art of acting at the right moment; bodily rhythms and biorhythms; healthy, unfanatical nutrition; herbal knowledge; healthy dwelling places; the power of the world of thought; the physical, mental and emotional effect of all these factors, and much more besides. Some of it is not to be found in any textbook; a few items, even, have never been published before. Perhaps for this reason one or two pieces of information will sound incredible or even bizarre at first reading – possibly because this is the first time that you have heard about them, or perhaps because they run counter to your convictions or arouse your prejudices.

And yet every piece of information, every rule, every piece of advice is based on personal experience – not just our own, but that of a large number of people, past and present, who are skilled in the art of healing. Little by little you will be able to share in these experiences yourself, because going about the daily round, trying out the rules in this book, will sharpen your attentiveness to nature and the things that surround us – will open you to hitherto concealed relationships between body, soul and environment. These insights will ultimately lead you beyond rigid laws and bring you nearer to a state which renders you incorruptible by and immune to the countless negative influences around you. Above all, you will be sheltered from the ever-present attempt to keep you in some kind of mental or physical dependence.

Sensing, watching, experiencing is the key to many things in nature which science cannot unveil – at least not with its restricted methods and from the high horse it loves to ride. Thus you should not expect a scientifically based work of reference, or a collection of patent remedies which relieve you of a task that you have to carry out for yourself. We are not trying to start up a new fashion, not advertising a new diet or way of life, or offering the thousandth universal remedy. No one should ever be made to think that he has to live *according to* something. Every human being is unique and individual. What is helpful for one person may well leave another unaffected or may even do him harm. Sometimes a particular method may help, while on another occasion the desired effect fails to materialise. No statistics of cures, no 'infallible remedy' is of any use to you, if something that has 'always worked' doesn't happen to work with you. You have to find your own way – each day anew.

We shall have achieved everything we wanted if we only succeed in awakening your *memory*: if you remember that you possess everything you need – all means, powers and capacities – in order to live a life that is really worthy of the name. Life! Let us not confuse a meaningful life with that chaotic alternation that has been drilled into us – of expectation and disappointment, numbness and pain, anxiety and relief, pleasure and frustration, stress and idleness.

Not for a moment is Man a foreign body on the earth and in the universe. Nature is not engaged in any struggle with humanity, but rather gives it everything it needs, as long as each individual learns to live in friendship with himself and with nature. This friendship can never be one that is prescribed by law. It is your own personal achievement, your own personal decision. The choice is always yours, no matter how hard people try to persuade you to the contrary. All of us – human beings, animals, plants, stars, planets, sun and moon, you and us – we are all in the same boat. And the only purpose of our lives consists in waking each other up and being there for each other – no matter how long humanity still needs in order to realise this. The best medicine for Man is Man.

Fortunately there are many people all over the world today who are well on the way to leaving behind the twisted thinking that has been imposed and foisted on us: the orientation towards material things, towards recognition and career, anxiety and security, the accumulation of power; towards those things that other people and institutions consider to be normal and right; towards the dreary and at times deadly ideology of "I only believe what I can see"; the numbing and crippling conviction that "there's really nothing that the individual can do". Many people today are beginning to live with more wisdom, common sense, measure and purpose; they sense what joy, serenity and inner peace are entailed in a life of inner independence and absolute responsibility for oneself. That deep and genuine satisfaction results from protecting one's fellow human beings and the environment – not as the lifestyle stemming from an enforced ideology or artificial morality, but rather as a crystal-clear insight into the actual nature of Man. They recognise what joy there is in living according to one's own inborn instinct – how effortlessly simple and clear life then becomes, even in the midst of the stormy squalls of fate. Many people know this already: that this authentic human nature exists and that one can turn to it at every moment of one's life – without needing first to have tormented oneself with endless theological, psychological or scientific studies. Everything true and essential is by its very nature simple and accessible to everyone in the world. God and his many friends in the visible and invisible worlds – they do not stand on ceremony.

Our time does not need any changes prescribed from on high, any new laws, any sermons of morality, and least of all any struggle against 'evil'. What our time needs is easy to formulate: *the awakening and arising of the individual.* We are not trying to hand you a sword, but rather a key. Nylon blouses, asbestos nor irradiated food have any chance of success if no one buys these things. Doctors, teachers, lawyers, politicians, businessmen who are no friends of humanity will not stand a chance if no one listens to them any more. Those fashioners of agrarian policy, who determine the legally admissible curvature of cucumbers and impose quite unnatural guidelines on agriculture without ever having planted a tree; those 'public servants' who fritter away our money by changing the length of postcodes; those politicians of every shade, who seek to manipulate people's feelings, thoughts and actions according to their own arbitrary whim and the extent of their fanaticism – their fear of life – they will not stand a chance if no one is taken in by it any more. Thus there will also be no shortage of information in this book, which concerns itself less with hard facts than with many of our instilled habits of thought that open wide the door to negative influences, and are much more potent causes of illness than any virus, bacterium or environmental poison.

It is our wish and our way, therefore, first and foremost to awaken in you the courage and unshakeable will to trust your own inner *instinct*, to live according to your personal feeling and intuition. That is our intention, and it is the birthright and the duty of all human beings. All we can do is open the doors. It is for you to summon up the sense of adventure and the courage to step through them. Never forget: it is *your* body, your soul, your life which are at stake. No one can or should live your life for you. What you feel and what you see: that is what you should live by – even if there isn't another person in the whole world who shares your instinctive perception.

The 'instinct' we are talking about here sometimes makes itself felt as a faint 'inner voice'. In every-day usage it is known under a great variety of names: intuition; heart; perception; feeling; inkling; conscience; feel; 'nose'; sense (often sixth sense). The power of perception which makes use of this inner voice knows what is really and truly beneficial to your growth – both inwardly and outwardly – at any given moment, and recognises the exact causes of problems and illnesses. The voice tells you what has to be done to effect a cure – whether in order to cure yourself the help of someone who is a friend of humanity is needed, or whether you can do it all on your own. It tells you when you should swim with or against the current, tells you what is helpful or harmful to you – often in contradiction to your own thoughts, hopes and fears.

All of us have allowed ourselves to be seduced or have even unconsciously decided – and not just in modern times, either – to turn our backs on this faint whisper of a voice, which tells us about all these things. As little children we were familiar with it, as with our best friend or guardian angel, and for a short period of our lives it almost never let us down. In those days we had no trouble recognising that the Emperor had no clothes.

Why did we allow the voice to become so faint? Because it is impartial. Because it speaks the truth, without regard for rank, name, and the consequences that flow from the naked truth it proclaims. Because it cannot be influenced or manipulated. Because its thinking is neither positive nor negative. Because it presents us with an unerring, brightly polished mirror. Because it sees things the way they are.

Whenever our sense organs let us down, it is this voice that shows the right way. It was the voice that inspired a human being with the thought of investigating the detrimental effects of asbestos. It is the voice that causes a human being instantly, without a moment's hesitation, to jump into the water and rescue drowning children – despite all personal fear, all mature consideration.

Which policy of our times, which national economy, which advertising company, which ideology could survive the dazzling light, the healing force-field of the truth? We have become so accustomed to confusing opinion with knowledge and living with lies, with the somersaults of the intellect, with the incessant roar of thoughts drowning out the truth, that the faint voice within us hardly has a chance to be heard. And in all our vain exertions to twist the truth into its opposite, we fail to see how our bodies are gradually undermined and debilitated – the perfect breeding-ground for all kinds of sickness and disorder.

And so we gradually lost our confidence in this voice, all too often hoodwinked by other, alien voices, by our own strident voices and by the voices of the 'experts'. Left in the dark, with the wool well and truly pulled over our eyes; in the shadows of life.

We are going to help you to put the brakes on and slow right down, so that in the silence you can pause for a moment and hear this voice once more and take its wisdom to heart. Help is often needed to do this, because it is quite unlike any other impulse within us: it isn't a feeling, in the sense of emotion, sentiment or desire; nor is it a thought in the sense of calculating, planning or hoping. Those who are familiar with it know that it sometimes comes and goes in an instant, like a brief chord of music or a sharp electric shock. Then again it can lead us through the pitch-darkness like a torch with inexhaustible batteries. What is more, you cannot learn this instinct as you might learn a craft. Often quite a long period of experimentation is necessary, with all manner of trial and error, before one can distinguish the inner voice from mere castles in the air, wishful thinking, and self-delusion and listen to it properly.

But there is one certainty that we can gladly give you: if you are convinced that you do not possess this infallible instinct, then that is only because you lack the courage to affirm it and trust in it. It is strictly a matter of nerve – and self-love. Access to this courage, to self-love, to instinct, is achieved through an unconditional acceptance of your responsibility for your own life, for every single step, every thought, word and deed, now and henceforward. Then success will inevitably follow. The abating of the storm in your heart and the peace that ensues will sharpen your hearing for the voice of the heart.

Even if instinct shows the way to apparent failure or error, to an uncomfortable or painful situation, it is still the only correct and possible way. For it is only through making mistakes – completely, whole-heartedly and without seeking afterwards for the culprit – that we can really learn from them and grow.

Obedience to this voice can transform a life from top to bottom. A door opens to a freedom which we seldom find these days and of which we are afraid: true freedom, which has nothing to do with 'freedom of choice'. It permits such rapid and certain judgement that one no longer has any choice, because the correct action from moment to moment is plainly visible. The decisions that one then takes, are based on such rock-solid certainty, that another alternative – let alone alternatives – simply doesn't exist. A person with this instinct – even in a wheelchair or behind bars – is free. And only such people will be able to help humanity surmount all the challenges that the future will bring.

The medicine of the future will be a mutual enrichment, a confluence of the most ancient healing methods and the best of modern medical science. An art in which magic and medicaments, loving touch and scalpel strokes, healing mental activity, prayer and meditation, after centuries of unnatural separation, finally melt into a unity which once again sees humanity as a whole. This is the only possible way.

Inner instinct, observation and direct experience showed our fore-fathers the way to natural and lunar rhythms, to a knowledge that deserves our grateful acceptance. We now propose to start acquainting you with a portion of this knowledge.

Johanna Paungger
Thomas Poppe

The Lunar Clock

For millions of years the moon, a bare, spherical chunk of rock, solitary and unwavering, has circled the earth our home – sometimes belying its existence, as when it turns its dark side towards us at new moon, occasionally almost obliterating the light of the stars, when at full moon it illuminates the night sky with the borrowed light of the sun.

The gravitational force as it flies past affects every point on the earth – and hence every human being, every animal, every plant, every atom on our planet. Because this energy has such manifold and profound effects, because the forces indicated by the phases of the moon and the position of the moon in the zodiac are going to accompany us through many chapters of this book, we should like to begin by telling you something about the origin and significance of the 'lunar clock'.

In the Beginning was Awareness

For thousands of years human beings strove to live in harmony with the manifold rhythms and laws of nature, in order to ensure their survival and discover God's purposes, which they inferred from natural events – the course of the sun and the moon, lightning and storm, the cyclic pulse of the seasons. They hearkened to nature and the harmony of the elements and unravelled their mysteries. Direct experience with sharpened senses, an unshakeable belief in a higher power, trial and error, sound common sense and a deep, directly perceived familiarity with the action of natural forces – it was by means of these that they discovered laws and the regular recurrence of particular influences.

The people of the eternal snows, the Inuit, live in the severest environmental conditions imaginable. Their language contains about forty different words for snow and ice, because their awareness learned to distinguish forty different states of frozen water. Only two of these forty types of ice and snow are suited to the building of igloos, their hunting huts. Indubitably the north American Indians of the forests and prairies were able to distinguish many more shades of brown and green than the city dwellers of today. Conversely, city-dwellers unquestionably have fewer difficulties finding their way about a strange town than Inuit and Indians. In all spheres of life experience and necessity sharpen our awareness.

Alongside his perception of the condition of things, Man investigated the dynamic relationship between this condition and the current moment of observation – the time of day, month and year, the position of the sun, moon and stars. He discovered that a great number of natural occurrences – the ebb and flow of the tides, pregnancy, the weather, the behaviour of animals, and many other things – were closely related to the movement of the moon.

It did not escape the attention of our forefathers that the effect and success of countless activities, some of them everyday and some of them less so, were subject to particular rhythms in nature – surgical operations, bloodletting, the application and effectiveness of medicines, felling timber, cooking, eating, cutting hair, washing and many other things. Operations and medications, for example, carried out on certain days proved to be successful, but on other days were useless or even harmful – quite regardless of the dose and quality of the medicines, regardless of the skill of the practitioner.

With the coming of a more settled way of life, Man became aware that such energies, varying from day to day, also affected all plants and individual parts of plants, and that a knowledge of this was of decisive importance in the cultivation, care and harvesting of crops. Thus for example medicinal herbs gathered at certain times are not as effective as when gathered at other times. Arable crops sown on particular days are faster-growing and hardier.

In a sentence: the effects and results of an action do not depend merely on the presence of the necessary skills and methods, but also decisively on the *time* of the action. So much so, that the correct action at the incorrect moment can thwart the success of the intention.

Numerous buildings of the ancient Egyptians, Greeks, Romans, Indians and Babylonians testify to the importance our forefathers placed on the observation of the heavenly bodies and the exact calculation of their movements. Insights into the congruence of, on the one hand, the seasons, weather, position of the stars, and, on the other hand, favourable and unfavourable influences on current intentions – would eventually join together into a usable tool that would also be of value to coming generations.

Appropriate, plausible terms for the observed influences and laws had to be developed; but above all there had to be a graphic system that would be valid always and everywhere and would enable one to look ahead to coming influences. Insofar as the forces recurred in harmony with the seasons and the movements of the stars, it was an obvious step to look around for a sort of calendar that captured these impulses each year anew.

Thus sun, moon and stars were transformed into the hands and face of a celestial clock. The reasoning is quite plausible: if a particular impulse – say one that is favourable for gathering a medicinal herb, the treatment of a particular organ, and the storage of crops – lasts exactly two to three days each month and the moon in this period always passes across the same stars, then the idea naturally occurs deliberately to group these scattered stars together and give this 'constellation' a name that graphically describes the characteristics of the current influence.

In addition to many other natural forces and laws, our forefathers isolated twelve impulses, each with a different nature and colouring, which recur in the course of the solar and the lunar cycles. To the constellations which the sun passes through (in the course of a year) and the moon passes through (in the course of a month) they gave twelve names: Aries, Taurus, Gemini, Cancer, Leo, Virgo, Libra, Scorpio, Sagittarius, Capricorn, Aquarius, Pisces.

On the basis of his awareness of the present moment and his comparative observation of the rhythmic pulses of nature, Man had created a star-clock for himself, by means of which he could calculate what the future held in store in terms of favourable and restraining influences on his intentions. This calendar removed a large part of the terror from the apparently senseless and random workings of natural forces. Many activities essential for survival could now be carried out more methodically and with greater prospect of success – sowing and planting, tending and fertilising, harvesting and storing – and, above all, many of the therapeutic measures taken by the medical practitioners within a community.

Numerous calendars in the past were henceforward designed according to the path of the moon, because the forces announced by the phase and position in the zodiac of the moon were of far greater importance for everyday life than the position of the sun. Even today many festivals are still adjusted to the position of the moon, as they have been for thousands of years: Easter, for instance, ever since the end of the second century has always been celebrated on the first Sunday after the first full moon after the beginning of spring. And even today numerous yearly calendars and farming calendars all over the world contain the signs of the zodiac through which the moon passes.

Forgotten in the Whirlpool of Modern Times

In the course of a few centuries knowledge about the influences indicated by the position of the moon almost fell into oblivion – so much so, that many people today react with astonishment and suspicion when they hear of it. There are many reasons for this, but one of the most profound is the advent a few centuries ago of a radically new method of observing nature which very nearly drove earlier modes of experience into the realm of superstition.

Until then our forefathers' inborn urge for discovery had been guided by a deeply-rooted insight: nothing in nature, they knew, is merely the involuntary pressing forwards and colliding together of blind, senseless forces. Nothing happens by chance. Whole peoples live through their heyday and downfall and then sink back into the darkness of history; and yet everything happens intentionally, purposefully – is full of meaning and significance both for the individual and mankind as a whole, steered by a power far too magnificent to be gauged by an imagination that is only directed towards short-term, material concerns. Even if on occasion the divine will appeared merciless and cruel on the individual level, our forefathers never doubted its existence. The statement, "The Lord gave and the Lord hath taken away" symbolised the unconditional affirmation of this will – affirming that all human beings were the children of a purpose. Untold generations lived and acted in accordance with this knowledge: until a new view of reality was imposed upon Man.

The investigative spirit of mankind – science, particularly western science – arbitrarily decided on a quite specific outlook and method for the study of nature and in the same breath declared invalid all other modes of experience. At the same time it found out how to examine individually a large number of forces that are involved in natural phenomena; it succeeded in taming these forces, replicating certain events and accurately predicting certain results.

Thus, seemingly overnight, there was no longer any place left in the universe for a higher will. Events, so the world was expected to believe, take place within a senseless, pointless void. The universe is nothing more than an enormous, automatically running machine. There was no room there for a god and the free will that he had presented to mankind; for past, present and future are merely 'lines in a screenplay written long ago'. Even chance events did not exist. Where mechanical laws hold exclusive sway, will and intention have no place. Without the protective and guiding influence of a force lying outside the automatic processes of life, the universe would one day either run down like a clock or else explode. And like a machine – thus runs the new 'confession of faith' – the individual human being is a necessary product of his inheritance and of the imprint of his past. He has the right, so to speak, not to be responsible for himself, since machines have no free will.

Scientists saw themselves as creators of a new future for humanity, a new world-order: in equilibrium; reasonable; enlightened; without superstition; without belief. Whatever could not be proven with the cold, heartless tools of science did not exist. On top of that, as if as a 'proof' of its validity, this impoverished science could and still can point to huge successes, not least in the field of medicine. All of us played along with this, cherishing the conviction that the title of Professor of Chemistry lent weight and validity to every word the bearer uttered – no matter how nonsensical and unrealistic it might be. Thus there set in what today is called professional blindness, so aptly lampooned in the university jingle:

> I am the great Professor Jowett,
> what there is to know I know it;
> I am the master of this college:
> what I know not is not knowledge.

And yet with its one-sided world view science has thrown the baby out with the bath-water: it behaves like someone who says to himself: "Yesterday I managed to bang in my first nail. So surely I can also use my hammer to repair this clock…" Modern technology and medicine have promised us ever faster solutions to all the problems of everyday life and let us carry on sleeping until now in the illusory conviction that the promise can be kept – if not today then surely tomorrow. Almost at a stroke the observation and observance of natural rhythms and many other laws seem to have become superfluous. Most of all, people have come to believe that they can dispense with patience, one of the most important capacities in mankind's dealings with nature. Finally knowledge concerning the wholeness of life persisted only in a few fortunate oases which deliberately did not surrender to the general tempo of industrialisation and 'progress' and the worship of the scientific viewpoint. It remained alive wherever closeness to nature, direct perception, intuition and faith made people immune against selfish influence, bias, cold self-interest and false prophets.

Many doctors allowed themselves to be seduced by quick successes and the promotional gifts of the chemical and pharmaceutical industry, into the conviction that from now on they could with impunity disregard the cyclic rhythms and wholeness of life. After all, someone who repairs machines only needs to worry about individual components and spare parts. The rapid removal of pain and symptoms, the repair of a part of the human unity, counted as a therapeutic success, after which one could sit back and do nothing. Someone who considers a gall-bladder to be the sole source of trouble and tries to repair it, can easily lull himself and his patient into the deluded belief that he has fixed something that has nothing to do with the actual owner of the gall-bladder. Helping people to help themselves, prevention and research into causes, patience and readiness for mutual, whole-hearted co-operation in the doctor-patient relationship – all of these have long receded into the background. However, there are grounds for hoping that a change is on the way. We are happy to observe today that many doctors have seen the signs of the times, partly through their own efforts, partly encouraged by vocal patients who have realised that they can no longer be satisfied with a visit to a repair workshop.

Like the doctor-priests, the shamans and medicine men of our forefathers, all skilled in the art of healing, many doctors today are acting once more on the insight that human beings are not machines; that they are more than a system of bones, nerves, muscles and organs that has got going after a fashion, held together by blind evolutionary chance; that body, mind and soul form an inseparable unity with each other and everything else around us – with other human beings, with nature, even with the stars. They are gradually recognising that illness arises whenever a human being – for whatever reason – can no longer maintain the vital, flowing equilibrium between the many elements of life – between tension and relaxation, between healthy egoism and devotion, between the indispensable ups and downs of fate. Many of them even know that the best medicine for mankind is love. The insight of these exponents of the medical craft is now leading back to holistic therapeutic methods, in which prayer and meditation, magic and healing touch take an equal place alongside the use of medicinal herbs, and modern techniques of analysis, surgery and physiotherapy.

However, there are other fields of therapeutic knowledge that still have no recognised place in official medicine: the effect of lunar rhythms, for instance, is demonstrable at all times, but still unsubstantiated by modern scientific methods. The question as to why a heart operation is less likely to succeed when the moon is in Leo must remain unanswered for the time being – sufficient reason, in the minds of many doctors, to ignore such knowledge entirely.

Not only science; all of us turn our back with a light heart on large parts of traditional knowledge – on the one hand because we have elevated short-term comfort to the highest good, at the expense of reason, measure and purpose, at the expense of acting with patience and far-sightedness. In the heated hustle and bustle of our times we swing incessantly in our minds between the joys and pains of the past and the hopes and fears of an imagined future. The present moment, the only place in which life actually happens and inner peace can grow, is lost behind a smoke-screen of habitual patterns of thought.

On the other hand, we ignore what has been valid and correct for thousands of years for the simplest reason imaginable: it is unknown to us. Perhaps you belong – whether as someone interested in your own well-being and in the health of your fellow-humans, or as a professional healer – to those courageous pioneers who wish to reconquer this knowledge, slowly, unhurriedly, little by little. For it is by no means too late to revive these ancient arts. Even if people are forever trying to persuade you that the individual has no influence over his own health and wholeness or the restoration of our environment: every single thought counts – every action, no matter how insignificant. You are much stronger than you believe.

There's a Treasure to be Raised

All the rules and hints presented in this book have their roots exclusively in our own personal experience – including the rules about the lunar cycle. Precise observation of Man and nature made our forefathers into masters of the art of timing. It would never have been possible to receive this knowledge and successfully pass it on time after time, if each successive generation had simply followed the rules without grasping their meaning, without finding confirmation for them in everyday life. A better word for such rules and laws would actually be aids to memory; since true laws are always rooted in truth, in the everyday reality of nature and Man, or else – in the case of moral or religious principles – they point the way to the genuine developmental potential of mankind.

There are undoubtedly many other rhythms and influencing factors in nature, but in the framework of this book we shall restrict

ourselves to our own knowledge and personal experience –
especially in connection with the forces that accompany the five
different states of the moon:

* New moon
* Waxing moon
* Full moon
* Waning moon
* Position of moon in a sign of the zodiac

Admittedly the search for causes still has to make do with
speculation, opinion and conviction, but for a long time now a
convention of language has been established with regard to lunar
influences. Thus for instance one says "the sign Pisces affects the
feet" or "the full moon influences the emotions". Almost everywhere in the book we have retained such expressions for the sake
of simplicity, even though they do not reflect the true facts with
complete accuracy – namely that the moon merely acts rather like
the hand of a clock.

In the course of its roughly 28 day orbit round the earth, the
moon always turns the same face towards it. When the moon passes
directly between the earth and the sun, its face is completely
shrouded in darkness. It cannot be made out then, because throughout the day it is almost next to the sun. On earth the new moon is
in force. In calendars it is generally marked as a black disc. There
prevails a short period of special influences on human beings,
animals and plants: for example, anyone fasting for a day now will
avoid sickness, since the body's capacity for detoxification is at its
highest.

The impulses of the new moon days are not experienced so
strongly and immediately as those of the full moon, because the
reorientation of forces from waning to waxing moon does not take
place so violently as it does at full moon.

Only a few hours after new moon the side of the moon facing the
sun comes into view; a fine sickle appears, and the *waxing moon*,

with its particular influences, gets under way. The journey of about a fortnight to full moon passes through the first and second quarters of the moon. Everything supplied to the body during this period in order to build it up and strengthen it is doubly effective for two weeks. On the other hand, the more the moon waxes, the less favourable are conditions for operations and the healing of wounds.

Eventually the moon has completed half of its journey round the earth. The side facing the sun now stands like a bright round disc in the sky: *full moon*. In calendars the full moon is marked as a white disc. Likewise these few hours exert a clearly discernible force on humans, animals and plants. Moonstruck people walk in their sleep, wounds bleed more profusely than usual, medicinal herbs gathered at this time display greater powers, midwives arrange extra shifts.

Slowly the moon moves onwards; the roughly fourteen day long phase of the *waning moon* begins (3rd and 4th quarter). Again we have to thank our forefathers for the discovery of particular influences during this period: operations are more successful, even someone who eats more than usual will not put on weight so quickly; everything that serves the flushing out and detoxification of the body is now more strongly favoured than during the waxing moon.

During the earth's year-long journey around the sun, the latter – seen from our viewpoint – remains for a month in each of the signs of the zodiac. The moon passes through the same signs during its approximately 28-day orbit around the earth; however, in its case it only spends two to three days in each sign. For us human beings, the current position of the moon in the zodiac exerts specific influences on regions and organs of the body; and these will be discussed in detail in the next part.

In this book we should also like to acquaint you with quite particular rhythms: rules for particular days in the year which are quite independent of the position of the moon. They are among the most puzzling things in heaven and earth. How are we to explain to you why fingernails and toenails stay healthy and strong if they are always cut on Fridays after sunset? We trust that there are readers who will be interested and curious enough simply to try out these astonishing laws. They are just as valid as all the other rules.

The Moment of Contact

There is one question that interests many people. How can it be that the correctly determined moment for an action, for instance an operation, often produces decisively positive effects, even in cases of chronic disorder, whereas only a short time afterwards a negative influence prevails which in the long term condemns the same action to failure? Is it not possible for the positive energy to cancel out the negative? For example if an operation on the face is carried out shortly before new moon it is much more successful than only a few days later during the waxing moon.

Perhaps the answer to this question will sound a little mysterious, but in it is concealed a basic principle of 'the art of good timing': *The moment of touching is the decisive factor.*

Touching implies 'coming into contact, taking hold of, concentrating, contemplating, grasping'. Whenever through my inward and outward will I come into contact with an object or a living being at a particular moment, whether it be with my hands, my tools or my thoughts, then at that moment I transmit force and fine energies. This happens every second of my life. The direction of my action, the ultimate goal I pursue with my hands or thoughts – whether positive or negative – will always become visible somehow in the material world, today, tomorrow or in ten years. The forces that are characterised by a moment in time – the phases of the moon and the position of the moon in the zodiac – sometimes work like a magnifying glass which bundles my intentions together and permits me to achieve a greater effect with them than if they were separate.

If a surgeon 'touches' the patient with a scalpel during an operation, there always flow into the effect and success of the action additional, fine energies – along with his thoughts, his mental attitude, his love for his work and his patient and many other forces, there are also the energies indicated by the position of the moon at the time. If a gardener touches a fruit tree and cuts it back, the beneficial or negative forces of the moon's position also flow into his action. Contact occurs whenever a good masseur thoroughly kneads his client's muscles, whenever a purring cat rubs around your legs and in so doing absorbs negative radiation, whenever you are cooking and think lovingly of the people who are eventually going to eat the meal, whenever a shooting star reminds you of your heart's desire…

The decisive factor in every contact is that sooner or later the *inner* intention of the contact comes to the surface – not the outward, alleged or feigned goal. If I apparently give someone a present, but inwardly I have a transaction in mind with the gratitude of the recipient as the commodity to be exchanged, then eventually the wedge that my self-interest has driven into my relationship with this person will become manifest. Whenever one touches out of love, one always generates love. When one touches out of self-interest, the only thing that happens is a transaction (or maybe not even that).

Countless inexplicable and contradictory experiences in everyday life – in medicine, in the garden and in nature and even in the household – find a plausible explanation in this fact, taken together with the cyclic influences indicated by the position of the moon. Take for example the fact that in hip operations one side is often more successful than the other. The principle of contact may be applied to all the rules that we shall be making available to you.

The Only Tool

You will perhaps have already gathered that the only 'technical aid' required for the knowledge of natural and lunar rhythms is a *lunar calendar* – a calendar that gives the *phases of the moon* and the *position of the moon in the zodiac*. You will find just such a calendar included at the back of the book.

From the thousands of letters from all over the world (up to now our books have been translated into eight languages) we have discovered what is of particular interest to our readers in connection with these calendars and what experience they have had with them over the years. We are now able to pass this experience on to you.

* Our lunar calendar is calculated according to the position of the moon in the zodiac. All the useful experience which we pass on in our books – in the domain of medicine and medicinal herbs and ecologically sound building, in gardening, agriculture and forestry – all of this is based on *this* calendar. As we now know, it is valid everywhere in the world. Because this book will be read everywhere in the world, the times for new and full moon have been left out, since these shift from one time-zone to another. The exact times, which are important for some activities, are contained in many conventional calendars, so they will certainly be found in a calendar obtainable in your region.

* We have frequently received queries because some regional lunar calendars exhibit slight differences from our calendar. You need not worry about this: most of these differences arise from the fact that many lunar calendars have been calculated by astrologers or astronomers, without any regard for lunar rhythms, which are for the most part unknown to them. If you have any doubt about the validity of a calendar, simply experiment with both calendars until you can be certain.

Ultimately, tiny discrepancies between calendars are not especially important, for a very simple reason: the transition between *forces* actually takes place *gradually*, not from one minute to the next, as some calendars want to make you believe. The influences indicated by the position of the moon in the zodiac overlap and merge, particularly when the calendar shows a sign three days in a row. Then the force of the neighbouring sign can still be felt on the first or can already be felt on the third day. God does not work in such a petty way that he compels us to perform a surgery (successfully) only up to 10.36 in the morning, while after that he condemns it to failure. And he has ordered nature in such a way that, for every suitable time that is missed or spoilt by the weather, sufficient alternatives are available in order to achieve results that are nearly as good. When it is a matter of an operation for which the patient is able to specify the date, then he should simply look out for the waning moon and steer well clear of the zodiac sign that governs the particular part of the body in question. Then differences between calendars are of no further consequence.

In any case people who have long used the lunar calendar and watch out for the right moment for their activities often no longer need to consult the calendar, because there are numerous signals in nature that indicate the change from one sign to another, once one has begun to pay attention to them: the penetrating light on air-days (Gemini, Libra, Aquarius), the active circulation during Leo, the differences in the way windows steam up on water-days and air-days, the slight headache when Aries arrives, the digestibility of a fatty meal during Gemini, Libra and Aquarius, and much more. People with intuitive gifts or 'green fingers' are often unconsciously guided by all these signals, which show us the most sensible way to proceed.

Nature does not allow itself to be forced into a rigid system and 'governed' according to a set of handy formulae, even if that is what our laziness cries out for. We consider that to be one of its most beautiful and life-giving qualities. The lunar calendar is a valuable aid, no less, but no more either. It is not intended as a substitute for your personal awareness and experience. On the contrary: it can serve as a key to the enlargement of your awareness. Out of this experience a force can grow that will be of use in all areas of your life.

* Note for readers in the southern hemisphere: All the rules concerning lunar and natural rhythms have the same validity for you – from South America to South Africa to Australia to New Zealand.

Slight exceptions are principally connected with the fact that the seasons are reversed where you are. Our winter is high summer for you, and when in your temperate latitudes the leaves are falling, we are being wafted by spring breezes. This difference is of especial importance in gardening, agriculture and forestry, for instance when deciding the right time for felling timber. This should be done mainly when the sap is at rest – in your temperate or cold regions between 21 June and 6 July, or in tropical regions during the period of greatest heat and aridity. With a little experimentation all the guidelines in the book can effortlessly be transposed to the southern hemisphere with its reversed sequence of seasons.

However, perhaps the most relevant difference for you is the external form of the waxing and waning moon in the sky. In the northern hemisphere the moon waxes from right to left, in the southern hemisphere from left to right. Since probably ninety percent of our readers live in the northern hemisphere, we have depicted the symbols for the waxing and waning moon as they are to be observed in the northern hemisphere – the exact reverse of what you see. To make matters simpler, look at it this way: when we talk about the 'waning' moon we mean the period between full moon and new moon – regardless of the form manifested in the sky or depicted in the calendar. When we talk about the 'waxing' moon we mean the period between new moon and full moon – regardless of its form in the sky or in the calendar.

Ultimately it comes down to your own common sense. Take the

information in this book first and foremost as a stimulus for the journey into the realm of natural and lunar rhythms. Build up your own experience, experiment, try things out. You will soon discover for yourself exactly what difference the 'topsy-turvy' seasons make down under. In the long run it is definitely more profitable to gain your own experience than to have every single step prescribed for you in a book.

I. From Head to Foot in the Rhythm of the Moon

Our bodies are our gardens, to the which
our wills are gardeners; so that if we will
plant nettles or sow lettuce, set hyssop
and weed up thyme, supply it with one gender
of herbs or distract it with many –
either to have it sterile with idleness
or manured with industry –
why, the power and corrigible authority
of this lies in our wills.

William Shakespeare: Othello

Many readers have a tendency to ignore the introduction to a book, so that they can get straight to the heart of the matter without lingering over what is 'superfluous'. If you, too, have skipped the introduction, we should like to ask you nevertheless to take your time and read it right now. We would ask you to let yourself be accompanied throughout the whole book by the feeling that finds expression there. Much of the concrete information and advice which we provide in the pages that follow will then take on a somewhat different complexion.

Motion in Equilibrium

Everything in nature is rhythm, sound, breath, light and vibration. Everything in the universe is in motion, nothing is fixed, permanent, unchanging. From all the suns right down to the smallest cell – everything is born, grows, passes over into maturity and death, only to wake anew to life in another form, another light. This also applies to us human beings.

In this eternal pulse, this passing in and out of being, everything is connected with everything else. No raindrop falls to earth without moistening a comet a light-year away. No thought passes away without trace: somewhere on a distant star it brings a flower into bloom – or right here in your own garden. How much more strongly, then, are we affected by the constant rhythm of the moon's journey around the earth. Right down to the level of individual cells the lunar wind is blowing and bringing all living creatures into vibrant motion. The ability to feel this and become a good sailing ship in this breeze can greatly assist a healthy way of life, a life in harmonious equilibrium.

A 'balanced life' means that one does not continually disregard the cyclic rhythms to which our body is subject or constantly try to swim against the stream. It means patiently hearkening to the rhythms of nature, the seasons and one's own body, learning how to understand their signals, and adapting oneself harmoniously, like a good surf-rider to their continuous ups and downs. A priceless ability, if one wishes successfully to weather the storms that life has in store for all of us.

On the other hand, a balanced life certainly does not mean being absolutely obedient to the wind and the waves and leading one's life by the calendar or the hands of the clock. Rigid regularity and inertia, a sluggish, monotonous, lukewarm ebbing away of time and life, are contrary to nature. Measured doses of disobedience, the occasional vigorous, joyful excess, whole nights spent in convivial company or working hammer and tongs – these are all at least as important for health – and staying healthy – as an ordered daily life. Every organ, every living creature from time to time requires mental *and* physical stimuli, shocks, so to speak, in order to push forward the limits of its developmental potential, in order to blossom into the wholeness for which it was intended.

Our body, the vehicle for our journey through life, is truly a marvellous thing. For decades it apparently forgives everything: faulty nourishment; lack of exercise; stress; prejudice; greed; excess of alcohol and nicotine and long-standing disregard for its natural rhythms. However, this robustness does not work wholly to our advantage. In the chaotic field of tension between past and future our short-term memory allows us quickly to overlook minor indispositions, disorders and important bodily signals. Often they are gone as quickly as they came, or else they hardly penetrate our day-to-day consciousness – a process that is vigorously helped along by medicines that soon deaden or eliminate these minor disorders: a migraine here, a strange ache in the stomach area there. So it is not easy for us to become alert to our body's signals, to search for the true causes and to change our living habits. So much has become cherished, comfortable routine that we do not want to give it up and we prefer to face emotional anaesthesia and serious physical disorders rather than learn to accept unconditionally the lessons of the body and of fate. Our modern education – through ignorance arising from unnatural and nonsensical curricula and the pseudo-enlightenment of science and the media – has withheld so much vital information from us and has stuffed us so full of superfluous knowledge, that today we know more about the inner workings of cars and supermarkets than we do about the function of an inner organ. We learn neither how to interpret bodily signals nor how to take care of the body and avoid illnesses – not to mention learning which rhythms affect it, how to accept physical illnesses as a form of message and lesson, and how to grasp the fateful meaning that sometimes lies hidden behind them. Our attitude to sickness makes us sick.

And all this despite the fact that in the West we have only recently lived through a period of fitness mania. Always fit, always beautiful, always on top form, always ready: this was and still is the order of the day. Instead of giving us a stimulus to get to know our own bodies, this ideal was transformed into a declaration of war on nature. Our bodies cannot always give of their best and be on top form. Nature in its kindness and generosity also gave us troughs in the waves, times to get our breath back, times for regeneration and learning; and we would do well to get to like them. It actually takes courage nowadays to be able to face downward movements with a cool head and calm submission – periods of weakness, physical affliction, failures in professional and private life, growing older, strokes of fate – to be able to accept these things without resisting, or deadening one's feelings or getting upset. We should bear in mind that such courage is always an entirely personal, individual achievement. Borrowed courage, whether through drugs or false words of comfort, is a delusion.

To pay attention to one's body, to give it what it needs, is a fundamental duty that we bring with us into the world. Anyone who does not spend a least thirty minutes a day on the genuine needs of his body will probably get more mileage out of illness than out of health. That is the truth, even if it perhaps sounds harsh.

However, the purpose of this book is to bring home to you how easy and enjoyable it is to submit to the rhythms of nature, out of friendship towards oneself, out of humility towards the beneficial transience of all beings and things. Many people like to preach "Love thy neighbour!" whilst, in an attempt to keep people under control, they hypocritically suppress the end of the precept: "... as thyself". They ignore the law of nature: only someone who is his own best friend can be a friend to other people. And the only person who can call himself friend is someone who sets no conditions, either on himself or on whoever he encounters.

At the start of our discussion of lunar and bodily rhythms, the table on page 32 is an important tool which offers you a survey of the various effects that are indicated by the position of the moon in a particular sign of the zodiac – the influence on parts of the body, food quality, etc. It contains the most usual symbols in order to facilitate looking up and reading off symbols in the various calendars and should be consulted while reading through the book.

Zodiac sign	Symbol	Body zone	Organ system	Element	Food quality	In waning moon	In waxing moon
Aries		head, brain, eyes, nose	sense-organs	fire	protein	April–October	October–April
Taurus		larynx, thyroid, teeth, jaws, tonsils, ears	blood-circulation	earth	salt	May–November	November–May
Gemini		shoulders, arms, hands, (lungs)	glandular system	air	fat	June–December	December–June
Cancer		chest, lungs, stomach, liver, gall-bladder	nervous system	water	carbo-hydrate	July–January	January–July
Leo		heart, back, diaphragm, circulation, artery	sense-organs	fire	protein	August–February	February–August
Virgo		digestive organs, nerves, spleen, pancreas	blood-circulation	earth	salt	September–March	March–September
Libra		hips, kidneys, bladder	glandular system	air	fat	October–April	April–October
Scorpio		sex organs, ureter	nervous system	water	carbo-hydrate	November–May	May–November
Sagittarius		thigh, veins	sense-organs	fire	protein	December–June	June–December
Capricorn		knee, bones, joints, skin	blood-circulation	earth	salt	January–July	July–January
Aquarius		lower leg, veins	glandular system	air	fat	February–August	August–February
Pisces		feet, toes	nervous system	water	carbo-hydrate	March–September	September–March

1. From Full Moon to Full Moon

I n the course of a complete circuit from one full moon to the next the earth's satellite describes a broad curve. The two main impulses are the *waxing* and *waning moon*, while in addition the few hours of the *full* and *new moon* are characterised by special forces, a knowledge of which can be extremely useful.

 *The Waning Moon*

During the period of roughly fourteen days in which the moon travels from full to new, there is a force at work on the body which supports certain intentions and preventive and curative measures, and at the same time acts as a brake and an unfavourable influence on others. The sentence to remember runs as follows:

The waning moon detoxifies and washes out, sweats out and breathes out, dries, consolidates, prompts to action and the expenditure of energy. The closer to new moon, the more effective the force.

All measures for which the time can be freely chosen and which have for their aim the *detoxification* of the body should always be arranged in the two weeks of the waning moon. A detoxification cure undertaken in spring using nettle tea, for instance, has a strong preventive and purifying effect and often lasts the whole year, while the same measure taken when the moon is waxing works much less well or not at all. The withdrawing effect of the waning moon is apparent even in the household: all cleaning, polishing and washing then is much more successful and problem-free than when the moon is waxing.

With its sanctification of the specialist, our age has caused us to lose sight of the whole picture. If for instance someone with a paranasal sinus infection marches off to see an ear, nose and throat specialist, the chances are that the latter will not recognise that the cause is to be found in a dental infection – perhaps a septic molar in the upper jaw – simply because his X-ray photo only goes as far as the lower edge of the nose. So many illnesses and physical as well as mental imbalances and disorders are exclusively symptoms of poisoning or irradiation of the entire body, starting out from a single point or several points in the body or the environment. Many of the inmates of mental hospitals are victims of such poisoning and could be leading normal, meaningful lives, if someone were to do them the favour of giving them a thorough detoxification.

All medical practitioners – from dentists to orthopaedic specialists – should therefore also think of detoxifying measures for each of their patients, at least as an accompaniment to therapies orientated to specific parts of the body. Which car-owner would ever think of pouring new oil on top of old year after year, or removing rust with a car-wash? What use is an aspirin to me if mercury from my teeth-fillings is wandering around in my blood? What use is a tranquilliser if inhaling lead has made me hyperactive? What use is psychotherapy if it is sleeping over a disturbance zone that has triggered off my mental problem?

Try to rely less on others and more on your own instinct and common sense: detoxify yourself – preferably when the moon is on the wane for the best results. In the course of this book you will get to know a lot of ways and means of doing this.

Another important aspect of the waning moon is the fact that during this period operations have a much greater chance of success and the healing phase is shorter. Wounds do not bleed so profusely; disfiguring scars that block the flow of energy in the body are left behind much less often. This subject is so important that we have devoted a whole section to it (see p. 152).

 The New Moon

On the day of the new moon the body's capacity for detoxification is at its highest. Anyone who makes it a rule to arrange for a *fast-day* at the new moon has already done a lot to prevent all kinds of illnesses.

Similarly this day is particularly suitable as the time to make a new beginning in many undertakings, as the starting point for throwing bad habits overboard, such as smoking or excessive consumption of coffee or alcohol. Strong withdrawal symptoms (which incidentally can make themselves felt even when giving up coffee) are generally kept within bounds; mentally, too, people react more calmly to the 'loss' – an important consideration, for even giving up harmful habits of thought can often have dangerous effects.

If you wish to take this information to heart, you should at the same time bear in mind that bad habits are often only 'bad' because people have persuaded us to think of them as such. We aren't try-ing to advocate 'slurping' one's food at mealtimes, but it can serve as a good example of how a sensible, important bodily activity has fallen foul of social rules that are divorced from nature. In public we wouldn't slurp our food either – like some old robber baron – but in the peace and quiet (well, more or less) of our own room we do it nonetheless sometimes, since this 'bad' habit actually has a point to it (see p. 148).

Often, too, bad habits are the outward expression of disoriented forces that only need a new goal in order to become valuable and useful for us, and by that token for our fellow human beings.

If you wish to give up a habit, look it quietly and calmly in the face, study it from all angles. Pay no attention to the opinion of those around you. If you decide to give it up, then don't go on asking for the reason. It's your will, and that's that. Full stop. Then choose a new moon day for the start of the 'new age'. It will support you in your intention.

The Waxing Moon

The waxing moon is the time of regenerating, absorbing and supplying:

The waxing moon, supplies, plans, absorbs, builds up, breathes in, stores energy, gathers strength, prompts to rest and recovery. The closer to full moon, the more effective the force.

During the two weeks of the waxing moon everything that you do to build up and strengthen your body and its organs, to fortify yourself in general, is much more effective than when the moon is on the wane. The body absorbs readily; it also puts on weight more easily with the same amount of food. However, you should note that restorative and strengthening remedies and methods are far more effective if the body has previously been detoxified. Otherwise what can happen is that you 'pour new oil on to old'.

All symptoms of deficiency can be remedied more easily while the moon is waxing than when it is on the wane; in particular minerals and vitamins are much more readily absorbed. Magnesium, calcium and iron preparations are much more effective. Perhaps you or your doctor have already noticed that the results of blood-tests (composition, pressure, etc.) can turn out differently when the moon is waxing. The effective absorption of iron preparations is of especial importance for pregnant women; when the moon is waxing they should pay particular attention to the instructions.

Accumulations of water in the body and legs are much commoner when the moon is waxing; and it is more difficult to flush them out with diuretic medicines. All symptoms of poisoning, from wasp stings to poison mushrooms, have a stronger effect at this time. (In contrast, when the moon is waning a simple blood-purifying infusion is often enough to put paid to a fairly mild poisoning. Even a drop of your own saliva can often be enough to make you forget a wasp sting.) However, when the moon is waxing the body is much better at absorbing all kinds of healing ointments.

The nearer to full moon, the less favourable are the chances of operations leading to a successful outcome and healing process, and the formation of scar tissue is more pronounced.

Full Moon

It is also advantageous to fast for a day at full moon, precisely *because* the body absorbs all kinds of substances so well – including the numerous artificial additives that turn up in our food. Water accumulates quicker in tissues on this day, and connective tissue becomes weak. The healing process after operations is at its least favourable; wounds bleed more profusely than at other times.

Experience with the results of inoculations has shown that one should not fix the date of an inoculation during the three days before the full moon and especially not on the actual day of a full moon. It is also important to treat inoculated children for several days as if they were recovering from an illness: no major sporting or other exertion, no running barefoot over cold ground, and so on.

The Phases of the Moon in Everyday Life

These, then, in broad outlines are the fundamental influences of the phases of the moon. You thus have a basic stock of information which will prove to be immensely profitable for your future physical and mental development. Armed merely with the knowledge of the effect of the phases of the moon, modern medicine could take a great step forward.

It is enough, however, if *you* take this step: if you gradually become aware in yourself of the different effect of the two major phases of the moon, you will be able to build the rhythms harmoniously into your everyday life. It's so simple: detoxify when the moon is waning, fortify when it's waxing. Still, you mustn't simply take on trust what is written in this book: observe yourself, watch, find out for yourself – you can notice these influences and recognise them yourself (have you ever noticed that when you take a hot bath while the moon is on the wane you sweat more than when it's waxing?). To be sure, it is difficult in modern times to adapt to this sort of rhythm. Almost all sequences of events, rituals and customs in private and professional life no longer make any allowances for the inherent impulses of nature; all too often we give in to the pressure and become convinced that we are compelled to forget and ignore natural signals, natural instinct and common sense. Yet such compulsion is often merely imaginary.

There is at least one thing you can do for a start: all strenuous daily work and hobbies (for nowadays the latter often degenerate into hard work) which are not subject to a fixed timetable, should be postponed a little until the moon is in its waning phase. Not all at once: slowly, little by little, closely observing the effects of this action, for nothing is more convincing than your own personal perception. When you feel how pleasant it is no longer to restrain your strength so much when the moon is waning, and when it is waxing to slow down more, to gather your strength, to prepare and plan – then you will begin to wonder how you were able manage for so long without using this knowledge and why you had never noticed it before.

Our body reacts if we *continually* force it to ignore its natural rhythms and needs. At first perhaps it is not perceptible, when we are still young and can shake off negative effects like water off a duck's back, or simply take an aspirin. But gradually these little impulses add up until they lead to a serious disorder. For that reason we would constantly like to remind you that this book is not a cure-all, full of instant remedies. The effects of ignoring natural rhythms are slow to make themselves felt, and likewise living in tune with these rhythms will be slow to show positive effects. If one sits back quietly once a day and briefly reflects which activities in one's daily life can be harmonised with the lunar rhythms, then one is bound to find solutions. We are not talking in terms of a feat that has to be achieved, but rather the result of an observation that opens up the way to correct action, by itself, without any effort.

2. A Journey through the Body

The two to three day sojourn of the moon in each of the twelve signs of the zodiac is accompanied by different forces which make themselves felt everywhere in the living world. Their influence on plants, animals, and human beings is clearly perceptible, in particular the effects upon body and health. Many people even are able to sense the transitional phase between two signs, for instance as a slight pressure in the head when the moon passes into the sign of Aries, which influences the head, or as an ache in the big toe when the moon is in Pisces.

In former times medical practitioners conscientiously followed the knowledge of the synchronicity of the position of the moon and the course of an illness – a fact which, surprisingly, is completely ignored in every work of medical history. Among them Hippocrates, the mentor of all doctors, knew all about the lunar forces and gave his students unambiguous instruction on the point: "Anyone who practises medicine without taking into account the movement of the stars is a fool." And again: "Do not operate on parts of the body that are governed by the sign through which the moon is passing."

In the table on page 32 you will find that each sign of the zodiac has ascribed to it particular bodily organs and regions of the body. Generally one talks of every sign 'ruling' certain bodily regions. This dominion over specific parts of the body goes so far that an embryo in the womb grows in phases that follow the position of the moon: the head in Aries, the neck in Taurus, arms and hands in Gemini and so on, for about ten full lunar orbits through the zodiac.

Concerning the position of the moon in the zodiac our medical forefathers acted according to the following principles:

• **Everything that is done for the well-being of those parts of the body and organs ruled by the sign through which the moon is currently passing is doubly useful and beneficial – with the exception of surgical operations involving those regions.**
Example: a reflex-zone massage of the feet with the moon in Pisces.

• **Everything that puts a special burden or strain on those parts of the body and organs ruled by the sign through which the moon is currently moving is doubly unfavourable or even harmful.**
Example: a chill in the neck region with the moon in Taurus.
Surgical operations in these areas should be avoided during these days if at all possible. Emergency operations are subject to a higher law.

• **If the moon is waxing as it passes through the sign, then all measures taken to supply nutrient materials and strengthen the region of the body ruled by the sign are more effective than when the moon is on the wane.**
If it is waning, then all measures taken to flush out and detoxify the region in question are more successful than when the moon is waxing.
The actual form of therapy used – medicine, massage, gymnastics, water therapy, etc. – does not matter so much as the ultimate intention that is being pursued by these means.

The following observation is particularly interesting: if the knowledge concerning the bodily regions ruled by the signs of the zodiac, together with the data in the table shown on page 32, is combined with the yearly course of the moon through the zodiac and the laws just enunciated, it follows logically that measures taken to heal particular organs and regions of the body will have differing effects in each of the two halves of the year.

For example: measures taken to detoxify a liver that is under strain (the liver is ruled by the sign Cancer) will produce better results in the months from July to January (when the moon in Cancer is always waning) than in the other half of the year.

Thus each sign of the zodiac has available to it forces that promote the flushing out of poisons for one half of the year and the supply of nutrient materials for the other half. This relationship was derived by keeping records of moments at which an application was especially helpful or simply had a good effect. Likewise notes were kept whenever an otherwise good method, administered in a favourable phase of the moon or during the appropriate sign of the zodiac, failed to achieve the usual effect. After years of observation the conclusion was reached that in autumn, for instance, certain applications lead more quickly to the desired result than in spring, and vice versa. When one has grasped this rhythm, the principle can be effortlessly transferred to other organs and parts of the body.

The Timetable for the Journey

The principle, starting point and effect of the forces indicated by the position of the moon in the zodiac are not all that difficult to describe; but we would like to give you a tool that is as comprehensive as possible, so that you may extract the greatest possible benefit from the lunar calendar. In addition to the discussion of the influences of the individual signs of the zodiac, you will discover the natural way to approach – and deal with –, a great many physical disorders. First of all we should like to present to you the timetable for the journey, the inner structure of the individual sections dealing with the signs of the zodiac.

Mental Invitations

A bodily illness or disorder is in many cases the echo, the consequence, the external symptom of a mental attitude, a constantly recurring sequence of thoughts; for instance certain conflicting desires, expectations or fixed ideas. Illness, then, is the visible smoke rising up as a result of the invisible fire in the mental world, the unwelcome weed sprouting up in the breeding ground of a negative lifestyle.

"It's a real pain in the neck", "it turned my stomach", "it makes my blood boil" are expressions that everyone knows. They are only a few instances among the millions which prove that we are all thoroughly acquainted with the connection between the inner attitude to life, between the mental world on the one hand and illness on the other – quite regardless of how much longer it will be before official medicine allows itself to be influenced by this inner certainty that we all have.

For example, stomach ulcers are considered, along with a lot of other illnesses (asthma, rheumatism, etc.) to be 'genetically conditioned'. That is almost never the case, at least not in the sense that the tendency to the illness is anchored in the genes. Science has only turned its attention towards the contents of our cell nuclei because it needs money for research and is practised by people who are seeking to gain control over aspects of life that we will never bring under our control, since God is the boss. Such people inevitably ignore the fact that in the case of 95 percent of all supposedly genetically conditioned illnesses it is not a physical defect that has been transmitted but a psychological *tendency*. Many patients gratefully endorse the scientists' judgement because it means they do not have to look the true causes in the face. The truth is this: in the main it is sickness-inducing attitudes to life, prejudices and ways of thinking that are passed on to children, not disease-causing genes.

If our inner certainty does not become lost in the veils of self-delusion, it emerges into consciousness and leads to a clear insight:

bodily disorders and illnesses are almost always our own doing. We ourselves bear the responsibility for the condition of our own bodies, and no one else.

The gradual realisation of this connection, the recognition of the actual cause of our problems, almost inevitably arouses feelings of anxiety and guilt, and often causes people to shrink away from this insight or even to resist it violently.

In everything that we make available to you in this book our starting point is that you honestly desire to stay healthy or become healthy once more. That is why, if we are to remain true to our intentions, we have to remind you of the real interrelations between body, sickness and health, mind and soul.

One example, chosen from many: you have fallen in love with someone who as yet is unaware of their good fortune. This has been going on for weeks. Perhaps there has not yet been an opportunity to tell them; perhaps you were too shy, or for whatever reason you were unable to declare your love. One day you come home tired and weary, your temples throbbing, and you think, "Two tablets, a shower and then straight to bed. Wild horses wouldn't drag me out tonight." The phone rings. It's the object of your secret adoration, inviting you out to go dancing.

What happens now in a split second to your tiredness, your headache?

By means of this example we are trying to start making a inter-dependence clear to you, and with time to bring home to you that there is no getting round a clear insight into this connection, if you wish to remain healthy or become healthy by your own efforts.

The bad conscience and feelings of guilt that often set in, when you go through this long process of recognition are quite un-necessary burdens. You need have absolutely no qualms about throwing them overboard. Of course, at first sight the realisation that we ourselves have dug the pit into which we have fallen seems hardly to be cause for celebration: someone who has lived for decades inside a cage and then discovers that all that time he has had the key in his pocket, may well be too proud to open the door. And yet a second glance should have you cheering with joy. Only a life outside the self-made cage truly deserves the name of *life*.

Feelings of guilt are the result of an upbringing in hypocrisy, supported by artificial moral concepts of good and evil, which make us more amenable to control and manipulation. And the result of being brought up in complacent passivity: illnesses 'out of the blue', caused by bacteria, viruses and unlucky accidents are more comfortable for our habitual ways of thinking. We can fight against them because they are intruders, aliens, coming from outside. On the other hand, anyone who has the courage to admit his own contribution to the illness stops fighting – because he knows that he is fighting *against himself*.

Have the courage to look into the mirror, and don't fool yourself. Of course, it is still up to you whether you conceal your innermost perceptions and insights from *others* (no one is expecting you to announce proudly to your boss: "Just imagine: I gave myself a stomach ulcer!"). But the central point is this: fooling *yourself* is the surest way to turn getting healthy by your own efforts into an unattainable goal. If illness offers you a welcome opportunity to give up responsibility for yourself, if it brings you more profit than health does, because you are afraid of the truth, then you had better not read any further. It would really just be a waste of time. In that case give the book to someone who loves himself.

In order to make these connections clear we shall also, in the course of discussing particular physical disorders, make apparent *which* thoughts and attitudes can make us ill – the more or less concealed *mental invitation* that we issue to the illness. Bringing these thoughts into consciousness and identifying the connection between them and physical disorders can in many cases set the healing process in motion.

Preventive, Fortifying and Supportive Measures

As has already been mentioned, detoxifying and fortifying measures taken in the region of the body ruled by the sign through which the moon is currently passing are doubly effective. Which regular, precautionary applications in our experience promise the best results in the given case? There will be no shortage of such tips.

We shall also be talking about the 'quality of the day': have you ever noticed that with the same conditions of outside temperature, pressure and humidity a stay in the open may be experienced differently at different times? Sometimes we reach without thinking for our sunglasses even though the sky is cloudy. Then again, sometimes we like to sit on a stone or on the grass, while on another occasion we daren't sit on the ground because it somehow feels unpleasant.

The solution to this puzzle could lie in the day-qualities – particular characteristics of a day which are connected with the sign of the zodiac that is currently in force. A knowledge of these can be of considerable use in precautionary health care.

We talk of *warmth-days* when the moon is in the signs Aries, Leo and Sagittarius.

These are often good days for an outing, and they feel the right temperature even if the sky is cloudy. On days like this you shouldn't be surprised if you feel thirstier than usual. Warmth-days have a drying effect, particularly the two or three Leo days, the driest sign in the zodiac. In Leo there is often the danger of strong storms suddenly brewing up with harmful consequences, especially after long heat waves (hailstorms!).

Light-days or *air-days* prevail when the moon is in Gemini, Libra or Aquarius. At this time the plant world can take in more light than usual, and the effect on us of these days is mostly pleasant, airy and benign. However, a person with sensitive eyes will sometimes find them uncomfortable: even when the sky is cloudy people sometimes feel the need to wear sunglasses, as the abundance of light is felt to be penetrating.

Cold-days or *earth-days* are Taurus, Virgo and Capricorn. When going on excursions at such times one should always take slightly warmer clothes and blankets, even if the thermometer is register- ing quite high temperatures. Particularly when the sun disappears behind the clouds, the earth feels cold to the touch, and the danger of chills and inflammation of the bladder is greater.

Water-days – Cancer, Scorpio and Pisces – never allow the ground to dry out completely, and the tendency to precipitation is greater. If you are planning to go somewhere on a picnic or to lie down on the ground after bathing, then don't leave the house without a blanket, and don't forget waterproof clothing or an umbrella. Incidentally sudden changes in the weather are particularly likely at new moon and full moon and during Gemini and Sagittarius.

Help with Healing

We shall be introducing you to a number of methods involving lunar rhythms that you can use, on your own or together with a doctor you trust, in order to deprive certain illnesses and disorders of the factors that feed them. If herbal applications are mentioned you will find more detailed instructions in the next part of the book concerning favourable times for gathering and processing them.

There will also be no shortage of pointers concerning *colour therapy*. Anyone who is keenly aware of himself and his surround- ings knows what a tremendous effect colours, patterns and colour harmony have on our psychological mood and hence directly on our physical well-being. But the fact that light and colour can be used as effective therapeutic remedies (for instance in colour acupuncture) is still relatively unknown. And so after our journey around the body we shall speak in a little more detail on page 136 about the effect of colours (in clothing, foodstuffs, etc.). We are talking here about *pure*, powerful colours, not blends or pastel shades. In our discussion of signs of the zodiac we shall state which colour is related to a particular sign. For example: Scorpio (sex organs, ureter) – red. You can use this colour information in order to imagine the bodily region in question wrapped in the colour belonging to it or else to wear a piece of clothing of this colour.

When you find colours recommended as the accompanying 'medicine' for particular illnesses, then these refer to the colour of the clothes or the individual garment that you can wear in this case, preferably over the region in question. It does not matter whether you wear the corresponding colour directly next to the body, for instance as a vest, or whether you wear it over garments of other colours. The effect directly on the skin is somewhat stronger, but the rays of colour picked up by the eyes have an equally favourable effect on the particular disorder.

Incidentally, with illnesses of every sort white is always a sensible colour for bed linen and pyjamas, since the body can then freely absorb the healing vibrations from the surroundings. Black on the other hand would be sheer poison, because it screens these vibrations off.

Four more important preliminary remarks before the journey begins:

* Firstly: perhaps while reading the following chapter you will fail to find precisely the illness or physical disorder with which you – or a person near to you – are currently wrestling. It was not our intention to compile a medical lexicon, and even then one often consults such books without obtaining exhaustive information. However, if you transfer to your particular case the numerous fundamental rules for maintaining and regaining health by your own efforts which have been covered so far and are yet to be covered, then there will still be enough material for you to do whatever has to be done: deprive the problem of the factors feeding it, detoxify the body and strengthen the immune system. In most cases that is already enough to smooth a path to relief and cure.

* Secondly: almost all natural and gently effective cures result at first in a so-called *initial deterioration*: the disorder, the pains

become worse after the application of certain naturally working remedies, massages or other measures – in particular following such things as homoeopathic applications or reflex-zone massages. This fact is often very inadequately explained even by competent doctors and practitioners. As a result many patients who are unprepared for this react with anxiety or distrust towards the healer and his methods, or they even look for another doctor who "has a better idea what will do me good". Don't lose heart: this apparent worsening is always a sign that the body is reacting, the therapy is working and there is a good prospect of long-term success.

* Thirdly: the transition between two signs always takes place gently. When for instance the Aries influence is coming to an end, the force of the next sign, Taurus, is already making itself felt; and in the first hours of the Taurus force, the Aries energy lingers on for a while. To be sure, the change of forces can be established mathematically to the minute, which is what many moon calendars do; but for you it is much more important to know that the previous sign goes on working for some time into the next one, and that sometimes the forces mingle – an important piece of information, especially when it is a matter of choosing the time for an operation (see page 152). Perhaps this is the reason why many incorrectly calculated calendars nonetheless give good results for their users: confidence in them and the overlapping of the forces lead to success.

* And finally: please never forget while you're reading that you are a free and independent individual. We are not prescribing or giving instructions; we do not presume to know what is helpful for you and what is harmful. Simply take all the information in this book as material that can serve as a basis for gathering your own experiences. And find a doctor for yourself who is a friend of humanity. There is bound to be such a person very close at hand. He would never dismiss what is written on the pages that follow with a supercilious smile. Together with you he would look for the best way to help you approach a difficult situation, a painful disorder or illness – with or without the help of the knowledge to be found in this book. The decision ultimately rests with you, not us.

To sum up in a sentence: regarding risks and side-effects of this book you should consult your own common sense.

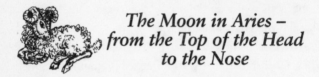

The Moon in Aries – from the Top of the Head to the Nose

In the human body the forces of the Aries days influence the area of the head down to below the nose. Many people experience the transition from Pisces to Aries with a similar strength to that of the change of forces at full moon. The forces take over from the somewhat watery sign of Pisces (with its effect on the region of the feet) and change to the often stubborn, dry fiery sign of Aries, with its influence starting back at the top in the region of the head.

• **Anything that you do in the two to three Aries days for the region of the head, eyes and nose has a doubly beneficial preventive and healing effect. With the exception of surgical operations carried out in this area.**

• **Anything that puts a heavier burden on head, eyes and nose in the Aries days has a more harmful effect than on other days.**

• **If you are able to fix the date yourself for surgical operations on the head, eyes and nose, you should avoid Aries days and the period from March 20 to April 20, and choose the time of the waning moon for the operation.**

What's in the air in Aries: Aries days are fiery *warmth-days*, their day-quality is dry-hot, their colour is indigo to bluish-white. In summer they often prove to be good days for an outing; sitting on the ground even for a long time does not immediately give rise to the danger of catching cold.

Herbs that are known for their effectiveness with headaches and eye complaints (eyebright) and problems with the nose and with frontal and nasal sinuses (hay-flower mixtures*), develop greater strength when gathered during Aries days. In the case of constantly recurring disorders it is particularly important to pay attention to the moment of gathering herbs. When stocking up, one should pluck them shortly before full moon and then dry and store them *after* full moon, regardless of whether Aries is ruling (see page 215).

The reason that headaches and migraines often occur at this time is because of the top-heavy, impatient Aries-energy. Often we have neglected our duties in the previous days or generally let things slide, and today of all days we try to "run our head against a brick wall".

Headaches/Migraine

The mental invitation for headaches: "It's getting more than I can take. – What a mad rush: it's making my head spin! – Sometimes I have the feeling I'm no longer my own master. – I'm afraid of not being able to meet the demands on me. – He/she/it is really getting me down."

An effective remedy against the harmful effects on your health of such a torrent of thoughts is simply to admit that something is getting too much for you, instead of trying to suppress it and fight against it. It is the insight that there are only twenty-four hours in a day, that you cannot split yourself into four and that all the hectic rush and panic is coming from within you, not outside. Observe

---

* mixture of seeds, flowers and grasses sieved from hay

yourself and try as much as you can to keep Aries days free of stress and pressure; and if that isn't possible then just let it all happen. Come what may, it's never going to cost you your head.

What you can do: Often a slight poisoning, whether mental or physical, is also responsible for your throbbing head. Certain combinations of food can also set off a migraine attack: for example wholemeal products taken with together with caffeine or cheese with grapes can sometimes be indigestible. The effect makes itself felt in both body and mind, susceptibility to headaches and migraine is higher, and in the longer term aggressiveness and impatience can take over. Both combinations have no effect on many people, but for some the consequences are serious, the more so since the causal relation is virtually unknown.

One very good measure for preventing migraine is to drink *a lot of water* on Aries days, and in general to go without coffee, chocolate, sugar and egg-white (a possible trigger for migraine). However, this piece of advice is only of use if you have learnt to trust the signals of your own body. Anyone who has mastered the language of his own body is able to form a clear picture of the things that are helpful or harmful to it. For one and the same disturbance of our well-being thousands of good and well-meant pieces of advice pour in from every side, thousands of medicaments, infusions and ointments might possibly be helpful. But if you listen within yourself, a single one of these remedies will be enough; sometimes you won't even need one at all. What helps "in most cases" depends on the individual, not statistics. But for that you definitely need a clear instinctive sense of yourself; the opinion of those around you is often not enough. In particular chronically ill people would be well-advised to look on their illness as a chance to learn, instead of passively placing themselves in the hands of the medical profession. However, if a doctor gives you to understand that he is not comfortable with your active attitude to your illness and your eagerness to learn about it – then vanish out of the door as fast as you can and look for a genuine doctor, a friend of human beings.

With the right approach one can avoid headaches on Aries days, thereby achieving much more than someone who without any insight takes a gallon of water and thinks "let's just see if it helps". It won't do any good. It may well be that this remedy has helped friends of ours often enough, but ultimately it is only a suggestion. It can't be made into a general rule.

In principle there is nothing good or bad about Aries days for the head region. It all depends what you do. Anyone who does hard intellectual work in Aries, for instance giving a lecture when he has no experience of such things, should not be surprised if he grinds to a halt with the feeling that his head has doubled in circumference and weight. Eye compresses for inflamed or exhausted eyes will do good service on Aries days. Observe calmly what these days bring for you, how you structure them, whether it regularly happens that "things get you down".

Bleeding from the Nose

The mental invitation for a nosebleed: "If only someone would pay attention to me. – Nobody loves me, nobody ever praises me."

The remedy for this is to love oneself and to become independent of the approval of others. Seeking for love usually leads to 'trade relations', not genuine love. The conviction that "I won't be accepted until I'm good" leads to dependence and enslavement. Only someone who lives as he feels and thinks, who lives as he really is, will have the chance to meet a person who accepts him for what he really is.

What you can do: A bleeding nose is a frequent occurrence particularly among children. Often they are a little weakened, over-taxed, or feel that they are unloved. Sometimes too tightly packed a timetable or too much hectic rush is enough to bring it on. A cold infusion of *shepherd's purse*, either drunk or used as a cold compress on the back of the neck, often helps immediately. In the case of repeated nose bleeding you should find out whether a hidden illness is present (high blood pressure, anaemia). Weakened nose veins could also be a partial cause.

Snoring

The mental invitation for snoring: "I won't let go. – What was right before can't be wrong today. – The way I see things, that's the way everybody has to see them, if you don't mind."

The remedy for this consists in seeing clearly that everything is in a state of flux, that the only thing you can be sure of is the past, and that one can confidently surrender to the stream of change. Constant alteration, development and ripening is our very nature, not standing still, holding firm and taking root.

Some people can never be happy just because everything passes away; they even envy others who have preserved a childlike delight in life and simple things. Such people are only afraid of three things: of the drive they feel firstly to hold fast to everything beautiful and crush it, then they are afraid of losing it, and then they fear the pain that inevitably follows from having to let go of it. Someone on the other hand who never holds tight grants freedom and peace to all living creatures and is able to take pleasure in everything.

What you can do: Almost everyone who snores regularly is sleeping in an unsuitable place (see page 305). Often moving the bed to a new position is all that is needed to reduce or stop snoring. Another proven remedy is to take a sniff of the finest healing earth.*

A neckerchief tied with a thick knot in the back, in order to wake the sleeper up if he rolls on to his back, is an old household remedy for snoring that probably has more disadvantages than advantages. In the long run which is more unhealthy: snoring or continually interrupted sleep?

* pulverised earth with therapeutic properties

Adenoids

The mental invitation for adenoids: "I can't stand the tension that's always in the air round here. I'd better keep out of it and not get in anyone's way."

Children who suffer from adenoids are often from family backgrounds in which there is a lot of subliminal tension and unexpressed negative emotion in the air. It is not enough merely to pretend to a child that it is welcome if it is not really welcome and loved. And the genuine feeling isn't on sale in any toy shop.

What you can do: Adenoids should only be operated on when the moon is on the wane and never when it is in Aries and Taurus. Success would only be short-lived and the adenoids would come back. Sometimes a displaced fourth vertebra in the neck with corresponding pressure on certain nerves causes adenoids to grow faster. An experienced chiropractor will be able to put matters right.

Colds/Influenza

The mental invitation for colds: "He's just sneezed right at me, I've caught it now. – I catch three colds every winter. – I've had it up to here! – It's all getting too much for me, I can't make my mind up! What he/she did/said really hurt me."

Such spirals of cold-inducing thoughts dissolve the moment one realises that it is precisely thinking "I'm bound to catch a cold" that prepares the ground for the cold or flu in the first place. Furthermore, every form of indecisiveness and false pride can have a knock-on effect resulting in a cold. "We really must weigh up all the factors before we can make a decision" – if you push this thought to its extreme, then you never will decide, because it is impossible to take all the circumstances of a decision into account. Without instinct and trust every decision becomes a torment. And what keeps us more alive than the unexpected?

What you can do: A sensible preventive measure would be,

regularly or whenever you happen to think about it, to position your toes *in your shoes* as if you were going to take hold of something with them. This exerts a strong, sometimes slightly painful and massaging pressure on certain points on the tips of the toes. This pressure stimulates the circulation of energy in the body, which has a favourable effect on colds that are just starting or are already in existence. Red-coloured clothing (stockings, underclothes, outer garments) is well-suited for severe chills and frequent colds (but not in feverish conditions!).

Lemons are generally useless for colds – all the preventive and healing power of most fruit on the market has already dissipated if more than two days have elapsed since it was picked. The danger of contagion during a wave of influenza or colds does not exist. You do not become ill because you catch it, but rather you catch it because you are already 'ill' – in other words: because your immune system has already been weakened in another way. Generally speaking, everything that strengthens the immune system is the most effective precaution against flu and colds. Bloodletting can also be helpful: against fever on the 26th day after new moon, for general strengthening on the 12th, 18th and 21st day after the new moon. (NB: pay close attention to the method of counting! See page 108.)

Sinus Problems

The mental invitation for sinus problems: Such disorders are often the physical symptom of an unexpressed irritation with someone in the vicinity: "She really gets up my nose!"

There are many possible solutions; however, there is no single one that we would wish to suggest to you. Unless you can make use of a recommendation such as: "Learn to love other people." Love cannot be produced on demand. You have to take the situation in hand yourself, above all by looking it straight in the face. Which of your expectations is the other person disappointing? What conditions have to be satisfied before your nose can report pleasant sensations? What happens if you give up your expectations and conditions?

What you can do: Especially in the case of chronic frontal and nasal sinus problems a zone of disturbance in the head region of the bed may play a part (see also page 305). It could also possibly be a hitherto undetected infection in tooth number 7 in the upper or lower jaw. Often a thorough course of dental treatment has proved helpful here.

Sinusitis is often the consequence of carelessly going around with wet hair when young. At least in winter one should never leave the house or school with damp hair. Nasal sinus problems often arise – like countless other physical disorders – from displaced vertebrae (the 2nd vertebra of the neck). An experienced chiropractor will be able to set this straight.

Eye Problems

The mental invitation for eye problems: "I've lost sight of my actual goal in life, and I'm afraid of the future (short-sightedness). – I daren't look. I'm not interested in what is near at hand and commonplace. The present has nothing to offer (long-sightedness). – I'm furious about what I see (dry eyes)."

Remedies: seeing the present as it is – how incredibly beautiful and how inconceivably horrible, sometimes both at the same time. Recognising the future as a figment of my imagination that only becomes a reality if I mentally invite it – for better or worse – into existence.

What you can do: Exercises for the eyes and eyesight, which are the topic of numerous books, are sometimes helpful as a precautionary measure and for weakened eyes, even in cases where glasses are already worn. Glasses often make permanent a weakness of vision which could easily be overcome with appropriate exercises and the ability to look reality in the face.

One old and effective remedy for exhausted and strained eyes is to moisten one's closed eyelids with one's own saliva, in the morning before eating. Two peppercorns, chewed before breakfast can quickly make bags under the eyes disappear.

Disorders of sight are often symptoms that accompany displaced vertebrae (the 2nd vertebra of the neck). In such cases an experienced chiropractor can often put matters right with a single treatment.

Conjunctivitis/Sties

The mental invitation for conjunctivitis and sties: "I'm furious and disappointed about what I see, but somehow I feel too helpless to do anything about it."

Rage and disappointment are always of our own making. No other person or situation is responsible. Both always match our own expectations, whether or not we were right to cherish them.

What you can do: Conjunctivitis is often the symptom of insufficient kidney activity. Particularly on Aries days you should be sure to drink enough, preferably just water (for further remedial steps see page 84).

Not infrequently the conjunctiva is slightly damaged by dust, a knock or freezing cold. Eye-baths with a lukewarm (!) decoction of *eyebright* can rapidly remove the problem. If eyebright is not available, then lukewarm tap water (no need to boil it) will serve quite well. Such baths work well during the waning moon and Aries days, especially if the eyebright was picked during the waxing moon and Aries days. *Camomile* baths are not at all suitable for the eyes, since the healing process is too quick and often a thick pus can form as a result. Apart from this camomile is an effective medicinal herb for inflammations of every kind.

These tips apply also to sties, and for purulent and non-purulent inflammations of the sebaceous glands of the eyelids.

Inflammation of the Cornea

The mental invitation for inflammation of the cornea: "I've never been so angry! – This mess is really getting me down. – I just can't cope with so much inconsistency."

The ability to experience intense happiness has a high price: namely the ability to experience intense sorrow. In actual fact it is no price at all. Both capacities derive from one and the same source – your instinct.

What you can do: Vitamin A deficiency can cause severe inflammation of the cornea. Take a lot of vitamin A, particularly when the moon is waxing: this lessens the disorder, often very quickly. However, the moment you detect any change in the cornea, it's absolutely essential that you should see your doctor.

Vitamin A is fat-soluble, and it is contained in all green parts of plants, in coloured roots (carrots) and in yellow animal fats (butter, egg-yolk). If you wish to meet your needs exclusively from vegetables, then a dash of oil should be added, otherwise the body cannot take in the vitamins – or only with great difficulty. Vitamin A affects the eyesight, the cornea and the retina, as well as the entire skin (hence the yellow colouring after an overdose of vitamin A) and mucous membranes.

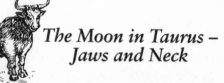

The Moon in Taurus –
Jaws and Neck

With the entry of the moon into the zodiac sign Taurus the region of the jaws and neck is more strongly influenced. This region of the body includes the teeth and jaws, the ears, the larynx and vocal chords, the throat and neck and, not least, the thyroid gland.

● Anything that you do in the two to three Taurus days for the region of the jaws and neck, for teeth, tonsils and ears, has a doubly beneficial preventive and healing effect. With the exception of surgical operations carried out in this area.

• Anything that puts a heavier burden on the neck region in the Taurus days has a more harmful effect than on other days – for instance a heavy strain on the vocal chords.

• If you are able to fix the date yourself for surgical operations on the neck region, you should avoid Taurus days and the period from April 20 to May 21, and choose the time of the waning moon for the operation.

What's in the air in Taurus: A person who is not otherwise especially concerned with his material security is more likely during Taurus days to start thinking that he needs a solid material foundation in life. Thoughts and reactions become more ponderous; it is easier to be obstinate.

Taurus is an *earth sign*, the day-quality is cool, earth-bound and somehow realistic; its colour is bright blue. During Taurus days one should always go out more warmly clothed than the thermometer would seem to require. A draught in the neck region at this time is the quickest way to get a stiff neck. Conversely a massage of the neck and shoulder areas during Taurus days could prove to be a real boon.

Although colds and inflammations of the throat are not infectious, one might well get this impression now, since Taurus has so many people going around with croaking voices and scarves about their necks. Which doesn't mean of course that one *is bound* to get a sore throat now. But there is certainly a greater danger of getting an inflammation of the throat.

Giving a speech on Taurus days can be agony for the inexperienced and may end in hoarse croaking. Just how effective even a simple tea can be against sore throats and tonsillitis is something everyone finds out who does himself this favour. Other medicines for throat inflammations, too, are especially effective at this time.

Particularly on cold Taurus days the ears should not remain unprotected. At this time they are more sensitive to draughts and noise. An eardrop of *Saint John's wort* oil now and then on Taurus days can often prevent earache, especially when the buds of Saint John's wort used for the oil were gathered on light-days (Gemini, Libra, Aquarius) or when the moon was waxing.

Sore Throats/Tonsillitis

The mental invitation for inflammations of the throat and tonsils: "There's so much I'd like to say but I daren't: sad things, beautiful things, angry things. – I'm afraid to express what's on the tip of my tongue. And it's hard to swallow it down."

The ability to express what one has to say, whether it is words of affection, grief or displeasure, is underdeveloped in our time – because one constantly finds that people neither listen to nor understand such words, never mind unconditionally accepting them. To express yourself honestly is always a risk; but all the same you should take that risk, in moderation. It is better to be misunderstood nine times and to be heard once sincerely and impartially than to remain silent ten times out of fear and mistrust.

What you can do: There are thousands of possible ways to deal with throat problems. Each can do some good if you apply the remedy with the right attitude. One of the most effective is not to be constantly criticising, whether mentally or verbally.

Don't ever have an operation on your tonsils during Aries and Taurus! This can lead to serious complications, secondary haemorrhaging, etc. Continually recurring sore throats, tonsillitis or stiff necks, may often be caused in part by displaced 5th and 6th vertebrae.

Earache and Inflammations of the Ear

The mental invitation for ear problems: "I don't like what I'm hearing at all. It's too painful. What my inner voice is telling me is true,
but I don't want to admit it, let alone act on it."

Children often have to grapple with ear problems because their
capacity for hearing the truth is still well-developed. Only gradually
do they learn to drown out their inner voice, and then they no
longer have to go to the ear specialist so often – but at what a price!

What you can do: For inflammations of the ear a hot, damp hay-
flower bag held against the ear is often extremely useful. Lukewarm
camomile poultices and a drop of *Saint John's wort* oil also serve
well, especially on Taurus days.

Hyper-function of the Thyroid Gland

The mental invitation for hyper-function of the thyroid gland: "All
my life people have been passing me by. – I've learnt this much: if
I'm going to count for anything in the world I've got to achieve
something – I'll only gain recognition if *others* approve of my
achievements. I've no confidence in my own judgement. So I'm constantly on the move, either in order to achieve something or else to
escape criticism."

Here is a secret that hardly anyone knows: nobody in the world
will ever be able to satisfy another person, never mind a lot of
people. You should act in such a way that you alone are content
with yourself. You only have to give an account of yourself to one
person, and that's our real Boss. He is immeasurably more understanding than almost anyone who walks the earth. You have the
right not to swallow everything that is put in front of you.

What you can do: When the thyroid gland empties too many of
its hormones into the bloodstream this results in nervous symptoms, restlessness, palpitations, perspiration, sleeplessness and diarrhoea. Unless treatment is given a state of total exhaustion can set
in. Infusions to purify the blood, drunk during the waning moon

between three and seven in the afternoon, seldom fail to be effective (see page 146). While the moon is waxing you can drink a daily cup of *watercress* tea.

Avoid eating red meat as far as is possible. Raw fruit and vegetables would be an effective additional measure; later on a basically vegetarian diet is a good method to curb the thyroid gland. Incidentally the 7th neck vertebra influences the thyroid gland, and displacements in this area put an added burden on glandular function.

Thyroid Insufficiency

The mental invitation for thyroid insufficiency: "There's something wrong with me, something missing. – For some reason no one has ever really cared about me and accepted me as I am. – If things go on like this, I'll give up. I'm suffocating."

Remedy: accept yourself as you are, without any ifs and buts, without tearing yourself apart. The radiance that you derive from this will, as it were, automatically attract people around you who also possess this capacity. For only someone who can accept himself unconditionally is able to see others as they are – and accept them.

What you can do: All measures for the treatment of thyroid insufficiency – poultices, blood-purifying infusions or medicines – should be taken when the moon is on the wane. However, if you switch to medicines that have to be taken regularly you will not be able take the moon into account. A fully adequate vegetarian diet is to be recommended. Incidentally, goitre is abetted by all varieties of cabbage and devalued, finely ground white flour. You will find the herbs that are suited to thyroid problems on page 223.

Dental Problems

The mental invitation for problems with the teeth – caries, inflammation of the gums, root treatment: "I simply cannot make my mind up, I seem to lack bite – so many alternatives, so little time, and when I finally make a decision I have endless doubts about whether it was the right one."

Decisions are like arrows shot from a bow. Nothing in the world can bring them back. Once the arrow is in the air we can calmly put the bow down and await the results of our decision. If the arrow hits the mark, that's good; if not, that's good, too. The bow is waiting for the next arrow, and no one in the world stands to lose anything worth mentioning.

What you can do: A lot. So much, in fact, that a whole section is reserved for this topic on page (156).

The Moon in Gemini – Shoulders, Arms and Hands

The Gemini-impulse affects the shoulders, the arms, the hands and also in part the activity of the lungs.

• Anything that you do in the two to three Gemini days for the region of the shoulders, arms and hands has a doubly beneficial preventive and healing effect. With the exception of surgical operations carried out in this area.

• Anything that puts a heavier burden on the shoulders, arms and hands in the Gemini days has a more harmful effect than on other days.

• If you are able to fix the date yourself for surgical operations on the shoulders, arms and hands , you should avoid Gemini days and the period from May 21 to June 21, and choose the time of the waning moon for the operation.

What's in the air in Gemini: The force of Gemini days is lively, moving in leaps and bounds; steadfastness and persistence are not its strong point. Chains of thought branch out inquisitively in every direction, leaving not one stone unturned. The day-quality is bright and airy; even when the sky is overcast the light can sometimes feel piercing. The colour is a lightish blue.

Gemini days are always a suitable time to do some good to the shoulder area; well-directed exercises and massage can work wonders at this time. Stiff muscles afterwards are probably a good sign, for this is how the body signals that it is busy with detoxification. Rheumatic complaints in the shoulder region respond especially well during this period to suitable ointments, possibly produced from herbs that were collected in Gemini or Taurus and when the moon was waxing. On the other hand wearing clothing that is too light in cool weather or driving in too strong a draught has a more negative effect at this time.

Those suffering from rheumatism sometimes have difficulties during the Gemini days, but the reason for this often lies in a complete change in the weather, which tends to take place in Gemini. Since the lungs are also influenced to some extent, methodical breathing exercises could be very useful at this time.

Shoulder Problems

The mental invitation for problems with the shoulders: "These experiences are a heavy burden for me to bear. – Sometimes I have the feeling I'm carrying the weight of the world on my shoulders."

Wanting to take upon oneself all the weight of the world is sometimes concealed arrogance; sometimes, too, it is a fear of the closeness that would result from shared responsibility and common effort. The inner solitude of the person carrying a heavy burden actually seems to weigh lighter than the vulnerability arising from open and honest relations. But what a blessing it is – to have the courage only to have time for people who accept me as I am and help to carry the load! They do exist.

What you can do: Physical therapy (massages, chiropractic measures, baths, etc.) are especially effective when the moon is on the wane in Gemini. In many cases pains in the shoulders vanish when a medical practitioner with acupuncture skills treats the meridian of the large intestine.

Rheumatism

The mental invitation for rheumatic complaints: "Why on earth do I work myself to death all year long? – Seeing that nobody loves me, I'm not going give anything of myself either. – Life has a really bitter taste."

As long as a service has to be matched by a service in return, giving by receiving, before one will give something oneself, only business connections can arise, never love and friendship. Anyone who believes that he was born with the right to the fulfilment of his expectations, will also leave the world again with this right intact – without ever having found a lenient judge who unreservedly grants him the fulfilment of this right. But someone who expects nothing receives everything.

What you can do: Rheumatic complaints of all kinds first of all necessitate a detoxification of the body. For this purpose there are a great many possibilities, such as *nettle* tea, taken as a springtime cure between three and seven in the afternoon when the moon is on the wane (see page 146).

In former times people used to line a whole bed with *ferns*. They were sewn in between two sheets and this was used as an under-blanket for the patient. If the patient suffered from cramp at night, his pillow was filled with common clubmoss. Some ferns are protected species now, however, they can be bought and they still do the job.

The 23rd day after new moon (NB: pay close attention to the

method of counting! See page 108) is ideally suited for bloodletting to counter rheumatic complaints. These can also often be caused by undiscovered dental infections, or displacements in the region of the 12th thoracic vertebra. You should also pay attention to these factors.

'Cold Hands'

The mental invitation for disorders of blood circulation in the hands: "That's too hot for me to handle. – I know I ought to tackle the problem, but I doubt whether I can do it."

As long as our world is based on hypocrisy and complacency, we shall always be burning our fingers, no matter what we grasp hold of. For there will constantly be a few or a lot of people there who want to find fault with us – since every person who gets to grips with something is a threat to those who do not want to – who do not want to face up to the meaning of their being here. Cold hands warm up through friction.

What you can do: Get to grips with whatever you always wanted to do, so that your circulation gets going. No price is too high! Bloodletting on the 12th, 18th or 21st day after new moon (NB: pay close attention to the method of counting! See page 108) is good for the whole body and thus for the circulation.

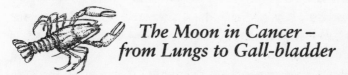

The Moon in Cancer – from Lungs to Gall-bladder

The force that is at work during Cancer days affects the chest, lungs, stomach, liver and gall-bladder. It often shifts our general state into one of slight restlessness, because the emotional world – as with all watery signs – takes on added depth and weight. Sometimes we suddenly see something that is otherwise held under lock and key inside ourselves, and then we start moving over unfamiliar ground.

• Anything that you do in the two to three Cancer days for the region of the chest, lungs, stomach, liver and gall-bladder has a doubly beneficial preventive and healing effect. With the exception of surgical operations carried out in this area.

• Anything that puts a heavier burden on chest, lungs, stomach, liver and gall-bladder in the Cancer days has a more harmful effect than on other days.

• If you are able to fix the date yourself for surgical operations on chest, lungs, stomach, liver and gall-bladder, you should avoid Cancer days and the period from June 21 to July 22, and choose the time of the waning moon for the operation.

What's in the air on Cancer days: The day-quality of the Cancer days is moist-cool, the colour is green. Anyone who suffers from rheumatism should not air bedding (duvets, etc.) over the window ledge or balcony during Cancer (or Scorpio and Pisces). The damp remains in the feathers, and this can have an adverse effect on the illness.

Often a sleepless night during the Cancer days is enough to make one wake up the next day with rings under the eyes and feeling totally shattered. The liver had a heavy workload and was unable to regenerate itself. Anyone who is susceptible to complaints of the liver, gall-bladder, lungs or chest can take advantage of Cancer days to do these organs some good. The stomach, too, occasionally plays up during Cancer days (wind, heartburn). A light diet is therefore advisable.

From July to January Cancer days always occur in the waning moon, and then for the next six months in the waxing moon. You will recall that when the moon is on the wane the system is flushed out, when it is waxing it is supplied with as much goodness as possible. According to this, cures aimed at healing or detoxifying the stomach and liver have more chance of success between summer and winter than they do between winter and summer.

Bronchitis

The mental invitation for bronchitis: "Somehow I don't like the set-up round here, but I'm afraid of expressing what I really feel. There could be too much damage and I could end up messing things up even more than they are already."

You want to tell someone where to get off? Go right ahead. Far better to make an honest end to the horror, than put up with the endless horror of hypocrisy.

What you can do: One proven remedy is pork fat, slightly warmed and spread not too thickly on a poultice which is applied at night until the bronchitis or cough has subsided. Also ideal for this purpose would be *marigold* ointment (for preparation details see page 218). This can drive away even an obstinate chronic bronchitis. Be sure to throw the first poultice away after use, and sterilise all further poultice cloths after they have been used once.

Bronchial Asthma

The mental invitation for asthma: "The whole thing is stifling me. – They're trying to take me over, but I'm fighting against it. – I shan't be able to breathe freely till the situation changes."

You should never accept a sacrificial role in life. Anyone who makes himself into a sacrificial victim will always be a plaything of his surroundings, of other people's interests. Everyone has the right to live *his own* life – for the simple reason that no one can do it better or with greater understanding. "You can only call yourself unlucky if you are an undertaker by profession and people stop dying." (Arabic proverb.)

What you can do: In the case of bronchial asthma an unsuitable sleeping place can also trigger off the complaint or make it worse. The numerous suggestions for cleansing rooms that have been polluted with harmful substances (see page 284) may prove helpful as a means to improve the air in the home and the workplace – an important measure for respiratory complaints of all kinds. For all problems with the lungs a bloodletting on the 24th day after new moon is particularly effective (NB: pay close attention to the method of counting! See page 108).

Heartburn
The mental invitation for heartburn: "I'm afraid."

No one can take away another person's fear. The only thing that helps is to gain for oneself the insight that when seen through a magnifying glass, a mosquito looks like an enormous man-eating dragon. So why go around with a magnifying glass in front of your eyes?

What you can do: *Healing earth* is a very good remedy for heartburn. An effective precaution is raw red potato, crushed and squeezed. Mix about three desert spoonfuls of the juice in your food. Additional remedies are raw apples, rusk and camomile tea, drunk slowly, pausing between gulps. Sometimes a displaced 6th thoracic vertebra is partly responsible for constantly recurring stomach-ache.

Inflammation of the Stomach and Stomach Ulcers
The mental invitation for inflammations of the stomach: "It's all so hard to digest. – I can't handle it all. I'm always having to adjust to something new. – It's all happening too quickly for me. – I don't think I'm good enough for it. Actually, when you look at it, I'm never good enough."

Be patient with yourself. Perfectionism is a deadly disease. Always having to be good blocks precisely those strengths that one needs for the reception of the new, for calm study and acceptance of the constant changes of life. In the fear of letting go of the old we forget what opportunity, what joy each new start brings.

What you can do: A change of diet is almost always the basic condition for a thorough cure. Restrict yourself for a while to predominantly vegetarian food. A good preventive method: crush unpeeled raw potatoes and drink the juice before every meal. It tastes bad, but it works well.

In the case of nervous stomach-aches which have no organic cause, get a medical practitioner who has gained experience of colour therapy to treat the outer side of the knee with the colour red.

Liver and Gall-bladder Problems
The mental invitation for liver and gall-bladder problems: " What I find really galling is that... – Everyone is making mistakes except me. It's the others' fault that it went wrong, I've nothing to reproach myself for. – I want to make a complaint! No wonder I'm so bitter (liver problems). – Don't try that on with me! Who do you think you're talking to? (gall-stones)?"

False pride is one of the most voracious diseases of civilisation. It carries off everyone that falls victim to it. The remedy? To get used to the fact that we are all mortal beings. Nothing works better than that. Nothing else brings more true joy in life, more gratitude, friendship and love.

What you can do: The great variety of possible disorders of the liver and gall-bladder makes it impossible to generalise. In most cases bed-rest is a good remedy, often even the pre-condition of a cure. Liver and gall-bladder regenerate best after midnight (see page 259). A sleeping cure is pointless if you rest during the day and become active at night. Basically warm to very warm compresses are needed in the region of the liver and gall-bladder, in order to promote the healing process. Make nearly scalding hay-flower bags and put them on for about two hours. Perhaps you may get the opportunity now and again to spend the night in a haystack – that would be an ideal accompaniment to the cure.

Herbal remedies to activate the gall-bladder (see page 221) should run for two full cycles of the moon – and no longer. The ideal conditions for success would be if the cure included the period from June 21 to July 22.

The colour yellow can have a positive effect in cases of liver damage. You should also consider a visit to the chiropractor: a displaced 4th or 5th thoracic vertebra may well be implicated in gall-bladder or liver complaints.

The Moon in Leo – Heart and Circulation

The hot-blooded, impetuous force of the Leo days influences the heart and circulation as well as the back and diaphragm.

• Anything that you do in the two to three Leo days for the region of the heart and circulation has a doubly beneficial preventive and healing effect. With the exception of surgical operations carried out in this area.

• Anything that puts a heavier burden on the heart and circulation in the Leo days has a more harmful effect than on other days.

• If you are able to fix the date yourself for surgical operations on the heart, you should avoid Leo days and the period from July 22 to August 23, and choose the time of the waning moon for the operation.

What's in the air in Leo: The day-quality of Leo days is dry and fiery; the colour is green. In summer in the northern hemisphere around Leo time, especially in August, the highest temperatures of the year prevail, sometimes with violent thunderstorms. It is very important to drink a lot at this time, since Leo has a powerful drying effect.

In general the Leo impulse brings the circulation up to peak activity. The back sometimes hurts more and the heart often plays up a little. An over-taxed circulation and sleepless nights can cause quite a lot of trouble during Leo; however, by the time of the next sign, Virgo, it's usually all over.

Many an inexperienced cyclists puffs his way to his destination during Leo, even though he has problems with his circulation or heart. Especially during Leo days one should not overstrain oneself. Of course we aren't talking about the normal physical activities of healthy people.

Leo is a very good day to collect herbs that have a curative effect on heart and circulation. Although it is the next sign, Virgo, that rules the digestive organs, anyone thinking of taking preventive and curative measures in the region of the intestine ought to start on this now.

Heart Problems

The mental invitation for problems with the heart: "I'm heartbroken about it. – I take no pleasure in anything any more. – Life is nothing but stress (heart problems). – Money rules the world. What does friendship count for (heart attack)? – I'll never manage to gain the love and appreciation that I need. But I'll never give up trying (coronary obstruction)."

The heart region houses the power of our love. If we do not allow this to unfold, for whatever reason, then in the truest sense of the word we strangulate the heart. We have allowed ourselves to be persuaded that love is a sentimental feeling. It is not: the essence of feelings is their constant variation; they are merely the accompanying symptoms of other things – thoughts and perceptions. One cannot build on something that is constantly altering like quicksand. Love is the thing that maintains us in life, that inspires us and restores us, that is always there – for you and for all of us. But only when it is given unreservedly, without ulterior motives and expectations. Amazing: the more one gives of it, the more there is! That's something science ought to try and explain…

What you can do: A contributing factor underlying almost all serious heart conditions is an unsuitable sleeping place (see page 305). A displacement in the region of the 2nd thoracic vertebra can lead to problems with the heart and circulation. A bloodletting on the 12th, 18th or 21st day after the new moon is beneficial and fortifying for the whole body. (NB: pay close attention to the method of counting! See page 108).

High Blood Pressure

The mental invitation for high blood-pressure: "I've been dragging this problem around with me for ages. Any minute I'm going to burst! But with the best will in the world I can't think of a solution. Above all it has to be a solution that lets me keep hold of the reins. – If I don't have everything under control I get scared."

The solution to a long-standing problem is often much more easily recognisable for well-wishing, impartial outsiders than for those actually labouring under it – in keeping with the maxim that it is easier to see the 'mote' in another's eye than it is to see the 'beam' in one's own. Why not accept the (very slight) risk and place your trust in such a person. Even if he shows you the way to the best of all possible solutions, you still have the freedom to reject it and remain as you are…

What you can do: The excessive consumption of stimulants and luxury items (coffee, alcohol, nicotine, sweets) has an unfavourable effect on high blood pressure. Naturally occurring herbs that effectively reduce blood pressure are: *mistletoe, garlic, wood garlic, onion* and *field horsetail*.

One very effective measure for dealing with high blood pressure is a bloodletting on the 26th day after new moon (NB: pay close attention to the method of counting! See page 108), or auto-haemotherapy likewise on the 26th day after new moon. A supporting and balancing effect can be obtained by regularly inserting days when nothing but fruit is eaten during Aries, Leo and Sagittarius, the fruit signs in the zodiac. Try to observe whether your blood pressure alters during Taurus, Virgo and Capricorn days, perhaps as a result of meals containing very salty dishes (see page 188).

Sleeping over a zone of disturbance, or in the wrong sleeping direction are also possible influences on blood pressure. You should always sleep with your head to the north or the west. If you live close to flowing water then you should sleep at right angles to the flow, regardless of the compass direction. People who sleep in the same direction as the stream often wake up exhausted the next day, whilst sleeping in the opposite direction often results in waking up with a heavy head.

Low Blood Pressure

The mental invitation for low blood pressure: "What's the point of all the effort: it's not going to work. – I don't reckon it'll come to anything. – You won't get anyone interested in that. – It's a sheer waste of effort."

It isn't difficult to look on the dark side. Just put on the appropriate spectacles and every rainbow will disappear. Sit around doing nothing because "there's nothing to be done" and the circulation will slacken off. But anyone who wishes to be able when autumn comes to gather in supplies to bring himself and his fellow human beings through the winter will think, feel and act differently – and in the end, God willing, will reap the harvest.

What you can do: Anything that stimulates your metabolism is useful: physical exercises in the morning, plenty to drink between 3 and 7 p.m. (most of us in general don't drink enough), a correction to your spinal column, avoiding heavy food, plenty of movement and, not least, autohaemotherapy by a doctor or medical practitioner.

A bloodletting for general strengthening on the 12th, 18th and 21st day after new moon is sure to have a favourable effect. (NB: pay close attention to the method of counting! See page 108.) Sometimes a displacement in the area of the 5th thoracic vertebra is partially responsible for excessively low blood pressure.

Anaemia

The mental invitation for anaemia: "My doubts are justified, wait and see. – You think that I'm trying to spoil your fun with my pessimism, but you'll thank me for it in the end. – If I can't be happy, neither can you."

Nowhere is it written that life is not supposed to be enjoyable. But it is written everywhere that combining duty and pleasure is a fine art. True: but it's a fine art simply because people have tried to drum it into us that work isn't supposed to be fun, and that happiness and pleasure are a luxury or even a sin. How much longer are we going to believe such nonsense, at the expense of our own health and freedom?

What you can do: Autohaemotherapy has proved to be an extremely effective remedy for anaemia, and numerous doctors and medical practitioners successfully apply it to the most varied disorders. If possible make sure that it takes place between 9 and 11 in the morning; and it will help even more if it is an earth day (Taurus, Virgo and Capricorn) during the waxing moon.

Gout

The mental invitation for gout: "I'm the boss round here and everyone dances to my tune; if they don't, they're sent packing, on the spot. No excuses or explanations".

The period of patriarchal master-slave relationships is nearing its end (even if it takes another century or so). Why? Because the gulf between the heart and elitist thinking is just as effective an obstacle to living and working together as physical distance. However, all global problems, particularly in the field of environmental destruction can in future only be solved successfully through genuine mutual co-operation on an equal footing. And the foundation stone for harmonious relations between peoples is laid by mutual trust at the lowest level – between neighbour and neighbour. There will always be wars and border disputes as long as fences and hedges are needed to maintain the peace between neighbours – rather than the insight and strength of loving thoughts which render all rivalry superfluous.

What you can do: An intensive purification of the blood is especially important with gout. Nettle tea is an effective preventive and healing remedy, taken regularly twice a day between 3 and 7 p.m., for fourteen days during the waning moon (see page 146). The sleeping area should also be examined for zones of disturbance and radiation (see also page 305).

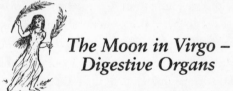

The Moon in Virgo –
Digestive Organs

The particular force of the Virgo days makes itself apparent in the activity of the digestive organs. It influences the large and small intestines, the spleen and the pancreas.

* Anything that you do in the two to three Virgo days for the digestion, the spleen and the pancreas has a doubly beneficial preventive and healing effect. With the exception of surgical operations carried out in this area.

* Anything that puts a heavier burden on the digestive organs in the Virgo days has a more harmful effect than on other days.

• If you are able to fix the date yourself for surgical operations on the stomach, the spleen and the pancreas, you should avoid Virgo days and the period from August 23 to September 23, and choose the time of the waning moon for the operation.

What's in the air in Virgo: Virgo days, with their dry-cool day-quality are the quintessential earth days. Their colour is yellow. This sign of the zodiac plays a very special role in gardening and agriculture. Almost all work in garden, field and forest is particularly favoured at this time.

People with sensitive stomachs and intestines often have problems with their digestion during this period. It isn't easy for many people to go without heavy or spicy dishes, but at least for these two or three days it would be a great advantage.

Herbs gathered during Virgo not only improve digestive activity, they also have a favourable effect on the blood, nerves and pancreas. In particular a blood-purifying infusion such as *stinging nettles*, gathered in Virgo, is bound to have a good effect. The winter store should not be laid down until September, when Virgo appears once more in the waning moon. An enlarged pancreas can be helped back to normal functioning by means of such a tea. The colour *orange* can have a favourable influence on digestive problems and poor bowel movements, especially if you wear it during Virgo days. Violet, on the other hand, stimulates the spleen and hence the strength of the immune system.

Intestine Problems
The mental invitation for intestine problems: "I simply don't have enough time to digest all that properly. And even if I had the time, I'd rather just look away and distract myself with something. – I feel so bored!"

The past has to be digested properly. And there is no greater adventure than to look reality in the face, unreservedly, without anger, regret or self-criticism. There's nothing to be lost, but everything to be gained.

What you can do: Many people with intestine and digestion problems have a tendency to take extreme measures. Usually what lies at the root of the matter, as so often, is impatience; the expectation of rapid results. However, modes of behaviour and eating habits that have been established for years cannot be altered overnight. And even if they could, the body only reacts slowly to changes: just as a ruined soil only gradually responds to natural methods of cultivation. It needs time to remember what is natural and readapt to the rhythms of nature. The intestine often has to relearn first how to recognise its own signals.

It is not uncommon that too much raw fruit and vegetables is the factor that triggers problems of the intestine. To be sure, such food is healthy, but often this is exaggerated. In general the diet has to be changed in order to deal with intestinal problems. Sometimes, too, displaced vertebrae are partly to blame, in particular the 6th and 12th thoracic vertebrae, as well as the 1st lumbar vertebra. A chiropractor will be able to tell you more exactly.

Constipation

The mental invitation for constipation: "The past has more to offer me than the present and the future. And besides, who's giving me anything? You won't get anything out of me. – Unnecessary? Nothing is unnecessary."

Remedy: the realisation that the last shirt has no pockets. The art of living consists in always travelling light, in one's thoughts as well as in the world.

What you can do: Take your time and read the next part of the book, because in most cases the basic evil is incorrect nutrition. In any case the composition of your diet ought not only to be 'healthy', it should also be in tune with your personal taste. Never stuff anything that is repugnant to you into your body merely because it says in some book that it's supposed to be healthy. Besides, there are numerous naturally effective remedies to get a sluggish intestine moving again. The harmfulness of continually taking laxatives should also be mentioned; anyone who deprives his muscles, bones and organs of their own essential functions need hardly be surprised if they go to sleep or even waste away.

A glass of *lukewarm* water, taken for instance at breakfast, can work wonders. A short bout of physical exercise has also proved very effective: in the morning before you get up, draw your right knee with both hands up towards your chest for one minute, then for one minute draw up your left knee, and finally for one minute draw up both knees. This exercise has cleared up even very obstinate cases of constipation, sometimes within two or three days. The effect probably derives from the gentle pressure from right to left setting the large intestine in motion – the natural route for digested food residues.

The colour *yellow* can have a favourable effect on sluggish digestion. Medical practitioners have achieved very good results with reflex-zone massage, in combination with colour therapy (possibly during Pisces days). In most cases patients can soon dispense with laxatives.

Diarrhoea

What you can do: Here, too, nutrition is the decisive factor. Doctors could preach whole books at you about diarrhoea and all kinds of other clinical pictures. We have no wish to replace this work or merely to repeat it parrot-fashion. In your own time, and without feeling you have to justify yourself to anyone, have a good think about exactly what it is you're in such a hurry to get rid of. Don't lose sight of the fact that not every physical problem is conditioned by mental factors alone. Could it just be that the Mexican soup you had yesterday was a little too hot?

Avoid the colour yellow in your clothing: it has a harmful effect in cases of diarrhoea.

Overweight

The mental invitation for overweight: "How can I protect myself from having my feelings hurt? I'll never forgive you for that (general)! – I've been completely drained. I've never had real love (arms). – Now I can do without your support, too. When I needed you none of you helped me (abdomen). – I'll never forgive my parents for that (hips). – I'll never forgive my father for that (thighs)."

Irreconcileability, the inability to forgive and hatred, are almost always the result of disappointed expectations and excessively high ideals. That is to say the other person is not to blame for your personal feelings. We are not born with a right to the fulfilment of our expectations, even if parents, peers, advertising, business and politics try to lull us to (nightmare-laden) sleep with the contrary assertion.

What you can do: Take your time and read page 173. *Diet Made Easy*. And never forget that no one is happy merely because he or she is slim – no one is unhappy merely because he or she is overweight. Unless of course you earnestly persuade yourself that this is the case. As long as the cash registers of the "Slim = Happy" philosophy go on ringing, you'll have no trouble getting a lot of applause for this belief. However, the fertile ground for real happiness is always cultivated in one's own heart and mind; here size and weight do not matter at all.

The trust placed in eating rules and slimming diets to remove non-pathological excessive weight is often exactly as great as the un-willingness to look its actual causes straight in the face. You should bear in mind that the only thing that a diet achieves is the increase in probability that your obesity will return and stick with you even longer. Overweight arose because of a habit – *your* habit. Only a clear insight into the nature of this habit of thought or behaviour will be able to guide you towards a change for the better – whether you now happily accept that you are overweight or happily melt away. Who is able to impart this insight to you? A prescribed diet? Another person? A book?

Perhaps this piece of information will help you. Coach drivers in travel firms pay close attention to the appearance of the landlords and landladies of the pubs and restaurants at which they're planning to break their journey. The more padding they have on their ribs the greater the probability that the drivers will let the passengers get out there.

On page 150 you will find more on the subject of *fasting* – a shorter or longer period without solid food, which has become fashionable in recent years as a means to detoxify the body or to lose weight.

Pancreas Problems

The mental invitation for problems of the pancreas: "Nothing in life gives me pleasure any more. Somehow everything is passing me by. There is nothing sweet any more to delight my tongue."

Many human tongues are so accustomed to bitterness that even the sweet things, the beautiful aspects that every day has to offer, are filtered out by their perceptive faculty. How to revive a deadened tongue, how to remove those dark glasses? Perhaps with the insight that we ourselves put the spectacles on. The decision always rests with me, whether to be depressed because my glass is half empty or happy because it is still half full. And as long as you can read these lines, or have them read to you, your glass is still half full at every moment of your life.

What you can do: As a preventive measure give up white sugar. White sugar consists of nothing. It contains nothing that your body really needs in order to stay healthy. All requirements for carbohydrates (the starch from cereals, vegetables, fruit, potatoes, etc., which is converted into sugar in the liver), can be more profitably satisfied from other foodstuffs.

There's nothing to be said against an appetite for sweet things, and if you need to satisfy it, then do so. It's enough if you know that it is an acquired characteristic, and that sweets are in the main only a substitute for the real sweetness of life, which we spoil with exaggerated expectations. The decision to learn from this insight is your affair. Incidentally, honey is not a good substitute for sugar. There simply aren't as many bees in the world as there is honey sold. On top of that they are mostly fed with sugar.

The Moon in Libra – Hips, Kidneys and Bladder

The somewhat neutral force of Libra days particularly affects the hips, as well as the kidneys and the bladder.

• **Anything that you do in the two to three Libra days for the hips, kidneys and bladder has a doubly beneficial preventive and healing effect. With the exception of surgical operations carried out in this area.**

• **Anything that puts a heavier burden on hips, kidneys and bladder in the Libra days has a more harmful effect than on other days.**

• **If you are able to fix the date yourself for surgical operations on the hips, as well as the kidneys and bladder, you should avoid Libra days and the period from September 23 to October 23, and choose the time of the waning moon for the operation.**

What's in the air in Libra: Libra days often give rise to the question, "Do you know what sign is ruling today?" – even among people whose instinct for the twelve lunar impulses is well-developed. The Libra energy is so neutral and balancing and often light as a feather, that it literally doesn't give any 'clear sign' of itself. Its colour is orange.

The day quality is bright-airy, and yet it is easier for inflammation of the bladder or kidneys to occur on these days, since even a damp pair of swimming trunks can put a strain on the region of the kidneys and pelvis. So you should take especial care to keep this part of the body properly warmed.

A good preventive measure is to have a lot to drink between 3 and 7 p.m., in order to give the kidneys and bladder a good rinse through. During these hours you should collect *white dead-nettles*, the flowers of which can be made into an excellent tea for the bladder. Exercises specifically for the pelvic region are also particularly beneficial at this time.

Kidney Problems

The mental invitation for kidney problems: "I'm really, really disappointed. I was planning to do so many things, but now I've failed. What will people say? I'm so ashamed."

For some people failures are the salt of life. Successes for them are merely the (almost superfluous) confirmation of a capacity; missing the mark on the other hand is a welcome chance to recognise what is actually missing – a chance to learn and develop: "Aha: so it doesn't work like that. Let's try something else."

What you can do: In cases of acute nephritis a bloodletting on the 6th day after the new moon would be very helpful. (NB: pay close attention to the method of counting! See page 108.) If you tend to have problems with your kidneys, bear in mind that tomatoes can cause kidney stones to form. Do not drink any more milk after 7 p.m. as this puts a strain on the kidneys and often triggers off troubled dreams. The 10th thoracic vertebra influences the kidneys: if it is displaced, it can also have an adverse effect on renal activity.

Inflammation of the Bladder

The mental invitation for inflammation of the bladder: "I won't allow anyone to take my convictions from me. Who is to say that I'll fare any better with new ideas? Who can guarantee me that? – I'm sick to death of all this new-fangled junk."

No assurance, no guarantee, no promise, no security will ever protect you from the truth: that things which yesterday were valid and well-tried may well be – and often are – useless and void today. Change does not care at all how long it takes you to come to terms with life's ups and downs – or whether indeed you succeed at all. And fortunately so; otherwise there would be no birth and no death, both of them liberating and enlivening events.

What you can do: Taking a lot of water or bland drinks, beyond the needs of thirst, has in the truest sense flushed away many a bladder inflammation. Of course a herbal tea specifically for bladder complaints would be even more effective. Gather the herbs for such a tea (for instance the flowers of *white dead-nettles*) between 3 and 5 p.m., and also drink it during these two hours. This is also the right time to drink herbal teas for the bladder which have been obtained from pharmacies.

A displaced 3rd vertebra is sometimes responsible for recurrent inflammation of the bladder. Consult a chiropractor.

Hip Problems

The mental invitation for hip joint problems: "Whenever important decisions are on the agenda, I like to let others take control. – I think I simply lack the stability to see it all through. – Whenever I come up against resistance or 'crosswind' I very easily lose my balance."

The stance I take in life, and the way I move forwards, how well-balanced I am, and how easily I am able to push the unexpected out of the way – none of that is ever dependent on external influences. One person gets a rude gesture from someone while he's driving in heavy traffic, and out of this his false pride fabricates a welcome excuse to demand his "right as an individual to live his own life" in a colourful courtroom scene. Another loses all his possessions in a fire and thinks and feels, after the first shock has passed, "Oh well, back to square one – that's the best way to stay alive and young."

What you can do: There are numerous ways in which to strengthen a hip joint that is under stress – exercises, regular setting by a chiropractor, sport, and much more. Anyone who is interested will take advantage of these possibilities.

If for a variety of reasons a hip operation is unavoidable, steer well clear of Virgo, Libra and Scorpio days, and choose a date when the moon is on the wane. Numerous teams of surgeons have discovered that hip operations – which often have to be carried out on each hip with an interval of several weeks – show varying degrees of success, and that on one side the healing process for the hip takes much longer, or even has to be reckoned a failure. In most cases the reason for this is to be sought in the wrong choice of date.

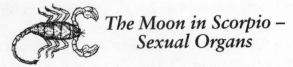

The Moon in Scorpio – Sexual Organs

No zodiac sign has as strong an effect as Scorpio on the sexual organs and urinary tract.

- Anything that you do in the two to three Scorpio days for the region of the sexual organs has a doubly beneficial preventive and healing effect. With the exception of surgical operations carried out in this area.

- Anything that puts a heavier burden on the sexual organs and ureter in the Scorpio days has a more harmful effect than on other days.

• If you are able to fix the date yourself for surgical operations on sexual organs, you should avoid Scorpio days and the period from October 23 to November 22, and choose the time of the waning moon for the operation.

What's in the air in Scorpio: The day-quality is especially moist-cool in Scorpio and not easy to cope with. Its colour is red. Mental and emotional energies tend to go deeper, awaken strange premonitions and guide feelings into hitherto concealed directions. Many people experience this force as something threatening and uncontrollable.

Expectant mothers should steer clear of all exertion during Scorpio, because it is easier for miscarriages to occur during these days, particularly when the moon is waxing.

The ureter, too, is especially sensitive during Scorpio and repays positive influences. Cold feet and failure to keep the region of the pelvis and kidneys warm can easily lead to inflammations of the bladder and kidney. Anyone who suffers from rheumatism ought not to air bedding (duvets, etc.) outside on the window ledge or balcony: moisture will remain in the feathers.

As a precaution, hip baths using *yarrow* can be of assistance at this time in a great many female disorders. It is an interesting fact that *all* medicinal herbs gathered during Scorpio are especially effective, regardless of their purpose. Gather them when the moon is waxing or full, store them (in bags, jars, etc.) when the moon is waning, and keep them in the dark. That will make them last much longer.

Infertility

The mental invitation for infertility: "I'd love to have a child, but... – Children would be too much of a responsibility for me. – I'm afraid of losing my freedom. – I'm scared of the liveliness of children: they'd turn everything upside down, all my well-worn habits. – How can one bring children into a world like this?"

Particularly in the first months of life but later as well, children are frightening creatures: in everything that they do, but especially in the way they look at us, they remind us. They remind us of all the things we have forgotten or repressed. They remind us of the things in life that really count. With one short glance they can destroy all the artificiality and falsity we have built up. You needn't worry: if the merciless determination is there to browbeat the child into believing what *you* hold to be right, it will gradually learn to bear the pain of giving up living in the truth. Then everything will be as it was. Unless perhaps you are determined not to take away the child's own instinct, and want to smooth the path for it to inner freedom. In which case having children is the elixir of life, a fountain of (almost) eternal youth.

What you can do: Among the main reasons for infertility and impotence is sleeping or working in an unfavourable place – a zone of disturbance (for remedial action see page 327). Sometimes it may be injuries and displaced vertebrae putting pressure on particular nerves (mainly the 3rd lumbar vertebra – perhaps due to sporting accidents or falling from a bike or a tree). In most cases a good chiropractor can quickly remove the problem. Here, too, there is a herb that can do the trick: *crane's bill*, prepared as a tea, is ideally suited for this. They say that the stork brings children: perhaps this is the basis of this wise old saying of all-too timid parents.

Impotence

The mental invitation for impotence: "I'm confident that parents, peers, magazines, television, films, women, church etc. have been telling me the truth about male sexuality. I acknowledge these laws and rules, particularly those in which meters, tape measures and stopwatches play a role. And I realise that I shall never be able to satisfy these standards 'How? How often? How long? When? Where? The demands are too high, the pressure is unendurable. I'll never be good enough."

Particularly in our big cities today, the picture that is being painted for young people trying to discover their sexuality is a picture of complete insanity, a caricature, a guaranteed way to a sex life of tension, anxiety and the compulsion to achieve – basically not a hair's breadth different from that of a hundred years ago. Morality, the compulsion to achieve and false 'freedom' push their way into sex lives with all the force of a steamroller, crushing everything natural, beautiful and in the truest sense of the word liberating, and effectively sealing off this source of joy and health. Hundreds of 'sex education' books leap into the fray, haggling with equal crudeness over formulae for happiness that have lost sight of the most important point: that in the domain of sexuality there can never be, nor should there ever be, any universally valid formulae. With one exception: every man and every woman has the right to experience sexuality, without any law, without norms and rules – as long as whatever happens is mutual.

If your picture, too, has departed from nature, then it is our whole-hearted wish for you that you will summon up the courage to exercise this right. That you and your partner will discover and live your sexuality in such a way that not a shred of expectation, pressure and law is able to upset the mutuality and genuine communion. If it's three times a day – good! If it's three times a year – that's fine! How long, how often, when, where, why – absolutely unimportant!

And if the pressure and expectation emanate from your partner, then you should silently ask yourself the question: "Where has love gone?" Without love there is no life – that much is certain.

What you can do: All the possible reasons that we have already mentioned in connection with infertility can also occur as causes of impotence. The same remedial measures are also valid here. One frequent trigger of male impotence and infertility, however, is the widespread conviction that after a certain age it is 'normal' if nothing happens in bed any more. That is absolute rubbish. It is only this conviction, not nature, that renders one impotent. And perhaps ignorance of the following information.

Why do you think it is that the testicles are located outside the body? It's quite simple: the normal body temperature of nearly 37°C is enough to condemn semen to infertility. The relatively cooler temperature of the testicles, as nature intended, keeps the semen fertile. Too high a temperature – caused perhaps by tight trousers and underpants, or perhaps something else – is fatal for the semen and fertility. The Chinese, the Arabs and many other peoples knew, and still know better than that: even today they still don't wear anything 'underneath'. In any case underpants are an invention of our century.

For this reason there is a very simple remedy that has helped countless men for whom deficient potency had led to self-doubt or even to 'retirement' from sexuality: *cold water*. Cold showers for the whole body, or at least the pelvic region, taken prior to lovemaking or regularly morning and night have often worked wonders. In many cases they are the secret of extending potency into advanced age – rather than any special little remedies or diets or inclinations.

Formerly men were recommended by interested parties and often for good reason to take cold showers and go for a run round the block in case they succumbed to an onslaught of erotic feeling. Doubtless this was sensible advice. However, you have just become acquainted with a sometimes desirable side effect of this: cold showers, especially in the area of the pelvis *increase* potency and fertility.

Menstruation Problems
The mental invitation for menstrual problems: "Somehow I find it hard to cope with being a woman – I feel uncomfortable about my

sexuality. The best thing would be just to ignore it. – Beautiful memories? I'm afraid I can't oblige. – Besides Dr XYZ wrote/said that one should... – I'm ashamed."

Being a woman in the present day and age is no easy matter since the natural, instinctive understanding of what that means has been swamped in a torrent of smart-alec books, articles and television programmes and talk-shows (the same applies to being a man). Almost all modern criteria concerning the differences between the sexes are artificial and far-fetched, far-removed from anything in nature, from any common sense – regardless who it is that cobbles these criteria together, whether psychologists, the church, politics, the media, etc. Such criteria bring about one thing only: discontented, unhappy women and discontented, unhappy men – ideal customers in our consumer society. So who could ever be interested in these criteria?

Have the courage to love yourself. Have the courage to act as you really feel – to act, if need be, against everything that the whole world is trying to persuade you to do. On every street corner or maybe even under your own roof, you will find false friends, both female and male, whose 'advice' is merely an attempt to sell you their own fear, their own view of the world. True friends will always encourage you to follow your own instinct.

What you can do: A tea made from *lady's mantle*, picked and drunk during Scorpio days, is not only a curative but also a preventive remedy. All antispasmodic infusions for menstrual complaints should particularly be drunk in Scorpio, and if possible picked then, too. In the case of missed periods, mud baths and increasingly warm hip baths or foot baths with herbs added are sometimes helpful. For herbs and herbal mixtures for menstrual complaints, see page 222.

 ## The Moon in Sagittarius – Thighs

The **Sagittarius days** affect the extended vertebrae (sacrum and coccyx) and the thighs.

- Anything that you do in the two to three Sagittarius days for the region of the thighs has a doubly beneficial preventive and healing effect. With the exception of surgical operations carried out in this area.

- Anything that puts a heavier burden on the thighs in the Sagittarius days has a more harmful effect than on other days.

- If you are able to fix the date yourself for surgical operations on the thighs, you should avoid Sagittarius days and the period from November 22 to December 21, and choose the time of the waning moon for the operation.

What's in the air in Sagittarius: The energy of Sagittarius makes one generous and prompts to far-reaching and sometimes thoughtless steps. Its colour is orange in the upper thigh and yellow in the lower thigh. The day-quality is dry-warm; sometimes these are fine, thirsty-making days, suitable for outings. However there are certain limitations: precisely on Sagittarius days the sciatic nerves and veins and the thighs make themselves felt with especial frequency. On top of that there are often pains in the small of the back down to the thighs, because during Sagittarius, as in Gemini, the weather can easily switch. So one shouldn't overdo it during Sagittarius and go on long hikes without training. Anyone who picks on Sagittarius to take the kids on their first major mountain walk, or perhaps even forces them into it, could very well put them off for a long time to come.

At this time massages are particularly beneficial and loosen up the muscles. Stiff thigh muscles, and deep-seated contusions can be quickly cured with a poultice of Swedish herbs (see page 149).

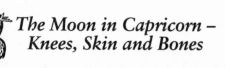

The Moon in Capricorn – Knees, Skin and Bones

The force of the Capricorn days influences the skeleton, particularly the knees, as well as our 'gateway to the world', the skin.

- **Anything that you do in the two to three Capricorn days for the knees, the skin and the skeleton has a doubly beneficial preventive and healing effect. With the exception of surgical operations carried out in these areas.**

- **Anything that puts a heavier burden on the skeleton, knees and skin in the Capricorn days has a more harmful effect than on other days.**

- **If you are able to fix the date yourself for surgical operations on bones (especially the knees) and the skin, you should avoid Capricorn days and the period from December 21 to January 20, and choose the time of the waning moon for the operation.**

What's in the air in Capricorn: The day-quality is earthy-cool, the colour is green, and the energy of these days prompts to persistent, serious, clear-headed work. Even on warm summer days the heat is often not felt to be unpleasant, and in the shade one cools off more rapidly.

A heavy strain on the skeleton in general and the knees in particular can have an especially noticeable effect during Capricorn days. With every movement heavy demands are put on the knees.

Anyone who has to climb a lot of stairs at this time will certainly long for evening to come. Just as in Sagittarius, you should not undertake any major mountain tours or the like, if you are a beginner or out of training. In particular sportsmen with a weakened meniscus should under no circumstances overdo it at this time. On the other hand, putting poultices on or rubbing ointments into the knee can have a particularly favourable effect during these two or three days. One can also do some good for other bones and joints at this time – for instance gentle stretching exercises, which should always be a part of any daily exercise routine.

A bloodletting on the 23rd day after new moon (NB: pay close attention to the method of counting! See page 108) has an especially favourable effect on the skeleton and is suitable as an accompanying therapeutic treatment with every form of bone and joint illness, such as rheumatism, multiple sclerosis, arthritis, etc.

In addition Capricorn days are suited to every type of skin care and to the specific treatment of skin diseases. Numerous inner disorders and imbalances are reflected first of all in the condition of the skin. This subject is so diverse and important that we discuss it in more detail on page 112.

Complaints of the Spinal Column
What you can do: Problems with the spinal column – from the base of the skull to the arch of the foot – are experienced by nearly 90 percent of schoolchildren. Why is that so? Ask the creators of our education system, who cram children during the most important years of their physical development and for inhumanly long periods of time into instruments of torture (i.e. unhealthy chairs and desks) – until eventually their spinal columns become accustomed to distortion and curvature. Perhaps because the ill-effects do not make themselves felt until later, the school can gaily wash its hands of the affair and dodge responsibility.

We also discuss the very important subject of complaints of the spinal column in somewhat greater detail on page 133.

The Moon in Aquarius – Lower Leg

The energy of the Aquarius days affects the lower leg and the ankle joint; it is a force that is particularly noticeable for people who have to spend a lot of time standing up.

• **Anything that you do in the two to three Aquarius days for the region of the lower leg has a doubly beneficial preventive and healing effect. With the exception of surgical operations carried out in this area.**

• **Anything that puts a heavier burden on the lower leg in the Aquarius days has a more harmful effect than on other days.**

• **If you are able to fix the date yourself for surgical operations on the lower leg, you should avoid Aquarius days and the period from January 20 to 18 February, and choose the time of the waning moon for the operation.**

What's in the air in Aquarius: The day-quality of Aquarius is airy-light, the mind moves a little erratically. Intuitive notions are heeded more often, impediments are not tolerated, even if only imaginary ones. The colour is light-blue, dark-blue on the ankles.

Inflammations of the veins are not a rare occurrence on Aquarius days. Time permitting you should lie down with your feet kept high and treat them to a salve (**comfrey**, etc.) gently rubbed in. Whoever tends to suffer varicose veins should avoid standing in one place for too long. On Aquarius days a prolonged shopping tour can spoil all fun.

Perhaps you know by now that your own saliva is a very special fluid. It works well not only for exhausted eyes but also for your legs: to get the energy flow going rub some of it into the back of the knees and softly massage in an upwards motion.

Varicose Veins

The mental invitation for varicose veins: "I don't feel at all at ease in my present position. – It's really all too much for me, but I lack the courage to make a move and change the situation."

The pain of having to stand still in a constricting and stalled situation often feels trivial compared to the fear of actually starting into motion, and making a fundamental change to the situation. What is more, the distressing situation is very often a socially acceptable, 'normal' one that many people round about have learned to tolerate. How can one acquire the courage to take that step into freedom in the face of so much 'good advice' from outside? Only through realising that you have to lead your own life, and that there's no one in the world for whom it's worth transforming yourself into a submissive slave. Helping and serving, though, are another matter: serving is the very stuff of all our lives, whether we're conscious of it or not. But *who* it is that you serve remains your free decision.

What you can do: Varicose veins are a sign of insufficient circulatory activity, usually accompanied by constipation. Standing for a long time, unbalanced physical exertion, and weak connective tissue are often contributory causes. A displaced 5th lumbar vertebra, can bring about disorders in the blood flow, cold feet, weak ankle joints and cramp in the calves.

The date for varicose vein operations should always lie in the waning moon. Avoid Capricorn, Aquarius and Pisces, but above all avoid Aquarius! Someone who has an operation on his varicose veins in Aquarius with the moon waxing might as well stay in bed and watch them grow back again. If a favourable date is chosen they will not come back, and the scar formation will also be very slight. Apply soothing ointments to the knee and rub them in carefully. Embrocations are more effective when the moon is waxing because the skin absorbs the ointment better.

In the case of phlebitis, cupping glasses should not be used, because there is a danger of blocked blood vessels (embolism). You are bound to have heard and read this a thousand times before: one of the most effective precautions against varicose veins is *movement*.

Cramp in the Calf

What you can do: A common cause of cramp in the calf at night is magnesium deficiency, which can be rectified with an appropriate diet or with magnesium tablets. A first aid remedy that is often effective is to stretch one's heels out and bend the toes upwards. *Common clubmoss* generally has a relaxing effect. For pregnant women with frequent night-time attacks of cramp it can be very useful when sewn into a pillow at the foot of the bed. Sometimes, too, locked toes or bones in the metatarsus are involved: in such cases a chiropractor can put things right.

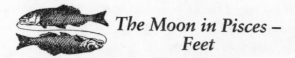 ## The Moon in Pisces – Feet

Pisces marks the end of the Moon's cycle through the zodiac, after which a new cycle begins. Aries began it with a force influencing the head; Pisces ends it with the feet.

• **Anything that you do in the two to three Pisces days for the region of the feet has a doubly beneficial preventive and healing** effect, in particular a reflex-zone massage. With the exception of surgical operations carried out in this area.

● Anything that puts a heavier burden on the feet in the Pisces days has a more harmful effect than on other days.

● If you are able to fix the date yourself for surgical operations on the feet, you should avoid Pisces days and the period from February 18 to March 20, and choose the time of the waning moon for the operation.

What's in the air in Pisces: The day-quality of the Pisces days is moist-cool; the colour is a bluish-white. Pisces forces sometimes cause the outlines of things to become blurred, and it is easier to take a look behind the backdrop of harsh reality. Many a firmly held point of view has loosened up during Pisces. Anyone planning an excursion during these days had better not forget his raincoat or sit down on the ground. At this time the earth hardly dries at all.

Admittedly the Pisces days only affect a relatively small area of the body, namely the feet and the toes, but in the truest sense of the word this area really is 'something else'. Everything that you allow into your body during these days has a much stronger effect than at other times – nicotine, alcohol, food, medicine, etc. A booze-up in Pisces at which the guests consume their normal quota, may well turn into a memorable event, when measured in terms of puffy eyes and thick heads the following day.

The reason for this effect is not known for certain. Perhaps it is because the feet contain the endpoints of all the body's meridians, and that a preventive, alleviative or curative reaction may be prompted in practically every organ in the body via the stimulation of certain points on the feet. The technique in question is known as reflexology; if you seek out an expert in this field you will be doing yourself a real favour. On page 150 we shall look into this in more detail. In any event Pisces days are ideally suited for it.

During Pisces days warts can be treated with considerable success. (However, do *not* undertake any surgical treatment of warts at this time.) At the same time it is essential to look out for the waning moon: if the moon is waxing it can happen that after treatment you suddenly have five warts instead of three. Another point to note is that especially during Pisces anyone who suffers from rheumatism ought not to air bedding outside on the window ledge or balcony: otherwise moisture will remain in the feathers.

Corns/Hardening of the Skin

The mental invitation for corns: "I'd rather grow a thick skin than let anybody shake my convictions. – Why do I cling on to these painful experiences? Well, I don't bear grudges, but... (a thousand reasons now follow)."

No one is free of anger, pain or grief, free of vindictive thoughts, when he encounters suffering or injustice. The only question is: how do I deal with such things? Do I collect and pile up negative experiences until they overwhelm me, until I view the present, however agreeable it may be, through a pair of dark glasses? Or do I take them for what they are: experiences that show me something about *myself*, that help me to learn and grow, and to which I can say good-bye without any remorseful or vengeful feelings, in order to be open and receptive to the new day? The choice is ours.

What you can do: Corns are often a sign of disturbed areas or an infected tooth. Someone who is knowledgeable about reflex zones in the feet will be able to tell from the horny hardenings on the soles of the feet, which particular organ is under stress.

Apply corn plasters when the moon is on the wane in the sign of Aquarius, and take them off after the next Pisces days (4 to 5 days later). As a precaution against corns and feet complaints, you should never wear new shoes for the first time in Capricorn or Aquarius.

Verrucas

The mental invitation for Verrucas: "Everything is stuck in a rut! No matter which way I turn there are no other possibilities in sight that might promise me a better future."

Not knowing which way to go is almost always a sign that one has not digested certain experiences and lessons in the past. Seen in this light the question is at bottom not "Where shall I go?", but "What avenues of escape are open to me? What way will allow me to carry on sleeping?" If I stop running away from myself, look my own reality straight in the face, and calmly accept what I see, then usually an alternative for the future will open up of its own accord, without any need for brooding and pondering.

What you can do: Using *garlic* during the waning moon, these particularly painful warts on the soles of the feet can be removed quite easily. In the evening cut a hole in a plaster and stick it over the verruca so that the latter remains uncovered. Cut a fresh clove of garlic in half, fix it with another plaster over the wart and wear this through the night. In the morning, if possible after taking a shower, remove the plaster, and each evening repeat the process with a new clove of garlic; stop when *new moon* arrives. Gradually the verruca will go dark, and eventually it will be a simple matter to remove it.

This completes the cycle of influences governed by the lunar rhythms. Anyone who looks into it and gradually perceives it within himself – even without using a calendar – will no longer constantly have to be on his guard. It is possible in the course of a month deliberately to give the body what it needs – from head to toe – and to pay particular attention to the regions of the body that are being influenced at any given moment. An easy exercise in harmony with the lunar rhythm: Aries – don't put your head under so much stress;

Taurus – on cool days don't go out without a scarf, and don't have any operations on your wisdom teeth; – and so on until you come to Pisces, the best time for foot baths and reflex-zone massages.

A few words about the implementation of the science of lunar rhythms in your everyday life: time and again we meet people who have made anxiety the be-all and end-all of their lives – who after reading this book no longer dare to go out in Leo, for example, for fear of over-loading their heart or circulation. People who say: "Yet another set of instructions *I have to* follow in order to stay on my feet!" Anyone who thinks like that has not understood us. Of course we cannot prevent anyone from treating this knowledge in such a fanatical manner. However, that is no reason for us not to publish it – as has sometimes been suggested to us. It would never occur to anyone to forbid salt because it can kill a human being when taken in large quantities. No one bans bread knives because they can be used for other, less innocent purposes.

We have confidence in your courage to take responsibility for yourself and your ability to make use of this book in such a way that it will become what it can be: an aid to being healthy by your own efforts.

At the close of this journey through the body let us mention a man for whom zest for life was not a distant goal but his very nature, who treated every day as if it was his first and last, and who once said: "When my pipe stops smoking, I'll be dead in three days" – which is what actually happened after 89 years. He was the grandfather of the authoress. We owe him a great deal. You will find a picture of him on page 336.

3. In Greater Depth

In the pages that follow we should like to acquaint you with a wealth of further experience and rules for a healthy life through your own efforts. They would either have burst out of the framework of one of the many chapters and sections in the book, or else they deal with a subject that deserves a heading of its own. This material, too, is based on long-standing observation and experience, as well as on traditional and tested knowledge that has shown itself in day-to-day practice to be as valid as ever.

Gain through Loss: Bloodletting

That blood is a very special fluid is something that was known long before medical encyclopaedias first described its qualities. It fulfils a wonderful variety of life-supporting functions – from the transport of oxygen and nutrients, through the transmission of information by means of hormones, to detoxification. Perhaps this variety is one of the reasons why flowing blood, whether on the grazed knee of a child or in a horror film sometimes sends a shiver down our spines, why nowadays we have almost too much reverence for this 'very special fluid'. At all events so much respect that most mothers reach for a plaster the moment a child sustains a minor injury. In most cases this is a regrettable over-reaction, for sticking on a plaster can often hamper a form of automatic purification that a light bleeding might have effected. In fact the body knows exactly what it has to do in order to cope with such trivialities. However, we memorise our mother's fright and replicate it the next time the bread knife slips a little. Such terror is often unnecessary, for anyone who has ever been a blood donor knows how much blood the body can yield with almost no discomfort.

Correctly carried out, a bloodletting is just such a deliberate loss: using a special knife, a medical practitioner makes a small cut in the vein of a human being or an animal (in the case of humans mostly in the crook of the arm), from which blood may flow freely. After a certain length of time – depending on the quantity or colour of the blood – the bloodletting is terminated. Why is this well-tried method no longer taught as a valid therapy in any university medical faculty today?

It sometimes happens that something that has been known for thousands of years in the domain of medicine passes so completely into oblivion, that when it is rediscovered we have to invent a new word to describe it – as for example in the case of biorhythms (see page 227).

Alternatively an ancient science, a tried and tested methodology, for the most varied of reasons can fall into such disrepute, that, although its name is not lost in the darkness of time, it nonetheless comes to mean the *opposite* of what the practice actually signified and achieved – as in the case of bloodletting. "The team had to suffer a bloodletting: half of the side transferred to other clubs": that's the sort of thing we sometimes read in the papers. Bloodletting today is a concept that is almost always equated with bleeding to death, weakening and exhaustion. Nothing could be further from the truth, when we are talking about genuine bloodletting, the intentionally produced loss of a small amount of blood.

This curative treatment, which has been successfully applied for centuries, is today considered at best a curiosity of medieval quackery that shortened many people's lives. Why has there been such a change of attitude? We can only guess at the reasons for it. But certainly one of the main causes is to be found in the fact that, just as was the case with the lunar rhythms, we do not know *why* it works so well. Why is it that a few drops of blood (generally about 100 millilitres, or one fifth of the amount that is drawn off at a blood donation) can produce such a decisive effect – an effect that cannot be explained in physical or chemical terms? Of course we may have our suspicions as to the inner mechanism of this effect, but we do not wish to waste our time with speculations. Instead of that, you should answer for yourself our simple counter-question: why should we deny ourselves this valuable enrichment of our therapeutic repertoire simply because the question as to *why* it works has yet to be cleared up? That it does work is our personally guaranteed experience.

A further reason why bloodletting was abandoned probably lies in the fact that formerly it was often used as a last resort, when someone was evidently close to death. So great was the positive experience with bloodletting, that people simply knew: if blood-letting didn't help, then nothing else would. Over-zealous doctors or anxious relatives in their panic no doubt often overdid things, letting blood repeatedly, or failing to observe the principles and the timing of bloodletting, which, as we shall see, are of central importance for its effectiveness. And yet on the other hand, when it's a matter of life and death, who is going to ask if the timing is right?

Now, because people commonly have a tendency when dealing with new information to display self-interest or short-sightedness, they are more likely to fasten on the fact that many people after a last emergency bloodletting nevertheless departed this life, than on the undisputed fact that bloodletting often was and is indeed the only possible life-saving measure. A bloodletting that heals and saves a life is forgotten after a few days have passed. A bloodletting that fails to achieve the desired effect leaves a deep impression in the memory, if people are looking for a culprit, or if they are looking for proof that this 'antiquated' method is worthless after all. Someone who has lost the ability to accept his fate will always seek for culprits – and find them – simply because it makes him feel more 'comfortable'. And that is how something that has worked well for thousands of years can get a bad name.

The good news is that despite everything there are still plenty of people today (in particular numerous vets – as they will admit off the record) who know about the healing and life-saving potential of bloodletting, because they have often been able to experience how severely ill people and especially animals can regain their health after bloodletting. Indeed many animal illnesses which today are held to be incurable are regularly treated with bloodletting and in a great many cases are completely healed. Only don't tell the university prof...

A third reason for the devaluation of bloodletting is the fact that *methodology and timing are crucially important for success.* Anyone who fails to take into consideration one of the few important elements of method and timing, will transform bloodletting at best into a superfluous measure, at worst into a harmful treatment that weakens the body. Without an exact knowledge of the method, bloodletting is a lottery. That is probably the reason why originally the art of bloodletting was a secret science, which was passed exclusively from one person to another, in part orally, in part in written form. One had to ensure that it was always carried out correctly, responsibly and at the right moment – with the exception of course of emergencies, whose timing could not be chosen.

Until recently, notes on the correct procedure for bloodletting only existed in the form of old Latin texts – i.e. the language of the Church, which previously through this commitment to Latin also pursued the objective of taking official medical knowledge under its wing and, by dint of its absolute power, only granting the general public access to certain parts of it. Either the people were judged not to be mature enough, or else the knowledge was considered too dangerous – for humanity or for the continued existence of the Church.

In this book we are happy to be able to pass on for the first time to the general public the knowledge of bloodletting and its curative power. The time is ripe for this. It will form a great enrichment of our medical knowledge, because:

> *Whoever takes to heart the rules and timing of bloodletting, will thereby gain one of the most successful methods of prevention and cure, of detoxification and decontamination – one that is practical and highly effective in dealing with a great many physical and mental problems.*

In which circumstances, then, is a bloodletting the method of choice – whether as a solitary measure or as an accompaniment to a more comprehensive therapy? In which illnesses can it bring about relief and healing?

For all people over 35 and not yet 77 years old who are in good health, an expertly performed bloodletting once a year is generally an outstanding preventive and detoxifying measure. Bad blood, constantly high cholesterol levels, allergies (often a sign of blood poisoning in the broadest sense), constant fatigue and exhaustion, rheumatism, depressions, problematic mental states of all kinds, high blood pressure – all these disorders and imbalances can be favourably influenced by a bloodletting; and this is by no means a complete list.

The key word is *detoxification*. Wherever a detoxification of the blood has a preventive or curative effect, a bloodletting can prove to be a powerful and in many cases a rapidly effective help. A bloodletting is equally sensible when it is a question of decontaminating the body. You can find out the more detailed context for this on page 305.

The Practice of Bloodletting

Effective bloodletting is dependent in the highest degree on correct timing and the observation of a number of basic rules for carrying it out. Most emphatically we would urge you as a patient to observe these rules for yourself and as a doctor or medical practitioner to comply with them:

• The most important rule: the blood must flow freely from the vein! It should neither be drawn off nor hindered from flowing in any way. If the bloodletting is carried out on a vein in the crook of the arm, the arm should be bound up as it would be in the case of a normal blood donation.

• The amount of blood can be between 80 and 150 millilitres (about 3–5 fl. oz.). Sometimes a slight change in the colour of the blood can be observed: stop the bloodletting at once, regardless of the quantity that has already flowed out.

• The bloodletting should take place on an empty stomach; however, the time of day is not important.

• As a preventive measure, or for general detoxification, blood-letting should be carried out once a year at the most (preferably in spring), between the ages of 35 and 77. In cases of illness or emergency the valid age limits are 28 and 84.

• The atmosphere during a bloodletting is not without im-portance: it should be calm and relaxed. We must allow the blood to leave the body, taking with it whatever we are trying to get rid of. No pressure, no compulsion, no exaggerated expectations.

Doctors and practitioners who are experienced in bloodletting know several regions of the body where the veins are suitable for bleed-ing. In general the arm veins used for a normal blood donation are also appropriate for bloodletting. In the case of preventive blood-letting, the right arm should be used for men and the left for women.

A bloodletting in accordance with these rules sometimes has

minor side-effects. One of these is an increased sensitivity to light for two or three days afterwards. Do not expose yourself to direct sunlight at this time and wear sunglasses; do not over-exert yourself, either physically or mentally; do not eat heavy foods, and take fewer milk products and other mucus-forming foods. Stay away from unfamiliar foods for two or three days.

Correct Timing

There are good days and bad days for bloodletting and its effects. When carried out on bad days, bloodlettings have a weakening effect on the whole body. As you can see from the table below, attention to the correct moment is of central importance, because sometimes good and bad days follow directly upon one another, or alternate one with another.

In order to adhere strictly to the rule you have first to find out the day and the exact time of the *last new moon*. Both pieces of information are contained in pocket almanacs obtainable in book shops; but they can also be sought in astronomical clubs and societies, or calculated from inexpensive shareware computer programs. The calendars included in this book do not contain these times, because they vary from time-zone to time-zone. It is most important, when carrying out the calculation that follows, that you do *not* take summer-time into account, if this is currently in force. For this reason you should check the calendar you consult to see whether or not the hour and minute given for the new moon takes summer-time into account. For the purposes of counting the new moon day is calculated as follows:

If the last new moon occurred before 12 midday (1 p.m. summer-time), the new moon day counts as day 1, the following day as day 2, and so on.
Example: Thursday, 16.9.1993, new moon at 4.11 a.m. = day 1; Friday, 17.9.1993 = day 2.

If the last new moon occurred after 12 midday (1 p.m. summer-time), the new moon day counts as day 0, the following day as day 1, the day after that as day 2, and so on.
Example: Saturday, 13.11.1993, new moon at 10.35 p.m. = day 0; Sunday, 14.9.1993 = day 1.

NB: You will sometimes find that day 30 coincides with the next new moon day. If the new moon occurs before 12 midday, day 30 drops out, so to speak, and counts as day 1 again. In other words, counting always starts from the new moon.

Even if the time of the new moon is very close to 12 midday, this has no bearing on the validity of the data which follows concerning the effect of bloodletting.
Example: New moon at 11.58 a.m. = day 1; new moon at 12.02 p.m. = day 0.

When you have worked out day 1 according to this data, you can read off which days are suited to bloodletting from the table on page 110. Next to some of these days there is an indication in brackets stating the purpose for which the bloodletting is particularly appropriate.

Blood donation is not the same as bloodletting! The effect of the former on the organism is much weaker, whether for good or for ill. However, the table does explain why some blood donors feel rejuvenated for a few days after the process, whereas on another occasion they experience a prolonged weariness. We have a piece of advice for blood donor services: it would be very advantageous for the quality of donated blood to dispense with the first 50 millilitres. Incidentally this recommendation in no way contradicts the fact that autohaemotherapy can be so successfully applied to a great variety of ailments. Precisely because the first blood that is drawn off contains information about the bodily disorder like a concentrated charge, it calls forth homoeopathically the exactly appropriate reaction in the body when this same blood is fed to it (see also page 142).

Bloodletting table

Day 1	bad	
Day 2	bad	
Day 3	bad	
Day 4	very bad	
Day 5	bad	
Day 6	good	(kidney activity)
Day 7	bad	
Day 8	bad	
Day 9	bad	
Day 10	bad	
Day 11	good	(anorexia)
Day 12	good	(for the whole body)
Day 13	bad	
Day 14	bad	
Day 15	good	(anorexia)
Day 16	very bad	
Day 17	very good (count carefully)	
Day 18	good	(for the whole body)
Day 19	bad	
Day 20	bad	
Day 21	good	(for the whole body)
Day 22	very good	
Day 23	good	(for the skeleton, multiple sclerosis and rheumatism)
Day 24	good	(for the lungs, and asthma)
Day 25	good	
Day 26	good	(with high blood pressure, against fever)
Day 27	very bad	
Day 28	good	
Day 29	bad	
Day 30	bad	

Bad Days in the Course of the Year

On a number of days in the year one should in general give up the idea of bloodletting, regardless of the result of counting up the days since the last new moon. These are the so-called 'Schwendtage' (Tyrolian idiom), the 'wasting days'*, which also have a role to play in agriculture and gardening. Thus on the following days a bloodletting tends to have an unfavourable result:

Month	Day							
January	2	3	4	18				
February	3	6	8	16				
March	13	14	15	29				
April	19							
May	3	10	22	25				
June	17 (very bad)	30						
July	19	22	28					
August	1 (very bad)	17	21	22	29			
September	21	22	23	24	25	26	27	28
October	3	6	11					
November	12							

Today once more there are numerous medical practitioners, and doctors, too, who practise bloodletting. For such courageous trailblazers a knowledge of the correct timing and methodology will assuredly be a considerable enrichment. If you think that a bloodletting could be of use to you, simply ask around until you find a practitioner who uses this method. Every good doctor and medical practitioner is someone to whom one can talk. Together with him observe the handful of essential rules, and nothing can go wrong. Everyone involved can only gain from the process.

---

* The implication is that such days are good for things like weeding or clearing up, but not much else.

Skin and Hair

"It's getting under my skin" – a frequently uttered phrase and only one of many signals that confirm our instinct in these areas – that the state of our skin tells us about the state of our body, mind and emotions. Almost all internal disorders and conditions of poisoning, bad blood and circulatory disorders may become discernible on the surface of the body. As if through a window, the disorder stares out at us from the skin. To experienced eyes (such as those of an acupuncturist) there's not a pimple that does not reveal by its position which organ it is that is currently detoxifying itself in this way. If you, in common with many people nowadays, are suffering from any sort of skin problem, you should first and foremost seek out and deal with the underlying causes. Scientific explanations are not so important for the natural physician. For him the important thing is whether the damage to the skin comes from outside (for instance from parasitic creatures) or from within. Thus the basic evil must be dealt with in exactly the same way as the change in the skin itself. Detoxification cures as an accompanying treatment can pull the rug from under a great many skin disorders. (See page 146.)

Skin Disorders and Diseases

Abscess

Sometimes an abscess breaks out like a little volcano, proclaiming an emotional hurt and injury, which the patient himself is unwilling to acknowledge.

An effective way to treat an abscess is to apply *coltsfoot* leaves, ideally gathered when the moon is waxing and dried when it is on the wane. Put the leaves in an enamel saucepan, pour a little water over them, bring the mixture to the boil and let it draw. Even just steaming the leaves will do.

Now lay the leaves while they are as hot as can be borne over the abscess, and repeat the procedure as often as acceptable. The dressing should remain in place for two to three hours, or overnight if preferred. Incidentally the abscess will open more easily and heal up more quickly when the moon is waning. In order to help it to heal, you should give up vinegar in your food for the time being.

Acne

Children and young people in puberty often suffer from acne because they do not feel accepted and find it hard to cope with their newly-awakened physical sensations. No wonder, when they have the example of the adult world before them and can see how unsuccessful the latter is at handling the most natural things in the world – the body and sexuality.

To treat acne from the outside is to fail to get to the root of the problem. Take a blood-purification cure of stinging nettles, as described in the chapter on detoxification (page 146). *Walnut* leaves or *dandelion* roots are well-suited for face-washes. Leave them in cold water for about twelve hours, then strain the water off and use it either warmed up or cold to wash the face.

Allergies

Attentive self-observation is of particular importance for people suffering from allergies: which thoughts, which foods, which pollens, which materials trigger off the allergy? What did I come into contact with shortly before its outbreak? In many cases suppressed or openly expressed anger plays a part ("I'm allergic to that person!").

In general when dealing with allergies the immune system has to be strengthened. For this a blood purification and stimulation of all the poisoned organs is useful – kidneys, bladder, gall-bladder, intestine, spleen and lymphatic system. At the same time a blood-letting can help, and a reflex-zone massage most of all. Drink a lot, especially in the afternoon between 3 and 7 p.m., and abstain from animal protein (especially eggs). There's an old unwritten rule that states that children, especially boys, should not be given the white of hen's eggs till they reach the age of five.

Allergy sufferers will profit from reading the next chapter about healthy diet, for the strength of the reaction caused by an allergenic foodstuff does not stay the same from day to day. Using the moon calendar it is possible to find out quickly what kind of influence is exerted by the specific food quality of the day: whether for example an allergenic substance has a stronger effect on some days than on others.

Our clothing dyes, pesticides, metals, about three thousand different kinds of finish, and last but not least remnants of detergent produce a great many allergic reactions. Make it a rule to give each newly bought item of clothing a thorough wash before wearing it for the first time, preferably when the moon is on the wane. Washing generally comes out cleaner at this time; detergents can be almost completely rinsed away, and dirt of all kinds dissolves more easily (especially on watery days: best of all in Pisces, but also during Scorpio and Cancer days). The waxing moon causes more foam to form and larger quantities of detergent remain behind in the washed item.

Of course it is not always possible to do all the washing that builds up in the household exclusively when the moon is waning. However, the results would convince you. When the moon is on the wane we use less than half the prescribed amount of detergent, and never have any problem with the washing machine furring up. If you find any calcium deposit in the filter, simply add a little vinegar to the water.

Skin Rashes

Skin rashes and nettle rashes can be effectively treated with *walnut leaves*, *ribwort* or *camomile*.

Leave chopped up walnut leaves in cold water for a day and use the strained off liquid for bathing or compresses. With ribwort you can crush it and rub the juice into your skin; or else you can make an infusion from it, and use it for bathing or compresses. Camomile is also very good for this purpose; and in this case if you use milk instead of water you might achieve better results. However, with festering eruptions, you would be better advised to use walnut leaves rather than camomile.

Cold Sores (Herpes Simplex)
Cold sores sometimes arise as a reaction to angry feelings, together with the fear of admitting to them inwardly. Many things may act as a trigger: certain foods (colouring, preservatives), cutlery metal, the edges of used glasses, too much sun, etc. Observe yourself: what did you do, think or feel just before the outbreak of the cold sore. Often with a little detective work you can get on to the trail of the cause in your particular case.

The *rescue cream* used in Bach flower therapy can serve well, if it is applied at the first sign of the condition. Colour therapy and colour acupuncture have also proved to be of value.

Itching
This condition can arise without there being any visible change in the skin and is sometimes a sign of liver disorder, nervous exhaustion or old age. In general itching skin is a signal from the body that it wants to rid itself of burdensome material, negative thoughts or irradiation. Therefore in this case, too, the need to remove the actual underlying cause should be brought into the foreground.

All detoxifying measures are more effective in the waning phases of the moon (see page 146). Drinking a lot between 3 p.m. and 7 p.m. helps the body to detoxify. During the waxing moon apply prescribed or home-made ointments in order to make it easier for the body to absorb the substances. Bathing with very warm, nearly scalding water, to which a little cider vinegar has been added, or with an infusion of yarrow can bring about an easing of the symptoms.

Skin Fungus, Athlete's Foot, Nail Fungus
Skin fungus in all its forms finds fertile ground in the refusal to let go of outmoded ideas. It thrives on nostalgic thoughts about bygone days, on clinging to the things of yesteryear, and on the fear of change.

Salt baths and ablutions are a good and effective remedy for obstinate cases of skin fungus and athlete's foot, however, only when the moon is waning. On the other hand, embrocations with alcohol (for instance Swedish herbs – see page 149) can do good even during the waxing moon. In the case of nail fungus cut or file the nails *only on Fridays after sunset* (this applies even with healthy nails). To heal the affected area soak a swab of cotton wool in some Swedish bitter or fruit brandy and paint it on to the cuticle and the strip between the edge of the nail and the skin of the toe. However, Swedish bitter colours the moistened parts brown. It doesn't look very nice, but it works.

Neurodermatitis
The principal sufferers from neurodermatitis are children who are under pressure, especially unspoken pressure, for instance from parents who may well insist outwardly that they do not demand a lot, and yet mentally are forever demanding achievements or cherishing exaggerated expectations.

We should like to reveal to you an old and very effective remedy for this skin disorder, even if it perhaps causes you to raise your eyebrows: moisten the affected skin area with the urine of a boy who has not yet reached his second birthday. If this is not available, then the child's or your own urine will serve almost as well. This remedy is also outstandingly helpful in cases of psoriasis and shingles.

Please also read the chapter entitled "The Science of Place" (page 305) and take to heart the advice on what to do about bad places. Many people suffering from neurodermatitis sleep or work over zones of disturbance. Particularly in the case of infants and small children you should try moving the bed straight away.

Marigolds, gathered during Capricorn or when the moon is waxing and then made into an ointment when the moon is waning, are an effective remedy for neurodermatitis (apply when the moon is waxing).

Warts
A little hatred here, a little hostility there: that's the soil in which warts can grow. Warts, moles and strawberry marks should only be removed or treated when the moon is on the wane, no matter what method you are using. If the treatment has not been successfully concluded by new moon, stop it nonetheless, and don't start it up again until next full moon. If you treat warts when the moon is waxing they come back again or even get worse. Treatments or operations during the waxing moon can turn out very unfavourably.

The sap of the *greater celandine*, which grows almost everywhere, even in cities, is an extremely effective and proven remedy for warts. Begin the treatment on full moon day and spread fresh sap on the wart every day. It's enough to break off one leaf: the sap is orange-coloured and seeps out of the broken stalk. Continue the treatment until new moon, even if the wart has already disappeared before that. Watch out for your clothes: celandine stains can only be removed with great difficulty.

According to an ancient custom, you can also try using an apple cut in half, which you rub on the wart. Throw the apple away afterwards, or better still, bury it. When the apple has rotted, the wart will have disappeared, too. This is a custom that in our experience has always worked.

Even rubbing one's own spit into the wart is a good method – in the morning, on an empty stomach; but it does not work so quickly as celandine sap. (See also the treatment of verrucas on page 100)

Bedsores
Two methods from olden times that have lost none of their efficacy are eminently suitable as precautions against bedsores: place a bowl of water with a fresh egg in it under the bed. Or: use a deer hide as an underlay for your bed. The result will speak for itself.

Care of the Skin and Body
All the hints and tips in this book for achieving a healthy life through your own efforts will at the same time assist you considerably in working from within for a healthy skin and strong hair. The whole secret of caring for your body and skin consists in moderation and regularity. If on top of that you take advantage of the current state of the moon, you will manage with very simple methods.

Deep Skin Cleansing
The best time for this is while the moon is waning – particularly when minor operations are required on lumps, pimples and the like. Scars almost never arise when the moon is on the wane. There is a wide choice of cleansing methods, but if you choose herbs you have to decide which effect you want to attain: anti-inflammatory (comfrey, coltsfoot), astringent (marjoram, ribwort plantain, centaury, etc.). We shall learn more concerning the characteristics of various herbs in the next part of the book (page 205 onwards). If on the other hand substances are to be fed to the skin, for instance by means of vitamin creams or firming or moisturising creams, then the waxing phases of the moon are more suitable. If you wish to pay attention to the zodiac sign too, then you should not miss the Capricorn days. These are suitable for every kind of skin care.

Here's an outstanding method for skin cleansing and treatment: place the cleansing or curative herbs of your choice in a bowl of water, stir them a few times in a clockwise direction and leave the bowl standing for a while in the sunlight. Use this water to wash your face and skin.

It would be an easy matter for cosmetic studios to check the difference between the waning and waxing moon: operations undertaken when the moon is on the wane (except on Capricorn days) would not leave any lasting scars behind.

Rashes, blisters, pimples, dandruff and scabs disappear much faster when treated during the waning moon.

A comment on the subject of *protection from the sun*, from which you may draw your own conclusions. Everywhere that the ozone layer has been damaged the incidence of skin cancer is on the increase. The strange thing is that among professional groups who work in the open air – builders, farmers, foresters and so on – the increase of skin cancer is relatively slower. As it happens, for various reasons most of these people do *without* light-protecting sun creams. Among other things this is because one of the desirable characteristics of such creams, namely a rapid, deep tan, is of no importance for them. These creams sometimes deaden the body's and skin's instinctive sense that enough is enough.

One final postscript on the topic of skin care: a large American cosmetics firm ordered an investigation as to which professional group among women had the best skin. The results were never published, because the winners by a huge margin were *nuns*, who used *no* skin-care substances whatsoever. Of course we would not wish to hide the fact that there were also other reasons why they came first: they have a healthier diet and their skin is definitely less subject to the strains of modern city and leisure living (too much exposure to sunlight).

Hair Care
People who pay attention to correct timing when looking after their hair can save themselves a lot of problems. Special preparations for

hair growth and dandruff would be superfluous, and baldness would never arise in the first place.

Go to the hairdressers a number of times when the moon is in Leo and observe what happens (this advice is of special interest to men). On the other hand it would be better to set permanent waves during Virgo days, because the hair would go too frizzy if it were set in Leo. Anyone who has no problems with his hair should have it cut during Virgo, because the cut and style will last longer. If you are unable to pay attention to the right date, then you should at least avoid washing and cutting your hair during Pisces and Cancer days.

One effective method for a good head of hair is *burdock root*. Use the boiled extract either to wash the hair, or else diluted as a final rinse. Dig up the roots when the moon is waning, or obtain them at a pharmacy. Equally good is *birch water*: fill a dark bottle to the brim with young birch leaves (gathered in spring). Fill up with corn brandy and leave the closed bottle standing in the sun for a month, so that it receives all the twelve impulses of the zodiac. The straining and transfer of the liquid is best carried out during Aries, Leo or Virgo days. Massage your scalp with this mixture, one drop at a time. Washing your hair with a decoction of birch leaves is also helpful. A very old and even simpler recipe for beautiful hair: place the birch leaves in fresh water, leave it standing in the sun and wash your hair with it.

This whole procedure also works with *stinging nettles*. Pick the leaves when the moon is waxing, dig out the roots when the moon is on the wane. Put the unwashed leaves and the thoroughly brushed roots (easy when the moon is waning) into the bottle, or else lay them in the water.

Whether it is stinging nettles or birch leaves, whether in alcohol, boiled or simply laid in fresh water, it's always what appeals most to your own feelings that works the best.

However, with these hints we are not offering any guarantee

against falling hair, since we often lose hair as a result of the side effects of medicines, hormonal changes in the body or psychological stress. After pregnancy or during the menopause considerable hair loss can occur, but this eventually eases off. For example we have experienced that after a patient had his amalgam fillings removed he suddenly had a new growth of hair, even though he was already going bald.

Care of Toenails and Fingernails

For the care of toenails and fingernails, for cutting and filing the most suitable time is any *Friday after sunset*. If you miss this moment don't try to catch up on your nail care on the following Saturday, as this is the most unsuitable day for this purpose. If they are cut or filed exclusively on Friday nights, fingernails and toenails become hard, robust and do not break so easily. Preparations for hardening the nails then become superfluous, since they always combat the symptom and not the cause. In general Capricorn days are suited to all nail care activities (incidentally keeping to the correct timing here also takes care of the teeth). From time to time lick up the dust from (unvarnished) filed nails: this acts as a homoeopathic remedy for a large number of physical ailments.

If you can't or don't want to observe the correct timing, you should at least steer clear of unfavourable days: avoid nail care during Pisces and Gemini days.

In-growing nails should always be corrected or cut when the moon is waxing; if they are treated when the moon is on the wane they always grow back wrongly. The exception to this is the complete removal of a nail: this minor operation is more successful when carried out during the waning moon (avoiding Pisces if possible).

Forms of Therapy:
From Movement to Homoeopathy

This section is about effective and successful forms of therapy which can also profit from a knowledge of lunar rhythms. If no explicit reference is given to these rhythms, then we merely give a short description of the method just as its purpose and value have been made available to us. In this case the correct moments for the application of the therapy in question can be obtained from the *Journey through the Body* in the previous chapter.

However, we are not making any comparative judgement about the value of the therapy, for you yourself must ultimately decide on the basis of information, advice and your own instinct whether it is sensible for you personally. Whether the laying on of hands or Professor XYZ's oxygen-therapy, whether massage, chiropractic or Feldenkrais bodywork, whether penicillin or Bach flower therapy – there are countless possible forms of therapy for each different (or even one and the same) illness or disorder. Every one differs from the others more or less fundamentally in terms of materials, time required, cost, the aim of the therapy, its philosophy and many other things. Often they differ, too, in the vehemence with which the assertion is made that this is the one and only possible cure. All these differences are utterly unimportant with regard both to statistics of successful cures and to recognition by 'official' medicine. No statistics in the world are any use in an individual case – and that is always what *your* personal case is. And there are countless remedies which would be effective cures in your case, but which are not recognised by orthodox medicine.

Ultimately the decisive factor here, too, is your personal instinct. Do you have a feeling that a certain form of therapy could help you? If so, then make your choice, regardless of whether you go to the GP round the corner, to a shaman or to a world renowned clinic somewhere thousands of miles away. Nothing and no one can help if you do not have any confidence in yourself, in the person helping you, in his method and in the right moment – whether you yourself choose this moment or whether it is dictated to you by fate. Whether the work is done with a chemical bludgeon, surgical operations or gentle, long-term methods, whether you are given an injection or hundreds of miles away the healing hands of a human being rest on your photograph – all of that is unimportant if you have confidence, if your instinct tells you that is how you want it and need it, and if your body responds to the healing impulse. Also decisive to a very great extent is the *correct timing* of the measure in question: all the rules presented in this book may be transposed without difficulty on to many different therapies.

And after you have made your decision have confidence in the way things take their course and accept your fate. Whether you go to a world-famous surgeon, homoeopath, medical practitioner, or faith healer – if he is a friend of humanity he will never offer you a guarantee that his method is infallible. All such people know that ultimately a healing is not their own work; healing takes place when the self-healing power of the patient, the capacity of the helper, correct timing, and not least personal fate all join forces and merge into a whole.

So, you are looking for 'proof' that a method is effective? Perhaps because you do not trust your instinct, or because you are afraid to face your fate? The fact that a particular method has helped your neighbour is not in the slightest use to you; nor is the fact that a method is everywhere recommended as efficacious – in the press and on television, by scientists and statisticians. Not even the fact that a remedy did you some good yesterday gives you any guarantee today that it will once again remove the same problem.

We know all that and hence do not belong to those 'proof-hungry' people who want to insure themselves against all and everything before anything necessary and sensible can be done. We are trying to convey uncomplicated knowledge in simple language, and to point towards certain natural rhythms that simply happen to work and have no need of any proof. So you do not have to wait until the scientists deign to prove that lunar rhythms, homoeopathy or chiropractic 'work'. You merely try the rhythms out and sense how everything takes its course almost by itself, quite simply, without any expenditure of time and money. You put your trust in your chosen method, your powers of self-healing, and the passage of time – that's all that's needed.

The incessant demands for proof are almost an illness, an addiction, an occupational therapy. At incredible expense proof is researched, while the results have been known for thousands of years. The main thing is that research is being done. Thus in 1992 a cardinal of the Roman Catholic church announces that an investigation has been initiated into whether the celibacy of the priesthood is still a sensible institution (given that it was introduced a long time ago, and was probably intended to prevent serious seekers after truth from having like-minded descendants. People who *know* are incorruptible, and no dictatorship could – or can – ever tolerate such people). In the same year in Germany an 'official' investigation begins into the use and value of Chinese acupuncture. In both cases things are being investigated whose value or non-value has been obvious for thousands of years. And all of that merely to save face. The results of these enquiries are 'generously' imparted to us, although the damage caused by holding fast to senseless practices or ignoring sensible ones need never have arisen in the first place. Is dying easier when it happens with scientific blessing? In the never-ending search for proof what is at issue is nearly always personal pride, trophies and decorations, not the actual question. Healers for example cannot allow themselves any deaths; their failure is a failure of their method, a black mark against them. On the other hand with orthodox medicine that's all right: their failure is 'inevitable fate'. The only strange thing is that they get the dead out of the hospital *at night*…

We know healers and diviners to whom numerous orthodox medical men turn for advice – always at night! The 'face' that a person wishes at all costs to save, and the addiction to proof are both symptoms of the worst disease that has ever visited our planet – the disease of personal pride. How often it has happened in recent times that a newly developed material, a new medicine, a new amalgam filling, etc. after years of use has shown itself to be harmful. The physical damage emanating from such material is many times greater from the moment that the deleterious effect is known or even only suspected in 'initiated circles' (manufacturers and scientists). Production, distribution and application are henceforth accompanied by anxious thoughts instead of the previous confident ones. The millions of amalgam fillings which are still being put in all over the world are much more poisonous for the body *because* all dentists now know about their harmfulness. (See also page 161.) This harm need never occur if only personal pride (and the fear of claims for damages) did not get in the way of the logical conclusion: "We made a mistake: the stuff is harmful in the long term; please don't use it any more."

This example can be applied in countless other cases – from celibacy, to aerosol cans to computer and TV screens emitting radiation. Such fallibility is so human, natural and firmly anchored in our being. Without detours and blind alleys there can be no learning. Taking the long view, what pleasure can I have in something that I have mastered 'perfectly'? What is the effect of someone who makes everyone feel that he knows everything and can do everything? Sometimes the only chance of curing the disease of pride consists in losing face as completely as possible, and learning by experience that there are after all people who can accept and love someone even without that 'face'.

Go and lose your face somewhere that you'll never find it again.

Then you'll quickly discover who your real friend is. Even if 'everyone' has left you in the lurch, do not despair. If you act as you really are then you send out a friendly invitation to the world, an invitation which one or two people, who are capable of accepting you as you really are, will eventually take up. Such people do exist and they are the only ones who deserve the name of 'friend'.

Trust your instinct and have the courage to distinguish between good food and poison – physically, intellectually and emotionally – without waiting for proof. That's the only way to live a poison-free life. You will very rapidly gain the power of discrimination through education and careful observation. People who are hungry for proof on the other hand do not see the slightest reason to do anything about physical or mental poisons as long as the challenge to furnish proof has not been met. And we assure you it never will be definitively met. The future will no longer allow us the luxury of first proving and explaining what is effective and obvious before we apply it. For financial reasons, too, we cannot go on squandering millions in order to prove that curative herbs actually cure, that calmness prevents disease and that the world is round. The answer to the question "Why and how does it work?" is practical and necessary when it is practical and necessary. Often it is not.

It is a human right not to be poisoned, mentally as well as physically – a right that concerns us all. But if you want to sue for damages your best chance would be to start with yourself.

Movement Therapy

All people are born with a delight in movement. Music is in everybody's blood. Whether the present moment finds you slender, strong, in the prime of life, athletic and a gifted dancer, a pear-shaped clumsy bear, or a stiff framework of skin and bone – living or rediscovering this inborn joy is a solid foundation for staying healthy through your own efforts. The reason for this is in thousands of books; but a single sentence would suffice to explain it: *anything that does not move falls into decay.*

There are numerous influences from childhood onwards that mar the happiness of this activity, so essential for life, and literally close down parts of our body – from signs that say "No ball games" and constant admonitions to "Sit quietly!", to the school desk, to the office chair and the compulsion to achieve. To be sure the greatest obstacles later are thoughts such as: "I can't do it; I won't make it; I'm no athlete; what if someone sees me like this!" – all of which start out from the conviction that movement, dance or sporting performance must always satisfy certain standards or external forms and alien requirements. Why is that there are so many books on physical training, all of them utterly useless and uninspiring?

This is because the real meaning of movement does not consist in doing something 'correctly'. So many teachers and therapists in this field convey the message, consciously or more often unconsciously, that with movement some sort of measurable goal has to be reached. "Bring your head between your knees; lift your arm above your head; keep your legs straight; no that's not right; oh well, you'll get it right in time..." – that, more or less, is the way the nonsense goes, making us forget what healthy movement and above all physical exercises for the sick are really about.

The sole aim of movement should be joy and flowing energy. If your arms can only move so far and no further – well and good! If you can only run so far, bend over so far, jump so far, dance for so long – that's excellent! You should never take another person, let alone a sport or PE instructor or a book, as a model for what you wish to, or even have to attain. And if anyone smiles at your 'style' then that means only one thing: pride goes before a fall.

Once again the only criterion for the success of your intention is your personal instinct. When you sense how even with the slightest movements a force is gradually beginning to flow, just feel this force. Straighten and stretch yourself for a minute (maybe right now!), just as you might in the morning after getting out of bed, and *feel* what is happening. Feel how the force is flowing and what pleasure that brings and how the pleasure and energy from the smallest movement and stretching spreads out over the whole body. And then only remember the joy and force – not how far, how high, how fast. Whether this joy then spurs you on to some kind of sport – to gymnastics, dancing, chopping wood, or aikido – is completely unimportant. It is not the method that makes the force flow, but your instinct and self-confidence. You should always bear this in mind.

What counts in sport and movement is never the external form. You should never overstep your limits and above all never overstep the 'pain threshold'. Each morning stretch what can be stretched, but stop short of 'breaking point', whatever that may be. And never compare yourself with anyone in the world. You are unique from the word go.

Every day doctors express thousands of admonitions that we should move more, do more sport – physical training, swimming, table tennis, hiking, running. We don't want to repeat them, because admonitions and proof are worthless. The only thing that helps is understanding. One old and valid rule of health runs as follows:

> Once a day work up a sweat.
> Once a day feel really hungry.
> Once a day get really tired.

Unnecessary maybe, but certainly of interest to the 'proof-hungry' or simply as an anecdote: the above rule recently received confirmation in a comprehensive study of more than 5000 people in the USA, who had reached their hundredth birthday in good health. The researchers had originally made it their aim to track down the secret of these people's longevity. What common factors could be observed? Did it depend on diet, lifestyle, attitude to life, abstinence, mega-garlic-ginseng, mysterious herbal elixirs? The result astonished the scientists: apart from one thing there was *no common factor*! Some of them smoked like chimneys, some drank half a litre of red wine every day; some were vegetarians, others got up at one in the morning to polish off a mighty chunk of bacon; some had fifteen children and seventy grandchildren, others lived like monks – and so it went on. In other words there was absolutely nothing that pointed to a universally valid recipe for health and long life. There was just this one exception: all of those questioned stated that they worked up a good sweat every day – by running, chopping wood, dancing, lovemaking, or whatever.

Movement makes energy start to flow. Flowing energy loosens blockages in the body, head and heart. Loosened blockages release joy and strength. Released joy helps us to stay healthy or get healthy – throughout body, mind and soul. Stiffening is the basis of death, movement the basis of life.

Massage and Bodywork

Shortly after the first world war a young doctor was working in one of the numerous over-filled orphanages in Europe. One day it occurred to him that the infants in a certain department seemed to be much happier and livelier, looked better fed, were less often sick and were generally in a better state of health than all the other children in the same age group. The young doctor's curiosity was aroused. At first his scientifically based medical training led him to the conviction that someone was feeding the children from private stocks – in addition to the daily diet of the orphanage.

However, after some time he discovered that this was not the reason for the children's superior condition. Their diet was exactly the same as that of all the children of the same age. There was only one difference: in contrast to the rest of the staff, the carer in charge of this hopelessly under-staffed home took the 'extra trouble' before feeding time of lifting each child out of bed, cradling it in his arms, stroking it and hugging it, and only then giving it its bottle and putting it back in its cot. From heart to heart via the skin – a way without detours.

Sometimes movement, experienced passively through the expert hands of a masseur can serve as the first stimulus towards healthy, self-motivated movement, both inwardly and outwardly. There are few physical illnesses or symptoms of psychological deficiency that cannot be relieved or cured by means of affectionate, more or less gentle physical contact – massage, bodywork (as certain forms of therapeutic contact are called today), lymph drainage, Feldenkrais massage, Rolfing, reflex-zone massage, etc. As far as the effect of manual treatments is concerned, almost all medical practitioners are in agreement on a number of fundamental points:

Firstly: most bodily processes are dependent on the unimpeded flow of fluids through the various systems of organs, and massage and work on the body can be an effective support for these circulatory flows. Every individual cell in the body must incessantly receive nutrients, oxygen, hormones, antibodies and other immune substances; and a great many harmful substances have to be removed. There is no tissue in the body that cannot be debilitated or ultimately destroyed by any lengthy interruption of these multiple circulations. Seen in this light massage is a very good precaution against all sorts of illnesses. It has a detoxifying and stabilising effect on the heart and circulation, and stimulates the activity of all inner organs.

Secondly: both muscles and connective tissue can often harden or become shorter or else they can swell up. As a result the posture of the body alters and restricts movement. After operations or other injuries, muscles can harden to protect an injured region, and connective tissue forms a scar over a wound. Much more often than not these protective and healing processes overshoot the mark, and the patient does not regain complete mobility or the usual feeling of well-being. Neglect, cramp, injuries, exhaustion, ageing and the countless physical stresses that many professions pile up on us – all of that can lead to hardening, shortening and swelling. For thousands of years massage and bodywork has been employed to relax muscles, relieve cramp and dispel states of exhaustion. Connective tissue becomes more supple, restrictions of the joints disappear and the scope for pain-free movement increases.

Both of these main effects of massage and work on the body can profit from correct timing:

For massages that serve to relax, ease tension and detoxify the most suitable time is when the moon is waning.

If a massage is intended to have a mainly regenerating and strengthening effect, perhaps with the aid of appropriate oils, it will achieve better results when the moon is waxing.

In these two effects are shown the mechanical aspects of massage and body work and the laws that apply concerning hydraulics, the elasticity and stretching properties of tissues etc.

Thirdly: massage and body work are not really forms of therapy in the sense used in orthodox medicine, but rather a form of education in perception. Nothing material is added, nothing is taken away; neither are there exact dosages and statistics of successful results. An experienced masseur is not dealing with locally confined problems with special tools in order to achieve specific goals. Rather he is cautiously creating for the mind of the patient a stream of information transmitted through the senses – new information which contradicts the existing mental picture of immobility and pain, and shows the patient that he is able to do much more than he thought. It is the client's mind that then takes care of the 'repairs' – the correct adjustment of a bodily posture, the more effective distributions of fluids, a better relationship between nerves and muscles.

Rubbing the skin, pressure on deeper tissues, movement of tissues – this is not only the way that all forms of massage and work on the body are carried out: it is also the way that our body becomes aware of itself – through this same movement and friction. This process remains unconscious as long as we feel at ease 'in our own skin'. It is only rarely, therefore, that we recognise from the outset the possible dangers of well-worn patterns of movement and posture, least of all during childhood. Even if later a disorder or illness throws us off course we seldom suspect that long-established ways of behaving could be the cause. Massage and bodywork, applied with affection and skill, can serve as the means to break the vicious circle of inadequate habits of posture and movement, and chronic tension and immobility. Massage and bodywork, sport and chiropractic, renewed friction and pressure, unaccustomed movements – these inevitably provoke new sensations that the mind can use in order to gain a new picture of the body, from which to create a new and more mobile version of it.

However much a person moves there is a strong force inviting him to go on moving just as he has always done. However, if he surrenders to the movements that another person has shown to his body, uninfluenced by his own impulses and reactions, then he can present his body with completely new sensations – sensations that bring home to him clearly just how his behaviour has come to trigger off various ailments and pains. Such moments of new sensation demonstrate that nothing can force him to stick forever to habitual patterns of behaviour. The mind is able to recognise that it possesses the freedom to decide whether to repeat them or not. Every doctor knows that such an insight is more valuable than any medicine.

Forms of massage and bodywork will in future assuredly take the place that they deserve in the palette of valid and effective forms of therapy. We do not have the option to stand still, either physically or mentally; to cherish the conviction that we do so, if only for a short time, is an invitation to inner immobility and physical disorder. Like clay, we either keep moist and elastic or else dry out and harden. If we wish to learn how to accept the body as a source of joy and to avoid whatever causes or increases pain, then massage and bodywork can be a valuable key. They can give us information about ourselves at a depth that no instruction, prescription or operation can provide – an inestimable gain.

Chiropractic

At every point in our life we are only a tiny millimetre away from a large number of more or less serious illnesses and disorders. That millimetre is located somewhere in our skeletal structure and marks the distance between for instance a correctly positioned vertebra, surrounded by relaxed musculature, and a permanently displaced vertebra held fixed by tensed muscles which have to compensate for the resultant distortion. The millimetre is to be found in a twisted pelvis that forces the whole musculature of the back to exert compensatory pressure on the vertebrae and hence on nerve bundles. It is to be found in arch of the foot which ultimately acts in the same way on bodily posture and hence on the general state of a person's health.

Rigid bodily patterns and distortions frequently develop as a reaction to adverse circumstances – accidents, operations, illness, anxieties that express themselves in bad posture (especially among children and young people during puberty), and the stress of everyday life. A twisted pelvis, permanently displaced vertebrae, an apparent shortening of the leg and the slightest shift of bones in the arch of the foot – leading to tensed muscles and heavy pressure on nerve paths – can form disturbed areas in the back which trigger off a great many chronically painful conditions and illnesses: from muscular tension, to ringing in the ear, disorders of sight, sciatica, slipped discs, migraine, disorders of the heart, digestive and respiratory systems – and many more, mostly secondary consequences of many years of stress on muscles and nerve bundles.

It verges on cruelty, the casual way in which we treat our

vertebral columns – and especially those of our children. Almost ninety percent of children display some form of posture fault, because far too little attention is given to this problem and in particular the long-term damaging after-effects – to say nothing of teaching the correct, relaxed approach to one's own body. By nature children move differently and much more than adults; that is why a displaced vertebra with them often straightens itself out as quickly as it came in the first place (through a minor accident, etc.). However, the older they get, the stronger are the influences on them inhibiting movement, as a result of anxious thoughts or the pressure to sit still in the daily routine of growing up.

And so as adults we come to terms with the lack of movement mentioned above, with a shortened leg and a bad posture, combating pains – important indicators of underlying causes – at first with pills and injections, until severer pains or in the worst case serious damage to the vertebral column, inter vertebral discs or internal organs finally brings us to our senses.

Our mind, too, our thoughts and attitude to life can literally force the spinal column to its knees. – Thoughts such as "My shoulders are not equal to the task: this problem is really weighing me down." or "I'm forever having to fit in with other people's wishes. I'm afraid: I twist and turn in every direction, and try to do justice to everyone." Expert eyes are able to read a person's entire attitude to life from his bodily posture. Is something weighing heavily on his mind, does he make heavy weather of everything, or does he travel light, because there's nothing worth taking seriously except the ripening of his soul? For almost every state of bodily rigidity there is a counterpart in our mental world that matches the physical mass and immobility. A rigid mind leads to a rigid body.

The merry trade in cramped muscles and locked vertebrae and joints could be largely brought to a halt, if – in addition to massage and bodywork – the art of chiropractic were also to receive the attention it deserves. An experienced chiropractor is like an architect, who knows the 'human building' inside out. He knows exactly how bones and muscles interact in order to achieve a minimum expenditure of energy and a maximum of strength *and* mobility. Unfortunately he is often only sought out when the pain – always the signal of a blocked flow of energy in the body – is already there, or even when the damage is already very advanced. Even in such a case his methods – a series of specific grips and movements – often prove to be a real blessing for his patient in straightening out displaced vertebrae and adjusting shortened legs.

We could wish that people didn't think for the first time of going to the chiropractor when the impairment to posture announced itself via pains or disorders of the organs, but rather that such a course of action should come to be seen as a worthwhile precautionary measure, even if the individual does a lot of vigorous movement and has no reason to complain about the consequences of a minor fault in his posture.

It takes long time for a fault in posture to become noticeable and to penetrate into our consciousness. It takes a little time for a displaced vertebra to settle down again in its natural position. That is why we recommend that you should go regularly once a year to a chiropractor or a doctor with training in chiropractic – and take your children with you. If he finds nothing wrong with your posture consider yourself lucky and go back to him the next year.

If he does discover something wrong he will first of all make sure that your muscles are warmed up (warm rooms, fango packs, etc.) then by means of skilful grips he will cause your skeleton to crack and creak, straightening bones and vertebrae from head to toe and removing any lopsidedness of the pelvis. Just what a blessing this is, for your particular complaint or for your general state of health, is something you will probably soon find out, usually only minutes or hours afterwards.

However, there now comes a decisive period. The muscles which have become accustomed to imbalance over the years have partially hardened, lengthened or lost their natural tone. They will try very hard to restore the old condition, the old faulty posture, the old pressure on the nerves. Thus sometimes it only takes a few days or even hours for the body to 'forget' the treatment given by the chiropractor. You should therefore back up the treatment with massages, warming, exercises, with focused training of those muscles that have come to forget the architecture of a healthy body. A good chiropractor will stand ready with advice and practical support, as you try to jog your muscles' memory.

Capricorn days are definitely the most favourable times for a visit to the chiropractor; but the time of the treatment is even more important if you have reason to believe that a particular bodily disorder is connected with displaced vertebrae. Then the rule that you already know applies:

Anything that you do for the well-being of those organs and regions of the body that are governed by the sign through which the moon is currently passing is doubly useful and has a doubly beneficial effect. For example: in cases of frequent migraine a chiropractic treatment during Aries is favourable.

Colour Therapy

Without light there is no life. And that means without colour there can be no life, for light consists of colours, as is testified by every rainbow – those countless drops of water that split light up into its colours. Harmonious colours have an effect on us similar to that of harmonious sounds and music. Colours and combinations of colours can enliven and inspire us, make us breathe more freely, spur us on, heal us – but they can also worry and depress us, and make us ill. Anyone who uses violet or black bed linen will have experienced what we are talking about.

"Even a cup of tea will force an answer from you if you drink it." – Thus runs an old and enigmatic proverb from Afghanistan. Its meaning will perhaps become clearer if we adapt it: "Even an ugly picture on the wall has an effect on us if we glimpse it out of the corner of our eye as we walk past." Light and colour make us live, light and colour can poison us, light and colour can heal us.

Look around and observe for yourself: how often in everyday life does the colour of something transform itself into the basis of a decision or a feeling? How often do we eat not the rice but the yellow of the curry, not the lettuce, but its green colour? How often is it the clothing of those we are with, the colour of food, cars and so forth that determines our behaviour? How often in the morning do we choose a piece of clothing according to its colour? Skilled advertising strategists know exactly what influences us, and they package the most poisonous stuff in mild green. And we help ourselves to it...

Observe and watch. For the brief information that follows is only a first stimulus. You will gradually develop your own instinct for what colours 'say' to you, what effect they have and which of their effects you want and need at this precise moment – whether in your clothing, the paint on your wall, a colour for meditation, in your food, and so on.

When we talk of the colours of the signs of the zodiac, we do not mean your birth-sign, but colours of the sign of the zodiac which is indicated by the position of the moon. Armed with this information you will be able to try out how you feel when you wear the colour of the current sign of the zodiac in some piece of clothing (for example yellow in the two or three Libra, Scorpio or Sagittarius days).

Red

Red is the colour of the pelvic region and the moon in the sign of Libra, Scorpio and also Virgo. Red influences the coccyx centre and stimulates creative, vital, earthy energies. It promotes passion and spontaneous action, and should therefore only be used with care and in measured doses. A pair of red pyjamas only makes sense if you take more pleasure in staying awake than sleeping.

In winter red socks and underwear are helpful in getting through even the coldest days.

Red activates the liver and supports the production of red corpuscles. If the red region, the zone of the pelvis is weakened, this weakens the whole body. Red, as the colour of the detoxifying and eliminating force, frees the body from constipation and is favourable in cases of iron deficiency. The level of adrenalin in the blood increases, sleepiness and lethargy become easier to overcome. It helps with colds and chronic chills. Red should not be used when inflammations are present. This colour is less suitable for people who easily become irritable.

Orange
Orange is the colour of the region of the abdomen, the lumbar vertebra (spleen) and the upper thighs, the colour of the moon in Virgo and also Libra. Orange puts one into an optimistic mood and awakens self-confidence.

It is suitable as the dominant colour in surgery waiting rooms and sick rooms. Anxious people should wear orange-coloured clothing, but not from head to foot. Too much orange can promote dependence on others. Problems of digestion and the skin and poor bowel movements are favourably affected by the colour orange, especially during the Virgo days. Orange increases the appetite and is thus helpful in cases of anorexia. The warming effect of orange relaxes and releases tension.

Yellow
Yellow is the colour of the stomach region and the lower thighs, of the moon in Libra, Scorpio and Sagittarius – the colour of intellectual, analytical powers, the colour of reason.

Yellow stimulates the digestive juices and helps with digestive disorders and constipation. It has a calming effect on the nerves and on conditions of mental and nervous exhaustion – a good colour in classrooms and studies. It can perform good service in cases of depression, particularly in clothing. Yellow functions as a sedative for the spleen, activates the lymphatic system and helps in cases of damaged liver. An over-taxed or damaged liver should be treated regularly with yellow, until confidence and the capacity for detoxification have been restored in the patient. It should never be used in cases of fever, acute inflammation, diarrhoea or palpitation.

Green

Green is the colour of the chest, heart and knees, of the moon in Cancer, Leo and Capricorn. Green has a balancing and neutralising effect. It is the colour of hope, harmony, healing and natural ripening.

Green influences the pituitary gland and thus has a regulatory function in the metabolism. It ensures an equilibrium between the liver and the spleen and has a regenerating effect on the muscles and connective tissue. It is beneficial and soothing for the eyes.

Blue

Blue is the colour of the shoulder and throat region as well as the lower leg and ankle, the colour of the moon in Taurus, Gemini, Cancer and Aquarius – the colour of creative power and deep insight, faith and devotion.

Blue can be used in cases of fever and has a generally cooling effect. It is thus also suitable for burns. It is unsuitable as a wall colour in a work environment, unless at the same time some warming colours also get a look in. Anyone who has to deal with a lot of people will be better able to deal with the negative thoughts of others if he has some blue in his clothing. Blue makes one calm and quiet and opens the mind to creative thoughts uninfluenced from without.

Indigo and Violet

Indigo and violet are the colours of the head region and the feet, of the moon in Taurus, Aries and Pisces – the colours of intuitive knowledge, deep perception and modesty.

Indigo affects the eyes, nose and ears; violet stimulates the spleen and hence the immune system. Violet also has the effect of purifying the blood and putting a brake on the desire to eat. It can have a calming effect on people who are active artistically, since it mutes the nervous system.

White

White is not really a colour, since it unites all the colours within itself. A person wearing white opens himself to all the forces in the surroundings. White walls have a neutral, unifying, calming effect. Sunlight is white because it contains all the colours: a short sun-bathing session every day, about ten minutes long, gives the body the possibility to regenerate itself and to collect from the spectrum all the vibrations that it currently needs.

Someone who uses white bedding and bedclothes during an illness will find it easier to pick up the healing vibrations and colours that he needs in order to recover. For this reason white is very suitable as a colour for walls and bed linen in hospitals, possibly in conjunction with beautiful pictures that promote an optimistic frame of mind. The walls in hospitals nowadays may be modern, however, the effect is left somewhat to chance if the colour scheme is not selected by practised eyes.

Black

Black is not a colour. Black swallows up colours and vibrations. Probably one of the main reasons for black as a colour of mourning lies in the fact that it shields the wearer from the thoughts and vibrations from the surroundings, and thus avoids weakening him further. Many young people nowadays wear black or dark grey: in so doing they are sending out the message: "I need inner stillness" or "Leave me in peace: the pressure is too great".

Perhaps these brief notes will clarify why *colour therapy* and *colour acupuncture* still number among the diversity of methods employed by numerous doctors and medical practitioners today. The age-old empirical science of acupuncture is based on the fact that our skin functions like an amplifier which passes on to the inside all the information it receives. Numerous precisely determined points and zones on the skin act like gateways to particular circulations of energy, organs and regions of the body. Their stimulation, for instance by means of massage, pressure, needles, electric current or simply radiation with specific colours has a favourable effect on the organ in question.

Colour therapy – using light rays which pass through coloured film, or coloured lamps (red light) – has proved its worth particularly in painful conditions of all kinds. It is used successfully with bone and joint pains, to speed up the healing of broken bones, damage to cartilage, follow-up treatment of operation wounds and transplants, with burns and ulcerated legs. (NB: ulcerated legs should only be treated when the moon is waning.) With almost all skin diseases, from cold-sores through eczema to allergic reactions, it can have a soothing and healing effect. Colour acupuncture has shown itself to be particularly successful with headaches and migraines. The advantage it has over classical acupuncture is that there is no damage to the skin and no danger of infection.

Incidentally, those who meditate with colours in order to heal should always keep the colours of the upper half of the body before their inner eye, even if the disorder is located in the lower half: for example the blue of the shoulder region when remedying a disorder in the lower legs. When the colour of the upper half comes into equilibrium that automatically affects the lower half of the body. Never concentrate on only one colour, but always go through all colours of the body.

Healing Like with Like:
Homoeopathy and Bach Flower Therapy

"**What did** I do to deserve that? Why is *always me*? Why am I always taken for a ride by false friends? Why do I always put my foot in it? Why do I always get to know the wrong people? Why am I always being exploited?"

These are questions that we often ask ourselves when fate delivers us a stroke of bad luck, perhaps in the form of an accident, a severe illness or a loss. You are not likely to believe this straight away, but the answer to all these questions is the same as the answer to the question: "How does homoeopathy work? What happens in my body, if I use Bach flower therapy?"

Homoeopathy, like Bach flower therapy, is extremely ancient; these therapies have not merely existed since their rediscovery by the people whose names are linked with them. The fact that "like can be removed with like" is something that many people know who have yet to hear the word homoeopathy.

Using the filings from one's own fingernails as a curative remedy or tonic, rubbing one's own spittle into the eyelids, the hollow of the knee or minor wounds, applying one's own urine to rashes or drinking it, burning or scalding minor burns a second time to produce instant healing without either blisters or scars – these and many other things have been successfully used and practised for centuries.

Likewise the therapy with flowers for particular illnesses or as a general tonic has been known for a very long time: the Navajo Indians of North America used to bend the heads of flowers into a bowl of water (without breaking the plants), expose them to the sun for a short while and then drink the water, with the same intention and effect that we know today.

Perhaps we shall be able in this brief section to make the purpose and great value of homoeopathic methods of treatment both accessible and plausible to you, and at the same time to reveal a connection that will unlock for you the meaning of a great number of apparently chance events in your life.

The most honest and precise concept in our language to describe misfortunes, unlucky accidents and distressing circumstances is the word *trial*. There is indeed a reason why we always get into the same difficult situations, why we always have to grapple with the same sort of problems: we did not take in and learn the lesson that is inherent in the apparent misfortune. And we may be sure that we shall have to endure the selfsame experience again and again *until* we either grasp its meaning or die.

This is the way life works and not otherwise. 'Nothing new under the sun.' We are not undergoing a process of learning but a process of opening. We do not learn through the 'acquisition' of knowledge but rather by opening ourselves to realities that have existed as long as the world existed. And there is not a single reality in the universe that does not exist *in us*. So what could there be for us to know that we do not already know? What is there to acquire that we do not already possess? The decisive factor is lifting the veil that conceals our own knowledge.

Only when I can unconditionally accept and learn to love everything that life can visit on me – every last experience, event, affliction and happy circumstance – will life allow me to take my own next step. Like always seeks out like. And like can only be overcome with like. I will continue making the same mistake until the mistake has been 'healed' – through acceptance, through the truth.

I shall continue to feel rage and anger towards certain events, people and things as long as I see them as something alien that does not belong to me, something that *is not me*. Only when I recognise that I am the one that I am fighting against and persecuting, will I be able to detach myself from the situation and continue on my way.

The proverbial wicked neighbour will continue to be wicked until I have accepted him unconditionally for what he is – until I have discovered the 'wicked neighbour' in myself. Until I acknowledge that I am just the same as he is. Whether after my insight I open the door to him or close it forever is a matter of personal instinct, not morality.

Anger over exploitation is something I shall continue to feel, and people will continue to take advantage of me, as long as within myself I am an exploiter – through the hope that it may one day prove worthwhile to let myself be used. Only when I have uncovered the inner exploiter will I cease to be exploited.

I shall remain an exploiter as long as I allow myself inwardly to be used and exploited – by my own greed and fear. Only when I have admitted my own weakness and susceptibility to manipulation will I be able to give up being an exploiter.

Something within me is constantly calling on me to live through the same thing again and again, because inwardly I am inviting it to happen – with the mirror image within me of what is confronting me apparently by chance in the outside world. If I see myself as a victim, I act as an invitation to every evildoer. If I am an evildoer I will always encounter victims. In either case everything remains as it was until I finally recognise myself in the other.

If I unconditionally absorb something alien, something disturbing, into myself – a deceitful partner, a constantly recurring mistake – and accept this as my own, my equal, then I can react with my whole being to this information, recognise myself in the stranger, and with the aid of this clear information about myself I can develop my instinct and do the right thing – say farewell to one lesson and make room for the next.

The secret of healing always consists in unconditional acceptance and receptivity, in no longer struggling against what is supposedly evil, alien, different. It consists in the clear insight that everything strange, repugnant and distressing in life is *myself*. When I discover the equivalence within myself of what is alien and 'evil' in the world, then it is no longer alien to me. It is only then that a transformation is possible, a healing. As long as I fight against what is strange, it remains strange and fights against me. When I embrace it and let it in, it becomes my own and can be resolved in understanding. In this same instant understanding hands me everything I need to tackle my problems at the very roots.

This is how vaccination works, how homoeopathy works, how life and love work.

In the process of vaccination the body takes in attenuated pathogens, reacts to the clear information that they contain, and thus gets a chance to deal with illness more efficiently (regrettably too seldom to justify compulsory vaccinations).

Homoeopathic remedies, Bach flower therapy, autohaemo-therapy and the information they contain is taken unconditionally into the body, which reacts to them and is able by means of this information and the mobilisation of its strength to free itself from the illness.

Homoeopathic remedies work like music on the radio: the orchestra is not there, the instruments are either back in their cases or on the scrap-heap, the physical, material component is absent. And yet on the radio the information for your soul, the effect of your favourite piece is just the same: it makes you happy. This despite the fact that on the face of it there is nothing there: not a single atom of the orchestra that played the music. In the same way there is 'nothing' in a homoeopathic remedy – nothing that can be weighed or measured. Apart from information. When will we ever grasp that it is happiness that makes us healthy and keeps us healthy – not the musical instrument and the musician, not the medicine, the tangible material element?

And if a remedy does not help, simply accept this as fate, instead of condemning the method, the medical practitioner or yourself.

Correct timing in homoeopathy: all remedies and methods directed at detoxification and removal are more successful when the moon is on the wane; all remedies directed at building up and strengthening when the moon is waxing.

The most favourable times for taking globules are Mondays and Fridays.

Autohaemotherapies should take place on earth days (Taurus, Virgo and Capricorn). A waxing moon makes this effect even better, because the body is more receptive to the information contained. Stop the treatment when it takes effect. It is not always necessary to proceed with the therapy according to a rigid pattern.

Bach flowers are almost always used for building up and general strengthening; for this reason they are often more effective when the moon is waxing.

Methods of Detoxification

There are numerous ways in which the body rids itself of harmful materials and metabolic products and radiation. The liver, kidneys, intestine, skin, lungs – all work in concert to rid us of everything harmful and superfluous. Anything that strengthens these organs is also strengthening the capacity of the body to detoxify itself. Many methods of detoxification are so successful and effective with the most varied disorders and illnesses that we recommend them again and again. In order to avoid having to repeat them every time, we have summarised them in this section.

Stinging Nettles: From 'Weed' to Medicinal Herb

A blood purification cure using stinging nettles can do a lot of good and bring about relief and healing in a great many ailments. For any healthy individual a spring cure of nettle tea will rapidly drive spring time tiredness out of his limbs. This cure stimulates the bladder and kidneys, promotes the activity of all the digestive organs and gives the body numerous minerals and vitamins. If you take this cure in order to get on top of a physical disorder or illness, you should prepare yourself for the fact that – just as with homoeopathy and many other forms of therapy – there can be an initial worsening of the symptoms: for a short time after the treatment pains or other symptoms become more acute, or it can even happen that the disorder can be displaced to another organ or area of the body. This is a good sign, and you should not lose heart because of it – quite the contrary: your body is signalling that you are on the right road, that it is responding and trying to supply the disturbed zone with new strength. Stronger symptoms and pains are ultimately only a sign that the body is expending more strength in order to break through the blockage in the flow of energy to the affected area – rather like the growing pressure that is exerted on a dam, the more water it has to hold in.

When the moon is on the wane, preferably in the afternoon between 3 and 7 p.m., drink as much nettle tea as you can, or take three soup-spoons of nettle-juice (obtainable from health food shops – only suitable for people in good health). Stop when the moon is new, wait fourteen days, and repeat the cure after the next full moon, until the ailment has got better or disappeared. As a cure for healthy people, two periods of fourteen days in the waning moon are sufficient; for detoxification in cases of illness or skin disorders three such periods are needed.

The stinging nettles are also best collected when the moon is waning. Only use young leaves, and dry and store them when the moon is on the wane. The plants must not be washed before drying. (Tip: if you want to use the fresh leaves, in a salad, for instance, roll them repeatedly with a rolling pin. This crushes the hollow stinging hairs and so they do not sting any more.)

If the moon happens to be in an earth sign (Virgo, Taurus, Capricorn), collect more nettles than you need for daily use and dry the leaves for winter. Used thus they have an especially good effect on the blood count. For healthy people, however, there is no need for a blood purification cure in winter. On the other hand a nettle tea now and then after a substantial heavy meal (e.g. at Christmas time) is a good idea.

The Power of Sunflower Oil

An old and effective method for the detoxification and strengthening of the whole body and at the same time decontaminating the teeth (see page 333) is known as an *oil mouthwash*. Each step of the method is important and should be adhered to closely in order to achieve the desired effect. This is how it works:

 * In the morning on an empty stomach and before you brush your teeth, take a soup-spoon of pure cold-pressed sunflower oil. We know that in the temperate latitudes of the northern hemisphere, from Russia (the land of origin of the method) to North America only sunflower oil achieves this beneficial effect. It is only in this plant that those powers are stored that can help this method to work successfully. Whether in other regions of the world there are other local oils that are more suitable, we do not know; but it is certainly worth a try.

* *Slurp* the oil, loud and vulgarly, like an old knight in the middle ages. This slurping fulfils an important function: it helps the entire body and all its internal organs to receive exact information, via the nerves of the taste buds and the brain, concerning what has just entered the body. The better tongue, nose and gums are informed, the better the body is able to tune itself. When the body receives the information 'sunflower oil' it knows that a substance has entered it on to which it can 'load' everything that is undesirable, particularly everything that has negative radiations.

* The important thing now is to keep the oil in the mouth *with-*

out swallowing any! Suck the oil through the teeth and cavities of the mouth, let it roll and slide, push it through the gaps between your teeth, slowly, casually almost, so as not to arouse too strong a flow of saliva. Do that for about fifteen minutes. (If you feel an irresistible urge to swallow before the time is up, make very sure you spit the oil out first.)

* After a quarter of an hour spit the oil into a wash basin and rinse both your mouth and the basin thoroughly. The oil has been transformed into a poison-laden substance: where it falls no grass will grow. Do not be surprised at the colour of the oil: it has now turned white.

* The most favourable time for such a cure: when the moon is waning and for a period of at least eight, preferably fourteen days.

Swedish Herbs

Swedish bitter is well-known and widely used throughout Europe as a detoxicant, stimulant and prophylactic, but it also has many other applications (treatment of minor wounds, poultices, stomach complaints, etc.). It is truly an elixir of life, a guardian of health, which should never be lacking in any medicine chest. The formula was handed down by the Swedish doctor, Samst, hence its modern name. It probably originally goes back to Paracelsus, who used the elixir successfully even on severely ill patients.

The following is the recipe for Swedish herbs:

10g aloes, 10g wild angelica root, 5g carline thistle root, 10g manna, 5g myrrh, 10g natural camphor, 10g rhubarb root, 0.2g saffron, 10g senna leaves, 10g Venetian theriac (*Electuarium theriacale sine opio*), 10g root of *Rhizoma zedoariae*.

These herbs, which you can order from a herbalist or chemist, should be put in a large dark-coloured bottle and 1.5 litres of pome fruit or grain brandy added (38% – 40% by volume). Leave the mixture standing in the dark at room temperature for 14 days, and shake once a day. Strain off small quantities for use in suitable containers, and keep these in a cool place. The longer they are stored the greater their curative power.

As a preventive measure against aches and illnesses take a teaspoonful of this Swedish bitter mornings and evenings thinned with some water or tea.

Fasting

Fasting is another useful measure for detoxifying and restoring the body. However, as a means of losing weight fasting is rarely successful in the long term. The causes of overweight remain unaffected, and afterwards the old eating and thinking habits usually re-establish themselves. If you wish nonetheless to fast, you should drink a great deal because all the detoxifying organs will be under very severe stress. You should also pay attention to correct timing: in general the waning phases of the moon are more suited, because the body's capacity for detoxification is higher. The Lent period of fasting is dependent on the phases of the moon, and a 'zero diet' at some time within that period is particularly effective. Likewise the period from the first day in Advent until December 24 is very favourable for living a little more abstemiously and detoxifying the body.

As we have already mentioned a detoxification of the body undertaken on a new moon day will last a particularly long time. Eating can put a brake on or even interrupt this process. At full moon, on the other hand, the body is especially efficient at taking in the materials supplied to it. Consequently it would generally be very advantageous on both these days to eat little or nothing at all.

Reflexology

Massage of the reflex zones of the feet, a method that actually belongs in the field of physical therapy, can be extremely useful for a successful detoxification of the body. Every bodily organ and every region of the body 'terminates' in a specific and discrete area of the feet. In a similar manner to acupressure (pressure on particular points throughout the whole of the body) it is possible through well-directed pressure and friction to arouse these zones and thereby to flood the relevant organs and regions of the body with energy and stimulate them to function normally.

Reflex-zone massage is even suitable as a diagnostic instrument. Generally those points on the foot whose corresponding organs are debilitated are more painful, or even identifiable by a thick callous. Thus with poor footwear we harm not only our feet but also our whole body.

Here, too, there often occurs an initial worsening of the symptoms, as was already mentioned on page 48. However, this is a good sign and should not make you waver in your resolve: skilfully carried out, reflex-zone massage is a genuine boon for those in good health and can bring relief and healing to the sick. In this instance correct timing is not all that important, but the force of Pisces days greatly assists the effect of this form of massage. On these days one should carry out massage with especial care, because people are more sensitive then. Anyone going for the first time to a medical practitioner or masseur for a reflex zone massage is probably well-advised to steer clear of Pisces days. Reflex-zone massages intended to stimulate organs of detoxification are generally more effective during the waning than during the waxing moon.

Of course there are numerous other methods of detoxification, which for the most part are no less effective. Here, too, it is ultimately your own instinct that decides. The method that appeals to you, in which you can place your confidence, is in most cases the most successful one for you – though it is impossible on the other hand to make general statements about its usefulness. Every human body is different, everyone detoxifies himself in a different way, each person has different toxic thresholds. Whenever someone says he swears by such and such a method, then it may well produce good results for him, but not necessarily for you.

Numerous medical practitioners have mastered the art of finding the method that is tailored precisely for your particular case. In particular homoeopaths achieve masterly results in the individual treatment of their patients. As we have said: your confidence is the decisive factor. Whether in a personally chosen method or in the advice of a medical practitioner – ultimately it is your own power of self-healing and your will to become healthy that tip the scales.

"Do not touch with iron…":
Concerning Operations on the Body

The famous Greek doctor Hippocrates (460–370 BC) wrote these words in his journal: "Do not touch with iron those parts of the body that are governed by the sign through which the moon is passing." He was thus stating, quite unambiguously, that a doctor should not carry out any surgical operations on regions of the body that are governed by the current sign of the zodiac. And so for example: no heart operations on Leo days, no hip-joint operations on Libra days, no operation on a knee-joint in Capricorn, etc.

Let us remind you of the rule:

Everything that is done for the well-being of those parts of the body and organs ruled by the sign through which the moon is currently passing is doubly useful and beneficial – with the exception of surgical operations involving those regions.

It is only at first sight that surgical operations appear to be an exception to the rule. Granted they are carrying out the *intention* of serving the welfare of the organ in question or of the entire body, but at the *moment* of the operation and the period immediately thereafter they have the effect of putting a severe strain on the particular region of the body involved. This applies in the same way to the removal of entire organs. An operation at the wrong time means that the body has to work harder to make up for the loss. The general rule for operations on the body runs as follows:

This applies to surgical operations of all sorts: given the choice, one should operate when the moon is waning. The period of the waxing moon is unfavourable, and the closer to full moon the more unfavourable it is. The actual day of full moon has the most negative effect of all.

Surgical operations on those regions of the body which are governed by the sign through which the moon is currently passing have a debilitating and stressful effect and are thus more harmful than on other days.

If you have a completely free hand in choosing the date of an operation, then pay attention additionally to the course of the sun and steer clear of the *solar* sign of the zodiac. Thus for example: no heart operations in August when the sun is in Leo. The corresponding times of the year for all regions of the body are given in the chapter entitled *A Journey through the Body*.

As we have mentioned, the transition between the signs of the zodiac happens gently. The change of forces cannot be pinpointed to the hour. If for instance two Pisces days are given in the calendar, on the morning of the first day there may still be an admixture of Aquarius influence in the day-quality; while in the evening of the second day Aries, with its influence on the head region, will sometimes already be making its presence felt. If the Pisces influence lasts three days, then the first day up to about midday is still strongly coloured by Aquarius; and on the third day the influence of the Aries impulse will probably already be quite strong.

For this reason we have sometimes stated that if the choice of date is up to you, you should also stay clear of the signs neighbouring the one that rules a particular part of the body; for example in the case of a jaw operation it could be advantageous to avoid both Taurus and Aries days.

Perhaps you are asking yourself a question of this sort: what about the negative influence of the Libra days if (as is the case from October to April) they fall in the waning phases of the moon (in themselves a favourable period), and I have arranged for an operation on my hip joint at exactly this time? In such a situation the basic rule is this: the favourable influence of the waning moon outweighs the negative influence of the Libra days. To stay with this example, here is a sequential list of the favourable and unfavourable influences on a hip joint operation:

Good:	waning moon, not in Libra
Fair to medium:	waning moon in Libra
Bad:	waxing moon in another sign
Very bad:	waxing mood in Libra
Most unfavourable:	full moon in Libra

This sequence can easily be applied to all other operations and regions of the body.

Why then is attention to the correct timing of an operation so important? As we have already indicated, every surgeon in the course of his practice will make this discovery or has even already collected parallel experiences: complications and infections following operations are much more frequent when the moon is waxing, and healing and convalescent phases as a rule last longer. Toward full moon there are often instances of severe bleeding that are hard to staunch. In addition, when the moon is waxing the process of scar formation does not run smoothly, and the danger of ugly, permanent scars is much greater.

This information is of especial interest for plastic surgery: after serious accidents multiple operations are often necessary in order to fashion a more or less acceptable external appearance. Many people, especially young people, are often reduced to despair when after numerous corrections and painful operations they are still horrified by their reflection in the mirror, or those around them constantly react to their appearance after an accident. In a world in which triviality and superficiality reigns, permanent scars can destroy a person's happiness. Attention to correct timing in this area can be of supreme importance.

However, scars often do not merely have aesthetic disadvantages: they act as zones of disturbance and energy blockages in the body and can do damage to the organism, especially when they disrupt reflex arcs in the hands and feet. There are many medical practitioners who have mastered the art of releasing such blockages, but it would certainly be a great advantage to nip the evil in the bud and prevent severe scar formation by choosing the correct moment to operate.

And so the most important rule is and remains: wherever possible carry out surgical operations *when the moon is on the wane.* Admittedly this information is still unknown to many doctors, because it does not yet fit into one of the many scientific pigeon-holes or into the hyper-organised procedures of hospitals. On the other hand, you are now in possession of this knowledge and can decide for yourself how your are going to handle it. The knowledge that a midwife ought to wash her hands also took centuries to gain acceptance.

One further word concerning *emergency operations*: you cannot of course select for yourself the date of operations after accidents or urgent situations that require immediate action. When an appendix threatens to burst no one is interested in the position of the moon. And rightly so. There is so much in our lives that is subject to our free decision – much more in fact than our anxieties would have us believe. And so much is determined by fate, condemns us to be mere onlookers, is taken out of our hands – likewise much more than we sometimes fear, because we lack confidence and above all the insight into the meaning of many of the events between heaven and earth.

If your doctor advises a quick operation, then heed his advice. Simply don't look at the calendar (in any case there's no time for that after an accident). Exercise trust, surrender to the situation and the wisdom of the being who has sent you this situation as an opportunity to learn and to wake up. And if you discover, either before or afterwards that the event occurred at the 'wrong' time, in terms of lunar rhythms, do not be afraid. Take a deep breath, breathe out and say to yourself: "Wherever the moon is, I trust my own powers of self-healing, I trust the people that are helping me, and sooner or later I'm going to track down the meaning of all this." Then you will have achieved more than many another person who has himself operated on at the right moment and thus cherishes the illusion that "nothing can go wrong". There are no guarantees in this life – with a single exception. We are all guaranteed as many lessons as we need. If not today, then early tomorrow morning at the very latest.

As for the question, how can you as a patient get your doctor to accept the date you suggest for an operation or change an unfavourable date that he has fixed, we would ask you to read the final section of this chapter. We have devoted the closing remarks of this part of the book to this important subject (page 165). Perhaps the thoughts and suggestions contained there will prove helpful in enabling the knowledge of lunar rhythms to become as widespread once more as it deserves to be.

Lunar Rhythms in Dentistry

What is the state of your teeth? No, of course you needn't have a guilty conscience if you are walking around with a few fillings, crowns or bridges in your mouth. After all, you aren't the only one: probably 90 percent of the population are just like you. The good news is that the effects of the lunar rhythms is also of use in the treatment and care of your teeth. However, the less good news is that a long-term alteration for the better in the condition of your teeth can only come about through patience and a certain degree of discipline in changing daily habits. Doubtless you have often heard that before, but that does not alter the fact that it corresponds with the truth. Nor can one expect any patent remedy from us that will render it unnecessary to get into the habit of taking daily care of one's teeth. At best the lines that follow may lighten this necessary trouble for you.

Truly it is small wonder that there are four-year-old children going around today with tooth fillings: in many respects the state of people's teeth is a sign of the general state of their health, a consequence of their eating habits and also of the fact that in our lives we have lost our 'bite' – forgotten how to make decisions without doubts and reservations. Anyone who is constantly afraid of the consequences of a decision will no longer dare to take time by the forelock, and very few of us grow up in circumstances that require us to 'bite through' difficult situations on our own initiative. This has its effect on the teeth in our mouth.

An unnatural diet, insufficient care, bodily disorders which also damage the teeth via reflex paths and energy paths, and our inner attitude: tooth decay marches in step with all other defects of civilisation. As a precaution against this a great deal could be gained by keeping to a natural diet, rich in vitamins and minerals. Of necessity such a diet should be started in childhood, or better still already during pregnancy. With a natural diet, even if daily cleaning took place without any kind of cleaning agent, the teeth would not be nearly so damaged as is often the case nowadays. Even sweets, whose greatest harmfulness lies in the psychological domain (see page 254), would have far less chance to attack the teeth. What we understand by a natural diet you will discover in the next part of the book.

Much too little attention is paid to the threat posed to the entire body by *infected teeth* – by sometimes microscopically small inflammations of the root of the tooth. From time to time such ailments can literally drive the affected person out of his mind. Numerous chronic disorders, illnesses and painful conditions – complaints of the spinal column, sinusitis, rheumatism, conditions of general exhaustion – have their origins in undiscovered tooth infections.

It is not uncommon in such cases for the person involved to wander from specialist to specialist without any organic cause being recognised. Often the restoration of one or more teeth – or the extraction of the culprit – can bring relief or cure. Unfortunately many root infections and zones of disturbance are not visible on an X-ray picture. In such cases an experienced medical practitioner will be able to find out whether the cause of the physical illness is indeed to be sought in a particular tooth or root of a tooth. Acupuncture, acupressure, reflex-zone massage of hands and feet are very good indicators of disturbed energy circulation between the teeth and various organ systems.

So, in what way can the knowledge of the effects of lunar rhythms be used in dentistry to the advantage of both patient and dentist? Let us now go through a list of common procedures of restoration and maintenance, whose success or failure in the short- or long-term is partially also dependent on the position of the moon.

Removal of Plaque

As a rule dental plaque is formed through inadequate cleaning habits. If it is not dealt with it can lead to caries, shrinkage and inflammation of the gums (periodontitis), and ultimately to teeth falling out. Any dentist can explain the correct way to clean teeth. In this process the cleaning agent is less important than the way in which you move the brush and the frequency with which you clean your teeth.

The favourable time for removing plaque is when the moon is waning, because new formation is thus kept within bounds. The ideal time would be Capricorn days when the moon is on the wane, but this is not absolutely essential.

Of course it isn't always easy to keep to the right time, let alone getting a dental surgery to conform with the lunar rhythms. However, you may find one or two helpful tips on the subject at the end of this chapter.

Crowns and Bridges

Any dentist would have no trouble checking out the influence of lunar rhythms if he sifted through his patient files for all cases in which crowns and bridges lasted a much shorter time than normal, and perhaps fell out again after a few months. A comparison between the date they were fitted and a calendar of the phases of the moon would confirm the following rule:

Whenever possible the fitting of crowns and bridges should take place when the moon is waning. They will last much longer than if fitted when the moon is waxing.

Inflammation of the Gums (Periodontitis)

The treatment of an inflammation of the gums by cutting back severely inflamed areas is only a temporarily effective measure, unless you subsequently get to grips with the cause. It all depends what cause you discover: if everything remains as it was – diet or insufficient cleaning habits, irradiation of the teeth, for instance through biting the nails (see page 333), etc. – then the inflammation will return after a short time and you will have to get used to the idea of an expensive denture. And even a (removable) denture becomes looser in time, if the gums are never massaged properly.

The favourable time for a treatment for periodontitis at the dentist's is when the moon is on the wane – avoiding Aries and Taurus days. The injured gums will then heal rapidly and bleeding will be kept within bounds. Such a treatment is a small operation!

Likewise gumboils should be treated when the moon is waning, and never during Aries and Taurus days.

In the case of mild gum inflammation (gingivitis), take a soft toothbrush and massage your gums firmly many times a day. Do not always use toothpaste for this, but dip the brush beforehand in sage tea. In the case of acute inflammation rinse your mouth with camomile tea and only brush lightly.

Extracting Teeth

When you want or need to say good-bye to a tooth – for instance a wisdom tooth, which sometimes almost requires an operation, or because of an infection in the socket – it is advantageous to pay attention to correct timing and it can save you a lot of after pains.

Choose the waning moon for extracting teeth, especially when it is a case of wisdom teeth or jaw operations, and steer clear of Taurus and Aries days. In addition you should if possible avoid the air signs (Gemini, Libra, Aquarius).

Gaps and sockets heal up quicker, and it is not unusual for the physical symptom or pain to disappear immediately.

Tips for Treating Teeth and Removing Amalgam Fillings

The fact that the body takes in all the substances that are fed to it more easily when the moon is waxing is sometimes a disadvantage. If carried out when the moon is waxing, a tooth filling of mercury amalgam (alloyed with zinc, copper, silver or gold) leaves behind more poisonous mercury in the blood than when the moon is on the wane. Gradually the realisation is gaining acceptance that mercury in the mouth – and hence in the entire body – is not exactly conducive to good health. However, we are not trying to prove here that amalgam is extremely harmful. We know that it is. And now you know it, too, if you didn't know before. In the USA amalgam that has been drilled out of teeth has to be collected from dental surgeries by a specialist waste disposal company in three airtight metal containers locked one inside the other and labelled with a skull and crossbones. In the meantime in many European countries special waste disposal firms are also taking care of this toxic waste.

Isn't it amazing? Amalgam is treated, quite correctly, as highly dangerous toxic waste and disposed of with special care; and yet people are still trying to make us believe that this rubbish in our bodies doesn't cause any harm.

It is scarcely credible, but even today dentists all over the world are putting in millions of new amalgam fillings – every day. From the point of view of the dentist, too, who breathes in the vapours resulting from inserting fillings, poisoning himself and his employees, it would make good sense to stop this madness. A dentist known to us grew a new head of hair after having his own fillings changed.

However, whether you continue to make yourself available as a guinea pig for this virulent nerve poison, mercury amalgam, is entirely up to you. If you make the wise decision to have your old amalgam fillings removed, then you should observe the following points:

* Have the work done *when the moon is waning*. At that time the body is not nearly as good at absorbing materials that have been breathed in or swallowed as when the moon is waxing.

* If possible do not have a lot of fillings drilled out at the same time, and never drill without damming in the tooth and taking precautions against swallowing (rubber dam). Only then can the resultant debris be sucked away properly. Rinse out as thoroughly as possible after drilling. Arrange with your dentist to have only a few fillings removed at each appointment, and only make a new appointment after a fairly long interval (one month later at the earliest).

* Get a medical practitioner or a doctor you can trust to prescribe a homoeopathic remedy tailored to your needs, which will help to neutralise the poisons that have been released (detoxification, auto-haemotherapy, etc.).

* Never begin the detoxification process until the last filling has been removed. Otherwise the detoxifying remedy would start to dissolve and break up the fillings that are still present and pollute the body with an unnecessarily large amount of poison.

If you drink a lot of (non-pasteurised, non-homogenised) *milk* before the fillings are replaced the casein contained in it can absorb the mercury that has been swallowed.

* As far as we know there is still no ideal material to replace amalgam. Either the durability is limited or the long-term effects of the replacement material are not yet known. To date the best medium to choose is apparently a very expensive synthetic glass with the trade name *Charisma*. Incidentally one prominent German toxicologist recommends not using any metal in dentistry whatsoever – certainly not several metals simultaneously. Even gold is supposed to have certain disadvantages; for instance when one has had to live for decades with amalgam fillings in one's teeth: gold, acting as an antagonist to mercury, is thought to prevent the amalgam stored up in the bones from being dissolved and expelled.

Care and Preventive Treatment of Teeth

It's been heard a thousand times before, but rarely heeded: keep to a natural diet, rich in vitamins and minerals, and clean your teeth regularly, if possible three times a day. Cleaning the teeth makes good sense at every stage in the lunar cycle. All precautionary measures for the care of teeth and gums which involve taking in substances – mouthwashes, supply of minerals, etc. – work well when the moon is waxing, because the body is more receptive at this time.

Incidentally, teeth can pick up harmful radiations. There is more on this topic in part IV of the book (page 305). At this point we would only mention that irradiated teeth have a debilitating effect on the gums and via the reflex arc on many organs and regions of the body that are connected with the teeth. The oil mouthwash method, described above (page 148), is also well-suited to the de-contamination of the teeth. Its effectiveness is practically independent of the position of the moon. Many people who had problems with their teeth or found themselves in situations of great physical exertion and exhaustion, have applied this technique with success. And to this day some of them do not leave the house without a small bottle of sunflower oil in their luggage.

Suitable natural *teeth-cleaning agents* are: sea-salt or various herbal teas (sage, camomile for severe inflammations, shepherd's purse for heavy bleeding of the gums), all of which not only remove plaque but also strengthen the gums – provided the correct brushing technique is used. Many dentists provide shepherd's purse extract, in case a treatment is likely to involve severe bleeding. Since time immemorial chewing bramble leaves has been recommended for bleeding gums – a very effective remedy.

What is comparatively less well-known is one of the best methods for daily teeth-care: beech wood ash. It works outstandingly well, and fulfils all the requirements that dentistry makes of a cleaning agent. Even advanced shrinkage of the gums can be halted by this means, if the correct method of cleaning and massaging is used. At teeth-cleaning time simply heap a thimbleful of ash on the edge of the washbasin and dip the moistened toothbrush into it until it has all been used up. At first it feels sandy and dry in the mouth, but it rinses out well.

Concerning *teeth-cleaning technique*: getting the correct technique for regularly cleaning the teeth across to children is another 'never-ending story' – quite apart from the fact that most parents have never mastered it and don't stick to it themselves. Adopting this habit in daily life is a tedious process, especially for the fidgety children of the video age; all the more so if on top of everything toothpaste has to be made to taste nice so that the little dears will submit to the wash-basin routine. But there is no way round this, assuming that one does not wish to start paving their way to a 'third set of teeth'. Brush your teeth after the main meals of the day and before going to bed. After the final cleaning nothing else should be taken: even a single gulp of lemonade is enough to ruin the good effects. Do not use a brush that is too big (better too small than too big), and always massage your gums in the direction of your teeth: on the upper jaw from the top down and on the lower jaw from the bottom up.

The decisive factor is *habituation*: it takes a long time for the gums to become inflamed, for caries to spread in the teeth. In this time we have got used to inadequate cleaning techniques, learnt to live with the rough feeling on the tongue of dental plaque, forgotten how good it feels to have smoothly polished teeth and healthy gums – almost as if the strange taste in the mouth, the rough surface of the teeth, the bleeding gums, the hypersensitivity to heat and cold were all a matter of God-given fate, inevitable phenomena of our civilisation. It took a long time for this state of affairs to set in, and patience and effort is needed to become accustomed to better cleaning techniques and to improve the situation...

If you are expecting advice from us as to how to get through this phase of habituation to good cleaning techniques, whether as a child or an adult, then we are going to have to disappoint you. The decision to do something about your teeth lies with you from the very first moment; and the same applies to your decision to hold out with your children and gently but firmly to counter their resistance.

You should bear in mind that the best replacement for amalgam fillings is a healthy tooth. The best remedy for shrunken gums is correct cleaning technique. The best remedy for inflamed gums is healthy gums. The best treatment for the wound after an extraction is not to have this wound in the first place. The best remedy for squandering your money on false teeth is simply not to need them.

Dealing with Medical Practitioners

We should like at the close of this part of the book to offer you some assistance in dealing with doctors. Perhaps after completing this little journey through the body you have gained some confidence in the knowledge of lunar rhythms, and are ready to test it out in your daily life and discover how useful it is. Possibly you are now considering the question: "How will my doctor or dentist react if I want to change an appointment because it falls on an unfavourable day?" or, more generally: "Is he at all open to this knowledge?"

Let us begin with a few facts and some questions that you can answer for yourself:

* Every day doctors all over the world prescribe medicines with a value of hundreds of billions of pounds and dollars. Two thirds of these are never taken. Half of them end up in the rubbish bin. What can we conclude from this?

* Almost everywhere in the world banks give young doctors fat

loans to start up their practices. What consequences does this have for the inner attitude of the doctor, for his practice and for his patients?

* In Holland 44 percent of patients leave after their consultation without a prescription; in Germany practically none do. Are the Dutch healthier?
* In Danish pharmacies there are 7,000 different medicines available. In the USA the figure is 100,000. Are Danish bodies built more simply than those of Americans?
* For a long time science has actually admitted just how important healthy, organic nutrition is for sick people, and what a blessed influence is exerted by a friendly atmosphere in a hospital. And yet what is daily life in hospitals really like?
* The soothing words and the gentle stroking of a male nurse, his love of humanity, can be a thousand times more curative than any medicine, any injection. How are nursing personnel paid in comparison with doctors?
* Everybody feels and knows: hate destroys – even one's own body. Love heals everything – even one's own body. Why is it that around this simple truth a whole branch of science, called *psychosomatics*, has been founded, which squanders millions of pounds only to 'prove' this truth, and then to develop patterns of behaviour that never do justice to the individual case?
* There are certain non-life-saving operations (gall-bladder, hysterectomy, haemorrhoids, tonsils, etc.) which doctors undergo up to 80 percent less frequently than the average for the population. The frequency of these operations among lawyers is equally low. Do doctors and lawyers, despite all experience and statistics to the contrary, really lead a healthier life than the rest of us?
* In the USA 75 percent of all patients additionally visit 'alternative' practitioners – homoeopaths, chiropactors, shamans, etc. – without informing their GP of these parallel therapies. Why is this?

All these facts and the answers that you have given are by no means a reason to revile doctors, let alone condemn orthodox medicine wholesale. They are all based on a single common factor: our ignorance and dependence.

If you personally begin to get to know your own body and your own mental world, with their individual rhythms and requirements, their weaknesses and their beauty, if you begin to accept yourself as you are, from head to foot, and if you love yourself, then you will never have any problem discovering the good doctor in your vicinity, the friend of humanity. And ultimately that is the only thing that counts. It is of no importance to you what kind of state modern medicine is broadly in today – far-removed from nature and alien to life. Admittedly, it has almost become a national sport to castigate orthodox medicine, but that isn't any use to you personally. The only thing that makes any sense is your own awakening to your body and the thoughts with which you influence it for better or for worse. Then you will have no problem finding good doctors and healers – they exist everywhere.

It is not difficult for us to understand why medicine has manoeuvred itself into its present blind alley. The fact is that it isn't easy for good doctors to become good doctors.

Modern medicine is a medicine of pigeon-holes: in its training syllabus there are meticulously categorised illnesses, but no whole human beings who eat, drink, think, feel and act – and who fall ill from their thoughts and feelings. There are bacteria and viruses, but no holistic view of the life-circumstances of a person, in which even a poisonous picture on the wall drawn by some melancholy artist can open the gateway to those bacteria. There are pills and medicines, but only rarely the tender, loving touch and embrace, whose effect is a thousand times more healing than any medication. There are scalpels and knives, but only rarely the readiness to get to know 'the gall-bladder case in room 768' as a human being. There are machines that can analyse every component of our blood, but only rarely is any instinct awakened for the curative power of loving thoughts. We see medical research that is almost exclusively interested in researching, funding research and 'the fight against disease', and contributes very little to a growth of confidence in the medical profession – and nothing at all to the ripening on the part of the patient of that vital self-confidence and sense of responsibility for oneself.

And then there is the appalling arrogance of it: for far too long a large section of the medical profession has been acting as an exclusive group that has developed its own secret language, always stays together and as an inevitable result fails to see the signs that it has been on the wrong track for ages. 'Staying together' always means staying blind. That is true of every professional group – medical specialists, teachers, lawyers, politicians – and in general of every human grouping that considers itself to be 'superior'. However, it is especially tragic in the field of medicine, because so many of us are directly affected by such blindness. Far too often we have been taken for a ride and used as guinea pigs. The all-too human tendency towards simplification has caused many people to greet the work of *every* medical practitioner with mistrust from the outset, and to abandon hope prematurely. Such mistrust is harmful for the individual and for the work of all good medical practitioners.

With our book we are trying to help reduce the number of victims of blindness and mistrust and to smooth a path back to the middle ground. To reawaken hope and trust – above all in your own powers of judgement and instinct – that is our aim.

In many countries in the world, medical training, health insurance schemes, politics and the public health service have entered into an alliance to make healing, and more especially preventive medicine, as difficult as it could possibly be for good doctors. Good doctors are interested in health, but the system only allows them to earn money – and good money at that – from illness.

In addition it is mostly financial resources and marks in school that determine who may become a doctor and who may not. Can you remember your own time at school? Do you remember the class swot? If we only open the way to medical training to people with the necessary cash and/or good results at school, we shall be making a colossal mistake. With very few exceptions, these are in fact the sort of people who shrink from life: people who recoil from precisely those experiences that would turn them into good doctors – namely getting to know life from head to foot, and showing love and understanding towards all humanity. It is as if we were to give a fine Swiss watch to a Ford mechanic to repair: why are we surprised when he reaches for a spanner?

For good doctors, on the other hand – just like good spiritual guides – nothing human is alien. There are countless hooligans and heart-breakers, truants and delinquents, who might have become the very best doctors, friends of humanity, because they are willing to get to know themselves and other people – to understand them and accept them unconditionally.

We can consider ourselves fortunate that many a classroom lout has after all made the grade, because he patiently followed the call of his heart – that after all there are many good doctors among the model pupils and children of rich parents, who have devoted themselves to life and healing with all their hearts. Unfortunately this circumstance is no particular credit to the training and selection procedures of the medical profession. Such doctors have become friends of humanity *despite* their training, not *because* of it. After much trial and error their hearts have opened to an insight into the real causes of illness. Primarily through self-knowledge, through humility towards the Boss of all of us up there beyond the clouds, and through personal experience, that seasoning which is the sole content of this present book. Such doctors even manage to slip through the constraints of politics and industry, of the health system and the professional lobbies, which make sickness more lucrative for the doctor than preventive work.

Fortunately everywhere that this book has appeared to date much has eventually begun to change. The number of doctors openly in favour of the knowledge of natural and lunar rhythms has grown. Many of them have been able to discover by experience what a beneficial effect its application has, especially on chronic clinical pictures – an experience that has made them immune to defamation in whatever form. Such doctors are no longer surprised if someone asks them to perform a blood test at a particular moment or to postpone a particular operation. With many of them the moon calendar is a permanent feature among their desk-top tools. However, they are still in the minority.

So what is to be done if as a result of personal experience you have gradually gained confidence in these rules, but your doctor wishes to perform an operation at an unfavourable moment or take other measures that are unsuitable?

* If you discover that your doctor has no understanding for your reasons for wanting a postponement of (say) an operation.

* If he is unable to explain his diagnosis, intentions and therapeutic methods in terms that you can understand, then change your doctor and look for a friend of humanity.

You do not have to justify yourself. You are not obliged to state your reasons. This doctor is simply going to need a little more time before he himself becomes open to what is self-evident.

You should always bear one thing in mind: a doctor can only help you to help yourself. He isn't a god. We have often heard, in the guise of a 'reasonable' argument against lunar rhythms, the sentence: "Supposing everyone came along with a moon calendar under his arm...." It probably is not feasible to integrate the knowledge of natural and lunar rhythms into contemporary medical practice overnight. And yet: alleged difficulties in the allocation of appointments in no way alter the validity of the rules of correct timing. From the outset it is up to you personally – and it is only to you, the reader, that we are addressing ourselves – not to put up with the lack of insight of other people or with other 'material constraints' – either in cases of sickness or in any other sphere of life.

II. Diet Made Easy

The secret of healthy nourishment:
Eat what tastes good to you,
Heed what you feel
And smoke your pipe in peace and quiet.
But how to awaken a deadened tongue?
How can I wash out blocked-up ears?
How can I still the turmoil in my head and heart?

F rom cauliflower to caviar, from roast beef to red cabbage, from coffee to cocoa – an immense variety of foodstuffs from which we make a daily selection that we allow to enter our body. The survival of the latter depends on it, certainly its health, too, and for many of us a fair bit of *joie de vivre*.

Contrary to what people have been trying to get us to believe for decades, it is by no means of decisive importance in this selection what amounts we eat and what ingredients comprise our food. If you are merely expecting from this chapter the thousandth guide to the 'correct' diet, if you want tables of vitamins, calories and ingredients, then you should pass straight on to the next chapter. We cannot help you with this, nor would we wish to.

The subject of diet nowadays fills thousands of more or less helpful books and manuals. Many of them sit on the shelf gathering dust because their recommendations cannot be translated into our daily lives, or because their authors have forgotten that "Man doth not live by bread alone": beautiful appetising pictures – without any nutritional value for your heart. That is why we shall be trying in this chapter to show you ways in which you can feed yourself, healthily and on your own initiative, and get hold of genuine, life-giving foodstuffs – without having to keep to senseless and often expensive rules. However, before we present to you the first basics of a healthy diet and a brief look at herbal lore, we should like to clear away some of the theoretical edifices that have plagued the subject of diet for several decades and caused so much confusion. Here as elsewhere in the book we shall not be doing very much to prove our words. It would only be a waste of paper. We are confident that we shall be able to awaken your memory about things you already know anyway. That is what we see as our task – here, too, in the sphere of diet.

In the Jungle of Dietary Rules

What do you think? Is it possible to live all one's life on half a cup of maize and half a cup of maize beer per day, and at the same time jog between 12 and 25 miles daily? Of course not, you will say. And yet even today the Tarahumara Indians in northern Mexico live on this Spartan diet, and have done for centuries. Once a week they even meet for a marathon run of 25 to 50 miles. After the run their heartbeat is even lower than when they started. When they are fed with a 'healthy and balanced' diet of vitamins and minerals, they get heart disease, high blood pressure, skin disease and caries – illnesses previously unknown in their tribe. Interested western researchers needed about a year to achieve the same physical performance on an identical diet. Almost without protest their bodies had come to terms with the spirit of inquiry.

Such examples may be found in their hundreds throughout the world – from certain Inuit tribes who feed exclusively on meat and fat, to Tyrolean mountain farmers who by prevailing standards live most unhealthy lives and yet live without illness to be 90 years old – to Indian fakirs who eat so little that, according to all the rules of nutrition, they should have ceased to walk the earth a long time ago. Nowhere in the world is there a form of diet that produces the same result for *all* people: namely the personal experience of living a healthy and energetic life. Do you recall the result of the investigation into 5000 centenarians? (See page 128.) There was no common factor in their dietary habits. What may be concluded from all of this?

For several decades we have been served up a series of old wives' tales, in the truest sense of the words – opinions and convictions streaming in from all sides, an incredible multitude of false ideas that people have been trying to drum into us for decades on the subject of correct nutrition – particularly in connection with the right diet for reducing overweight.

"This diet gives you the certainty that you are eating healthily, or that you are becoming slimmer because of it." – Thus, or words to that effect, runs one such old wives' tale. We are surrounded by a jungle of slimming cures, cooking recipes, and dieting tips, in books, on radio and television and especially in magazines. Confusing, contradictory and yet always 'in line with the latest scientific findings', i.e. with the built-in guarantee that yesterday's latest scientific findings are already old hat today. The day before yesterday roughage was considered 'superfluous' and removed from our food; now we are magnanimously informed just how essential it is for life, and it is marketed very effectively. Foodstuffs are now artificially enriched with vitamins and other essential ingredients, which previously were removed from them at great expense. Undoing the damage wreaked through splitting up and tearing to pieces the unity that is an edible plant is today being sold to us as 'progress'.

The day before yesterday they tried to hammer the idea into us that potatoes and spaghetti were the great fatteners; yesterday potatoes had become the number one slimming diet; today pasta has been elevated to the status of a power-food. Fat (cholesterol) on the other hand has become the villain of the piece (the only strange thing is that a human being cannot survive without fat). About thirty years ago nutritional science established the daily requirement for protein; today it only recommends about one fifth of that amount.

And what sort of nonsense will they be whispering in our ear tomorrow? If we cannot summon up the courage to use our very own, personal instinct for what is sensible and in keeping with nature, regardless of what everyone is saying, we will constantly be torn this way and that from one correct diet to another, from one guide to the next. What is the point of all this? Why do we need diets, raw fruit and vegetables, macrobiotics, why so many guide-lines and laws? There is only one reason: so that cash registers keep ringing, book sales keep rising and researchers keep researching.

The reality looks quite different: the diet that will keep you healthy and glad to be alive is one that you yourself will have to discover by your own efforts. It may vary from hour to hour, day to day, age to age and even from place to place. And in order to become slimmer, supposing this is at all necessary, the only thing you need is a change in your *mental attitude* to eating – but never a specific diet or pattern of nutrition.

Throughout history, too, physicians have spoken about correct nutrition, without necessarily using the word 'diet' or a word with that meaning. They always urged us to adopt a sensible, harmonious form of nutrition, which, particularly with the addition of various herbs, had both a preventive and a curative effect. (In this chapter we are not discussing diets specifically prescribed for illnesses: these are sensible and important and should be respected.)

We would emphasise that there is no single guidebook to healthy nutrition, no diet, no medical advice that has validity for all time. There is absolutely nothing to which one could hold, nothing that would give us absolute certainty. A diet that is correct for all humanity simply does not exist. The diet that is correct and healthy exclusively *for you* does exist; but you will find it neither in women's magazines, cookery books and medical manuals, nor in guidebooks for natural food. Even alcohol, cigarettes, white sugar, white flour, devalued and lifeless foodstuffs: though they may have no constructive and strengthening influence on the body, their usefulness or harmfulness varies greatly from person to person and from moment to moment and is sometimes negligible. Whether it is a selective diet, giving up sweets, giving up meat or a strict diet of raw fruit and vegetables according to Professor XYZ's method, nothing will satisfy you in the long run – that we can guarantee you.

Only your own instinct can decide: your heart and soul must be able to sense an inner harmony with whatever it is that you are taking in, if you are to be able to enjoy and digest healthy food and drink. Whenever and whatever you eat and drink, enjoy it in peace, without having either the ingredients, calorie content or fat content calculated for you, thus driving away your healthy appetite. Your personal, natural perception will very rapidly make plain to you the natural limits of quantity, calorific content, etc.

Once and for all, forget all diets and patent formulae and pay some heed to what your body has to say to you from day to day.

You are unique, and no one knows you better than you yourself do. And never fight against fits of craving for food, but try to track down the real cause and work with loving care against it. No one ever became slim, let alone happy, through prohibitions, self-castigation and lamenting, but rather through re-thinking and taking action. The lunar calendar will help you a great deal in this.

There is only one question that you should ask yourself before a meal: what effect is this meal, this food, this cup of coffee going to have right now on me, my body, my mind the strength of my immune system? In other words: am I taking in *vital energy*? You won't find the answer to this in any guidebook in the world. *You* are the expert: find out for yourself which foodstuffs or stimulants are helpful or harmful at which particular times. Only personal instinct can determine this – in the truest sense of the word, your sense of taste.

1. The Six Pillars of Healthy Diet and Digestion

I*n the field* of nutrition, too, you can win back much of the autonomy that so many 'interested parties' are trying to take out of our hands. Quite independently of all the current rules and laws for healthy diet we should like to offer you six stimuli which, taken together, will achieve one thing: awakening a feeling for the correct diet in your particular case. Find your own rhythm, let your actions be uninfluenced and independent, and you will be sure of success. On your way to this instinctive feeling – to the development of an unmistakable sense of taste which can effectively disregard all guidebooks and tables – you will find the necessary provisions on the ensuing pages. These comprise the following:

1. The way to the heart is through the stomach
2. The personal nutritional rhythm
3. Eating what our own land provides
4. Eating with our eyes, nose and tongue
5. The correct combination and sequence
6. Paying heed to our bodies

1. The Way to the Heart is Through the Stomach

Two American heart specialists, Meyer Friedman and Ray Roseman, investigated a group of tax consultants over a period of six months. The consultants were requested to keep an accurate record of their diet, because the two researchers wanted to establish what effect nutrition had on the heart and circulation. With the beginning of the month of April, the most industrious period of the year for tax consultants in the USA, their cholesterol level rose steeply, reaching heights well above the average – even though they had not changed their eating habits. After the submission of tax declarations at the end of April and the consequent slackening off of the workload, cholesterol levels also sank back to normal – without the help of any medicines, therapies or changes in diet.

So: *what* is the role played by diet in raised cholesterol levels?

During a study in the seventies rabbits were fed high-fat food in order to investigate how heart disease arises. In all the groups of experiments the findings coincided – with one exception: in one particular group there were, surprisingly, 60 percent fewer disease symptoms. There was nothing in the bodies of the rabbits that gave any indication why they were better able to assimilate the 'heart attack fodder' than the other animals.

It was only by chance that it was finally discovered some time later that the student whose job it was to feed the rabbits liked now and then to take 'his' rabbits on his arm and stroke them lovingly for several minutes. Subsequent studies on other animals confirmed this connection.

So: *how* did the student prevent heart disease?

By means of these examples we want to remind you of something that we all experience every day: what happens in the hearts and minds of all involved before, during and after cooking and eating has at least as great an influence on the quality and health value of the food, and hence on our bodies and state of health, as the mere quantity and composition of the food ingested and the timing of the meal – if not much more. The thoughts and feelings that accompany you while you cook, sit at table and eat your meals, determine to a great extent the benefit and food-value that the ingested food has for you. It's as simple as that.

The best food, the healthiest diet, is transformed in your body into poison, into superfluous fat, into general debilitation, if the atmosphere in which you cook and eat is spoilt – through lack of affection during the preparation, fear of overweight, through stress in whatever form, and so on. "Just watching is enough to make you fat!" Anyone thinking like that is quite right. His thoughts are what transform food into superfluous fat.

"The way to a man's heart is through his stomach." The proverb states the plain truth. If conversely we say that "Lack of heart also passes through the stomach", it may not yet have quite the same proverbial force, but it is no less true. A meal at Grandma's is not only good because she cooks with the old recipes and because she knows her relatives and all their likes and dislikes. The loving work she puts into the preparation, the loving thoughts about the children and grandchildren transmit pure vitality into the food as it is cooking, regardless of what she is cooking, how much she serves up and how long she has been cooking.

A piece of bread and butter gladly given, without the expectation of anything in return is a thousand times more healthy and strengthening than the best six-course banquet whose only object is to impress the guests.

A carrot peeled lovingly and with kindly thoughts (because one knows that he or she likes to eat carrots) is far better for the digestion and the whole body than a carrot bought at the best health food shop in town and which was only bought because it was supposed to be 'healthy'.

Even freeze-dried instant coffee is healthier than the best freshly ground coffee, if the heart that stirs the spoon does so with benevolent thoughts towards the recipient of the cup of kindness.

You may gain some idea of what is to be made of the 'latest scientific research', if you consider what would have happened if one of the tax advisers had gone to the doctor during the period when his cholesterol level was high. He would have been given the full treatment – perhaps with such good advice as: "You'd better change your diet, otherwise you're in danger of a heart attack", with suggestions for his diet, and in the worst case with drugs. What would have happened would be what happens incredibly often in cases of a high cholesterol level – as every doctor knows: despite all medication, in spite of keeping to all the dietary prescriptions and regulations, the level does not go down by the time of the next appointment. On the contrary: often it is now higher than it was at the beginning of the treatment. Why? Because a feeling, because *fear* has caused the cholesterol level to rise. The anxiety of the tax adviser about missing an appointment. The anxiety of the patient who has to swallow unfiltered the panic-mongering words of the doctor ("I regret to have to inform you…") – an influence that many doctors exert, often unconsciously, and that frequently has a weakening effect even when examining healthy patients (pre-cautionary visits, mass screenings, etc.). On top of that the medicine would have blocked the innate ability of the body rapidly to lower the cholesterol level of its own accord – its natural reactions would have been disturbed.

The only effective remedy, namely the perception that the high cholesterol level was stress-induced, that pressure and anxiety are always self-made, that at any moment in one's life one cannot do more than one is actually doing, that inner tranquillity normalises the cholesterol level and influences the effect of food in our bodies – such a remedy is only rarely prescribed and even more rarely accepted.

"I can't monitor the attitude with which the food is produced in the canteen/restaurant/ready-to-serve food store!" Yes you can monitor it, and you do so every day. Follow up the effect that the food has on you. How do you feel afterwards? And then let your instinct decide whether next time you wouldn't rather have an open sandwich with fresh herbs that you yourself or a well-disposed fellow human being has prepared, instead of bolting down any old meal that has been unlovingly cobbled together or some food from the automat. Just how good the food can taste in a restaurant where the cook is in love or happily married is something we know from personal experience.

In every action, not merely eating and cooking, good intentions are more important than calculating intelligence. We eat atmosphere, love, thoughts and feelings. It is through these that our health improves or deteriorates. As long as a person is dependent on superficial externals, as long as he does not trust his instinct, he will only be able to guess at the difference between Grandma's soup, made from lovingly, naturally grown tomatoes, and ready-to-eat microwave meals, made from chemically sprayed, forced greenhouse tomatoes. The difference is real, nonetheless. Perhaps you are one of those people who have the courage to try and sense the difference once more, without immediately demanding 'proof'. You will not get the proof until later, and for many people that will come too late.

2. The Personal Nutritional Rhythm

Have you ever noticed that the same food seems saltier on some days than on others? That sometimes your favourite dish tastes really excellent and has no unpleasant after-effects, while another time it weighs heavy on your stomach?

Whether a meal agrees with us or not, whether it makes us put on weight or not, is often also dependent on the current position of the moon. When the moon is waxing the same eating habits and quantities much more frequently give us a feeling of fullness, and we put on weight more easily than when the moon is on the wane. At this time the body is much better at absorbing not only medicine, alcohol, nicotine, ointments and even sunlight, but also food. Supposing you have problems with your weight you should observe your eating habits when the moon is waxing. There's absolutely no need for good solid plain cooking to make one fatter, but if it is consumed too often when the moon is waxing, it will certainly push your weight up more easily. In spite of that, there's no point eating nothing but grain and lettuce at this time. As in all things the golden mean is the best way.

Conversely, when the moon is waning one can often eat more than usual without immediately putting on weight. Likewise the body will not take immediate exception to a few sumptuous meals. Even meals eaten directly before going to bed will not have the same 'weight' as when the moon is waxing.

Sometimes a habit can rapidly be changed if a good reason for this is plainly obvious and you have an insight into the causal relations. All your strenuous efforts will be over once you understand the language of your body: try to track down the difference between the waxing and the waning moon and, as far the effect on your diet is concerned, eat what you normally would during the waning phases of the moon and shorten your stride somewhat during the waxing phases.

If additionally you insert a fast day or a fruit-only day at both the new and the full moon and perhaps eat no meat on Wednesdays and Fridays (this old rule has lost none of its validity), then you will have arrived at the ideal slimming programme, effortlessly, all by yourself, without any special diet. At full moon the body stores up too much and at new moon the body's capacity for detoxification is at its peak; on this day it directs all its energies towards cleansing and detoxifying; and, freed from the task of digesting food, it can get to grips with its reserves and the poisons that have accumulated within you.

However, another essential influence on diet and digestion is not merely the phases of the moon, but the forces indicated by the position of the moon in the zodiac.

Again and again these days the talk is of the necessity for a balanced diet, the idea being to meet as well as possible the statistical daily nutritional requirements: proteins, carbohydrates, fat, minerals, vitamins, etc. This idea ignores the fact that certain basic forms of our food – fat, protein, carbohydrate and salt – are not assimilated by the body in the same way every day.

As many parents know, children, whose natural instinct has not yet been watered down so much as it has in adults through sweets or compulsive eating, often go through marked phases of 'eating like a horse': all day long they simply can't get enough generously filled sandwiches, or they stuff themselves with pancakes or highly savoury things.

The fear that in such phases their diet could become unbalanced is completely without foundation. Firstly the fit usually only lasts for a few days; and secondly in the course of several days the body does after all get everything it needs. A meal should never contain everything that is 'healthy' and necessary for life. Formerly as a matter of course people used to follow a form of selective diet because they knew about the varying receptivity of the body from day to day. Only rarely did vegetables, assorted side-salads, meat, cheese and raw fruit and vegetables appear at the same time on the table. It is only in modern times, where food is often misused as a sort of visiting card or badge of prosperity, that we have allowed the true reason for the simplicity of former days to slide into oblivion. With what results can be seen from the large number of diet-induced diseases of affluence. The advice to chew our food slowly is sensible not merely because the stomach can digest meals better if they are thoroughly chopped up. By virtue of slow chewing all the organs of digestion receive precise information, via taste buds, brain and nervous system concerning the type of food that is heading their way, and are thus better able to attune themselves to it. The chaos of information that is triggered off by a profusion of foods and artificial flavourings on the plate deeply disturbs the task of preparing for what has been taken in. With clear, simple information our sense of taste can react much more precisely and the stomach, pancreas and gall-bladder can adjust themselves much better and more exactly.

What were the influences that our forefathers used to watch out for before they served a meal. The following table describes the mutual effect between the position of the moon in the zodiac and the 'food quality' of a day.

Zodiac sign	Food quality	Part of plant	Organ system
Aries	protein	fruit	sense organs
Taurus	salt	root	blood circulation
Gemini	fat	flower	glandular system
Cancer	carbohydrate	leaf	nervous system
Leo	protein	fruit	sense organs
Virgo	salt	root	blood circulation
Libra	fat	flower	glandular system
Scorpio	carbohydrate	leaf	nervous system
Sagittarius	protein	fruit	sense organs
Capricorn	salt	root	blood circulation
Aquarius	fat	flower	glandular system
Pisces	carbohydrate	leaf	nervous system

When the moon is in Aries, Leo and Sagittarius, fruit days prevail in the vegetable kingdom: as a rule these days are especially favourable for the sowing, growth, care, harvesting and storing of fruit. Such days have the best protein qualities, with particular influence on the sense organs. During Taurus, Virgo and Capricorn, the root days, the best salt qualities prevail, and these are favourable for nourishing the blood. Gemini, Libra and Aquarius, the flower days, display the best fat and oil qualities, influencing the glandular system. Cancer, Scorpio and Pisces, the leaf days, possess good carbohydrate qualities and influence the nervous system.

What then is meant by 'food quality' – for example, when the moon is in Pisces and carbohydrate qualities are predominant. Olive farmers know that on some days they can get almost twice as much oil from their fruit as on other days. Many of them know the connection precisely and always consult their moon calendar, in order to reserve the oil days, Gemini, Libra and Aquarius. At harvest time, tea planters in China always follow an agricultural calendar that takes the course of the moon into account.

Simply expressed: the lunar calendar – the course of the moon through the signs of the zodiac – shows in intervals of two to three days varying impulses affecting food and the capacity of the body to utilise this food. In certain ways the carbohydrates in a portion of spaghetti behave differently on a carbohydrate day, in Cancer, Scorpio and Pisces, than they do on other days: the ability of the body to make the best possible use of this spaghetti is not the same for all people and from one day to another. In other words: the harmonious interaction of vegetable foodstuffs and the body, and thus health and well-being, are also dependent on the time of the meal.

Even less than is the case with much of the other information in this book, these influences cannot be transformed into some kind of handy system or formula which you can follow unerringly from now on. Only your own personal observation will open up for you the full impact and value of the knowledge of the food qualities.

Let's take an example: suppose you like to eat a vegetable stew with sausage. Although you always like the taste, you notice that its effect can vary. On certain days you rapidly get an unpleasant feeling of fullness, flatulence or similar uncomfortable sensations. Note down the date, and also write down the times when it tasted especially good and there were no side-effects. After a short time you will discover that the same food qualities, the same sign of the zodiac is in force when a meal is easily or not so easily digested. Was it on root days that the meal in question lay heavy on your stomach a number of times, or was it on fruit, flower or leaf days? You should also observe the effect of meals in which carbohydrates (bread, flour-based food, etc.), fat, fruit or savoury food predominated.

On the basis of this personal perception it is very easy to build up a list of 'good' or 'bad' days for each particular type of food. We are unable to provide such a list or make precise suggestions, because every person reacts differently to the food qualities. There are many possibilities:

* Some people like fatty meals and digest them well precisely on the *fat days*, Gemini, Aquarius and Libra, while other people don't even like the smell of fat on these days. Pay close attention to what you find particularly tasty at this time and how it affects you. You may possibly discover that fatty food agrees with you least of all precisely at this time, and you may have to alter your weekly menu if, for example, your glandular system is disturbed. If your cholesterol level is very high – regardless what the reason is – then note carefully whether it is changed by eating fatty foods on these days, or whether, conversely, going without fatty food precisely at this time brings the level down.

* Some people find bread, for example, particularly easy to digest on the *carbohydrate days*, Cancer, Scorpio and Pisces, while for others even two slices are more than they can take. If you find that you particularly like flour-based foods on these days and at the same time are fighting a running battle with weight problems, then your sensation of hunger is being directed towards the wrong things, for one reason or another (see *overweight* page 81). In such a case try the following experiment: for several months only eat easily digestible bread that is rich in roughage on Cancer, Scorpio and Pisces days, and avoid all dishes with a high carbohydrate content (cereals, potatoes, etc.). Perhaps even this small adjustment will be enough.

* Some people enjoy salty food during the *salt days*, Taurus, Virgo and Capricorn, more than on all other days; whilst others refuse even slightly salted things. A low-salt diet is indicated in many

bodily disorders and illnesses (e.g. high blood pressure). If this has been prescribed by the doctor, then these days are often especially awkward for some patients, because Taurus, Virgo and Capricorn strengthen the (for you) harmful effect of salt. Unfortunately it is often precisely on salt days that you have a particular craving for salty things. Anyone who now acts on the motto "just this once" can completely undermine the results of a whole month's moderation. Anyone who has recognised such an effect within himself will be able with a little discipline to take counter-measures against this appetite.

* On the *protein days*, Aries, Leo and Sagittarius some people can digest fruit or eggs especially well, others especially badly. Observe whether your weekly menu contains a noticeably large or small amount of protein or fruit and what effect this has on you.

Be patient: after only a few weeks or months you will be able to find out by means of the notes you keep and the comparisons you make with the moon calendar at the back of the book, exactly what effects the various food qualities have on you personally and what is particularly good or bad for you and on what days. Your very personal profile could then look something like this (or exactly the opposite):

"On Aries, Leo and Sagittarius everything connected with fruit is good for me. On Taurus, Virgo and Capricorn days root vegetables and salty things are not so good for me. On Gemini, Libra and Aquarius days fatty dishes have less effect on me than at other times. On Cancer, Scorpio and Pisces days I can't get enough pasta, bread and other foods containing carbohydrates."

Such a personal list can become an important tool, especially for people with allergies: a food that triggers of allergic reactions does not cause the same amount of harm on all days of the month. With the aid of the moon calendar, it is an easy matter to find out whether and in what way the current food quality affects the conflict between body and foodstuff. Giving up a particular food for a few days in the month, which may well become necessary as a result of your notes, is clearly not as hard to bear as a life-long dietary regime.

If your food has already been planned for days ahead, or if canteen meals are what await you, then to be sure your list will not at first sight appear to be much use to you. But even then you can still find out whether it agrees with you or whether something lies heavily on your stomach or whether there are unpleasant side-effects – valuable insights for later, when you are able to decide on your menu for yourself or when you want to feel free to give some meal or other a miss. Perhaps you will even find ways to contribute to making the food in the canteen gradually conform more with the real needs of the employees.

Generally speaking there are no fattening or slim-making foods. Every person has his own highly individual approach to food and drink – as indeed he does to whether the moon happens currently to be in Aries or Capricorn. Thus a person who sometimes only feels like eating salad or fruit and another time only wants bread and root vegetables, has no need to be afraid that his diet is one-sided: perhaps it merely means that he is someone whose instinct has awakened.

3. Eating What Our Own Land Provides

You will get to know another basic pillar of healthy diet if you follow this advice: in your daily diet place the main emphasis on *locally grown* food. There are two main reasons for this piece of advice:

Firstly: everything that grows and thrives in a particular region of the world contains all kinds of protective and nourishing elements which are needed by the people living in that region – provided that the plants and animals grow up largely unharmed by chemical fertilisers and poison sprays. This characteristic is not merely confined to the material contents of home-grown plants; their power is also the result of a specific radiation which they possess and which cannot be destroyed by domestic processing and cooking.

Local plants and animals are able to deal with all the influences in the particular environment that can weaken human beings – bacteria, radiation, air pollution etc. This capacity is transferred to those who eat them and strengthens their immune system.

Vegetable or animal foodstuffs that are imported from a distance derive from plants and animals that have adjusted to different conditions and constraints than those found locally. So much so that if they are consumed in large quantities they can in many cases have a really detrimental effect in the destination country. When potatoes were introduced to Europe and chosen as a basic food-stuff, for many decades thereafter a great many people died from illnesses of immune deficiency triggered off by the fact that their organism was not adapted to this particular arable crop.

Just how far-reaching is the capacity of plants to adapt to specific environments may be shown by just one example that is representative of all plants and animals. Gobernadora (*covillea tridentata*) is a Mexican plant that grows on limestone crags on a wafer-thin layer of humus. If we examine its chemical composition we find that it contains about twice as many substances in it as are found in the soil in which it grows – materials that it did not produce itself but absorbed from the surrounding air. As with Gobernadora, so with all plants and animals: they take in every-thing that goes to make up the entire environment – both positive and negative. The body uses the positive element to build itself up and strengthen itself; the negative element – radiation, bacteria, certain poisons – it uses as information which it processes as it would in the case of a homoeopathic remedy (see page 142).

We are all familiar with the fact that local produce is healthier than foreign: why is it, do you think, that a *fino* sherry drunk in a bodega in Seville tastes much better than the same bottle in London or Sydney? Why does hot Mexican food agree with us better in Oaxaca than in Manchester or Vancouver? Why does fish and chips in Italy or hamburger in Mexico lie more heavily on our stomach than at home in Bristol or Washington?

The proverb tells us: "When in Rome, do as the Romans do."

No matter where you happen to be staying, strike up a friendship with the (as yet) unknown, and try eating the local food. Doubtless it will take some time before your body on its travels has adapted to circumstances abroad, and that also applies to the ability to digest an unfamiliar diet. And yet it is precisely through consuming local foodstuffs that you will be able to assist the process of adaptation effectively. Take a close look at the typical holiday-maker abroad, who only asks for the 'usual' (and gets it, too, because the guest is king). What do you see there? An agile, relaxed, healthy person who is genuinely interested in the strange and new?

Of course, tongues and tastes can be trained: anyone who for years and decades has known nothing but sprayed, artificially fertilised and devalued food, from agricultural factories and breeding establishments, processed by the food industry, will not immediately understand this piece of advice, for his body will not be able to recognise the difference straight away. Many children nowadays go "Yuck!" when they are given orange juice from freshly pressed oranges for a change – instead of the yellow, sweet, sticky stuff that they're used to (5 percent orange juice, 95 percent habit-forming substances and water). What is known only to a few people is that long-term 'loyalty' to any particular product of the fast food or ready-to-eat industry is often aroused by means of certain ingredients that trigger off a sort of physical addiction.

Here, too, it is the golden mean that leads to the goal: obviously you do not have to give up those beloved bananas, those exotic vegetables and fruits, that Argentine steak. But the watchword is measure and purpose. For the sake of your health, place the main emphasis on what is local. At least the fresh herbs that you use should always come from round about, best of all from your own herb garden (which can be grown very successfully even on the window ledge of a town flat). This little powerhouse of nature will not let you down, when it's a matter of staying healthy through your own efforts.

Try this experiment: a systematic 'diet' lasting several weeks with natural, biologically grown foods would wake your body up and remind it of its real needs. And perhaps you will even make a surprising discovery: you are now able to eat less, because the natural sense for when you have eaten and drunk your fill will return, and because the body now signals much more quickly that it now has what it needs. Just think how quickly it will now be possible to reduce weight, almost without noticing it and without the slightest self-castigation!

Here's another experiment for you to try: cook your food for longer than usual but at lower temperatures than is indicated or usual. Treat the food as a living being that has only lived in order to serve you: "Live and let live". Leave out all artificial flavouring, pre-prepared seasoning mixtures and the like; cook in enamel pots and pans using wooden spoons. At the very least do not leave any metal cutlery in the food during or after cooking. Only use carefully measured amounts of fresh herbs in your cooking or for seasoning. And then treat your nose and tongue, all your senses and your whole body to this little feast!

Science tells us that pressure cookers can conjure up healthy meals because the ingredients are largely conserved. However, we do not feed ourselves on what chemical analysis has to tell us, but on vibrations, colours, sounds and love.

The second reason for the advice to use local foodstuffs is this: in so doing you are making a decision to support your own agriculture and thus helping the recovery of your own country and in the long term its inhabitants.

What is happening in almost every state in the world in the sphere of agriculture shows, to put it mildly, a deep contempt for mankind. What is called 'policy' in this area is unworthy of the name. At best it is practised by people who have no confidence in nature, and therefore leave all decisions to scientists and statisticians – people who for their part know neither nature nor humanity. At worst it follows exclusively 'economic' interests.

Lurking behind such 'policy' is usually anything but a concern for natural foodstuffs, or concern for the welfare of farmers and consumers. In Europe, for example it is paving the way for the covert intention gradually to eliminate agriculture and in particular small-scale farmers and to transfer the production of food 'on a grand scale' to countries more suited to it, such as the USA. Numerous development aid initiatives in the past and the present served no other purpose than to increase the dependency of third world countries (Africa, Asia, Central America, etc.) on our lifestyle. Here is the latest example of this: only recently a tribe was discovered in New Guinea, consisting of 79 members, who had never come into contact with civilisation before. "As a first relief measure," reported the newspaper, "they have been sent clothing and cooking utensils." There is an old proverb that runs: "God preserve us from well-meaning fools, and send us clever adversaries."

What madness, too, in agriculture: in every country in the world it is precisely the small farms and businesses that are our future hope for genuine foodstuffs, because they alone have the ability to produce food of high quality in harmony with natural laws and without harming the environment. Agricultural mega-concerns are often unwilling 'for economic reasons' to foot the bill for raising and nurturing crops and animals in such a way that the food derived from them really is food and not just so much padding with which to stuff, bloat and fill our bodies.

The knowledge that in all our food wholeness and inner harmony have to be preserved has almost slipped into oblivion in this age of super-canteens and ready-to-serve dishes. The fact is that genuine food has to be allowed to grow without artificial fertilisers and poison sprays. There cannot be high quality foodstuffs if these are torn apart by chemical or mechanical effects. All the important accompanying and complementary materials, vitamins, minerals and trace elements, right down to colour and aroma, are either severely damaged or eliminated.

The ways and means of a misanthropic agricultural policy are complex: their effects are not only visible in butter mountains and the destruction of fruit: storage costs are artificially kept higher than transport costs. Certain prices are kept artificially low. The motto is buy rather than produce yourself. In Europe in many cases farmers have to pay to get rid of milk, after years of heavy subsidies for the dairy industry. In Austria milk is exported abroad, where it is processed into butter, which is then re-imported and sold at a much higher price than it costs in the butter-producing country. Almost everywhere the pattern is the same: political decisions bring farmers, via pricing 'from above' and promises that can only be kept in the short term, to a point where they are dependent on certain products and methods of cultivation. Then the policy changes, and dependence on prices and quantities purchased drives numerous small farmers into ruin. The agricultural factories grow.

The list of examples could be extended indefinitely, but the important point is simply the inescapable conclusion: healthy, high-quality food, produced by small businesses with loving care and in harmony with nature, is clearly not wanted by the powers that be, since everything is done to pull the rug from under the feet of those trying to bring it to our table. The argument that after all hardly anyone nowadays would want to be a 'small farmer' is stupid. Anyone that transforms fertile soil into a desert can hardly complain that nothing can grow there. Anyone that gags a person should hardly be surprised if he is lost for words. There are always enough people with strong hearts and hands, for whom the happiness and satisfaction of producing quality and health in tune with nature is far more important than the number of days holiday they get, the size of their fields and stalls, and the number of programmes on TV. However, politics is almost exclusively oriented to what is good for the 'big folks' and creates hardly any incentives or favourable conditions for what is natural and beautiful. What can one call an EC policy that gives farmers money to give up their farms and let fields lie fallow, and then on top of that tries wherever possible to get the public to see this as an 'environmentally friendly action'? We trust that you will be able to find for yourself the words to describe such magnanimity.

We are all painfully aware of the consequences of this policy because we all suffer under it. However, not everyone knows just how great is the power of the individual. Not everyone knows that every single one of us with his own thinking and actions can gently take countermeasures to put the brakes on this faulty development and give it a new and positive direction. You are the customer; you are the king.

By deciding for local produce you can work against this downward trend and gradually gain control over what appears on your table, over its origin and quality. You can take a hand in determining whether countless unnecessary shipments of goods continue to pollute the air, whether our countries dry up and become fallow land or industrial wastelands, or whether the earth is there for us – just as God wishes and we need it to be. Of course, an unthinking consumer *only* wants an apple. He's paying for the apple – goods for money, end of discussion – irrespective of whether the apple has travelled half-way round the globe or simply comes from the orchard of a farmer in his home village. The main thing is the apple, and no maggots, but the fruit farmer knows that there are no apples without a tree and that a tree needs space and care. Just because the end user does not have to worry about the tree, this does not mean that he should be indifferent to the tree – likewise the soil in which it is rooted, the sun wind and clouds above it, its vitality and the strength that it has absorbed and concentrated in each of its fruits. Without a tree there can be no apple. Maybe the customer will never in his life get to see the tree that produced his apple, but he would never get to see the apple either, if the tree weren't growing somewhere.

A great part of the fears and dependences of our time arise through thinking without due regard to interrelations. But what is fear other than 'not understanding'?

Many people also think: "The more exotic and faraway the land my vegetables come from, the more my guests or family will be impressed. Who can I possibly serve things that were grown just around the corner, to say nothing of those tiny apples from the farm nearby?" There is an excellent remedy for such ideas: never go to eat where such ideas are at home, and don't get yourself invited by such show-offs. Cook for yourself the things that grow round about, and only invite real friends. Then everything will taste just fine to everybody.

There are two questions that you should eventually ask yourself if you decide to follow our suggestions. First of all: where can I obtain healthy, naturally grown foods?

There is no point cursing about sprayed and worthless food. You should have the courage not to buy things that you have sensed and recognised to be worthless. Day in, day out advertising brings home to us only one thing: not that we have a right to precise information, but that we can be effortlessly seduced – among other things into the belief that something is healthy because it comes in a green package. If you have always eaten only imported, sprayed, irradiated and devalued greenhouse fruit and vegetables, treat yourself for once to the pleasure of preparing and eating your favourite dish made from local organic produce. When you have tasted the difference you will know why it is time for a rethink. Perhaps you will also take heart from the fact that you are not compelled to eat nothing but cabbage in winter. There are a great many arable crops and other foods that are very suitable for storing. In addition in temperate latitudes the body is well-tuned to the seasons and does not absorb fresh vitamins so well in winter. An apple a day would be enough. Once you have decided on this course, you will not have much difficulty, perhaps in collaboration with friends and neighbours, in gaining access to sources of genuine foodstuffs. Find the shop, the vegetable stall, the farmer who can deliver food that really nourishes you and your family. These things are available near at hand.

The second question is: how can I grow healthy food for myself? Unfortunately there is not sufficient room here for a short gardening course; but this much can be said: anyone who has a garden of his own knows all about variable results in the yield. Even under identical conditions (soil, climate, care) it can happen that the yield is sometimes good and sometimes not so good, or even downright bad. Someone who would like in future to dispense with chemical fertilisers and sprays will be pleased to learn that by applying the art of doing things at the right time one can greatly assist this intention, indeed one can sometimes even fully realise it – whether as a market-gardener or farmer, as a garden owner or even when you only have a balcony or window ledge to call your own. The moment of harvesting is also of decisive importance in connection with how durable the produce is and how suitable for storage without artificial preservatives and poison sprays. When this present book goes to press there may not yet be an English translation of our previous work on the effect of lunar rhythms in garden, field and forest (Paungger & Poppe, *Vom richtigen Zeitpunkt*, Munich 1992), but this will certainly make its appearance soon. Keeping to the lunar rhythms will greatly assist you in dispensing with chemicals and thus bringing healthy food to the dinner table.

Nature has seen to it that no one has to travel far in order to obtain what his body needs. What our heart needs is even nearer, not a hand's breadth away...

4. *Eating with Eyes, Nose and Tongue*

Whether cooking is done with love or not, whether meals are eaten at the right moment, whether the food is local or imported, at every moment of your life you have a further choice between a meal that affords you vitality and food that tends rather to weaken your organism.

Eat with your eyes, nose and tongue. Let colour, smell and taste decide what may enter your body and what may not. In a word: listen to the music in your food.

Whether it is a Beethoven symphony or authentic folk music, Indian sitar or Eric Clapton's guitar – almost everyone knows a particular type of music or individual pieces or melodies which gladden the heart and help to get over many a mood of depression. Music does not always have the same effect: from time to time even a favourite piece can be boring or lose itself without trace in the organs of hearing and the convolutions of the brain.

The same applies to eating: eyes, tongue and nose are the 'ears' with which we sense and assess our food before it vanishes into the depths of our stomach and digestive organs. You should give these ears a chance at every mealtime: listen to the music of eating, look at the colours, smell the aroma, take you time tasting it – and have the courage to trust completely what your sense organs tell you. In a fraction of a second your whole body, not just your brain, reacts to this information either with "Yes, that is just the thing for me right now" or "No, that isn't the right thing for me just now". The latter judgement can either mean "This isn't the right moment for this particular dish" or "These foods are in general unhealthy for me and don't agree with me".

You should trust this judgement. Little by little your instinct will develop and even render you no longer dependent on the moon calendar or the food qualities, because your body will in any case know about its own rhythms and needs. It is simply that everything has been done to train this instinct out of us.

Trust your instinct: from one moment to another, from one meal to the next, from one hungry feeling to the next, it will not let you down, if you seek to discover for yourself what does you good or otherwise at any given moment. This instinct will allow you gaily to say good-bye to the conviction that there is anything that is always good, that always helps. "A diet of raw vegetables and fruit is always good. Camomile tea has always helped me. Butter is harmful/healthy for everyone" – these are thoughts that you should neither take on board nor spread abroad. What your instinct tells you can never be generalised. What is right and good for you can be useless or harmful even for your own children, especially if you try to force it on them.

5. Sequence and Combination

The choice of sequence and combination of foods has considerable influence on their effect and digestibility.

Perhaps this ancient wisdom will surprise you: you should always eat raw before cooked. More or less in this order: fruit or nuts before lettuce and raw vegetables. Then sour milk, bread or milk, if these form part of your menu. And only then, finally, foods that are somewhat harder to digest, such as high-fat foods, meat, cooked vegetables, eggs and cheese. Sweet foods should always come at the end. If you have been accustomed to another sequence or have been eating raw and cooked food at the same time, try this sequence for a few weeks. The result will speak for itself.

What you chop up together on your plate, the combination of vegetables, for instance, is equally important. Every farmer and gardener knows this: the correct community of plants in the area under cultivation contributes a lot to smoothing the path to natural agriculture. Mixed cultivation, as it is called nowadays, is of inestimable value, because the plants help each other to keep pests in check and deter them at the outset.

Plants that are in tune with one another in nature also enter into harmonious combinations on our plate. Two types of vegetable on one plate are not easily digestible for everybody. Someone who has a sensitive stomach ought not to eat individual foods simultaneously but one after the other. Vegetables that do not form a harmonious plant community in the garden do not belong together on the plate either.

The basic rule consists in bringing crops that grow below ground and those that grow above ground into a well-balanced relationship. Any imbalance in this regard (for instance, *only* potatoes and onions or *only* tomatoes and beans) has far-reaching consequences that affect the whole human being, both his body and his prevailing mood. Even alcoholic drinks which are obtained from arable crops – vodka from potatoes or whisky from barley, brandies from pomes or from stone fruit – have completely different effects on body and mind.

You will be able to find out in many gardening books which plant communities are favourable in the garden and thus on the dining table. An excerpt from the manifold possible combinations is given in the following table:

Vegetable	Favourable next to...
potatoes	cabbage types, spinach, dwarf beans, kohlrabi, dill
carrots	onions, spinach, lettuce
cucumbers	onions, runner beans, celery, beetroot, parsley, lettuce, kohlrabi, cabbage types, dwarf beans
peas	celery, lettuce
celery	dwarf beans, spinach, onions, runner beans, tomatoes, leeks, kohlrabi, cabbage types, cucumbers, peas
spinach	tomatoes, runner beans, kohlrabi, carrots, potatoes, cabbage types
tomatoes	celery, spinach, onions, parsley, cabbage types, kohlrabi, lettuce, leeks, dwarf beans, carrots
lettuce	onions, tomatoes, runner beans, dwarf beans, radishes, dill, peas, cucumbers, strawberries, carrots, leeks
onions	tomatoes, strawberries, cucumber, parsley, lettuce, kohlrabi

Unfavourable both in the garden and on the table are: beans next to onions, parsley next to lettuce, cabbage next to onions, beetroot next to tomatoes, potatoes next to onions, tomatoes next to peas, red cabbage next to tomatoes, peas next to beans.

If potatoes are part of your staple diet and play a central role in your meals, you should always add fresh parsley, chives or other herbs. Many herbs contain strong powers that are able to counterbalance the heavy, 'subterranean' emphasis.

6. *Paying Heed to Our Bodies*

It is important to listen attentively not only to the music in food but also to the music in the body. Rightly understanding its tones and signals, learning its language is a necessity for healthy diet and digestion, and for maintaining health through one's own efforts.

Rule number one is never to eat more than the feeling of hunger dictates. The body needs about five minutes to signal that it has overstepped the limit. Thus if you already feel full during a meal then you have been eating five minutes too long. It would therefore be highly advantageous to stop while you still feel a marginal sensation of hunger. This will generally disappear after a short time. (The exception to this: your appetite is aimed at appeasing another, psychological hunger. In that case there is no food in the world, be it ever so delicious, that will really satisfy you.)

During colds, for example, hunger is mostly absent, and rightly so. Don't eat anything, or at least anything heavy or in excess of usual amounts, and have a lot to drink. Every animal if it is ill or wounded instinctively does the right thing: it stops taking solid food and rests. Each digestive process uses up some energy first before the body places the energy once more at our disposal. The body signals to us in due time when it needs renewed energies, and this moment generally comes much later than we think.

Rule number two concerns the digestive and elimination processes. There are few subjects in the area of preventive health-care and treatment of illness that are dealt with so superficially – so neglectfully – as our digestive processes. A sure sign of this is the state of many public toilets. Only in the rarest cases are these places that one likes going to because the atmosphere there is conducive to relaxation, to giving oneself up to one of the most natural and 'liberating' processes in the world – these places that even a prime minister goes to on foot.

An equally sure sign of the state of our foodstuffs and the generally disordered digestion for which these are responsible, is the incredibly high consumption of toilet paper in western countries. Formerly for the best of reasons it was taken for granted that medical practitioners and doctors immediately enquired about the composition of their patients' stool, and drew firm conclusions from this as to diagnosis and therapy.

Even in the parental home and at school natural rhythms of digestion are trained out of us. Parents consider something an 'achievement' which ought never to be seen as such. At school digestive processes have to wait until the lesson or even the morning or afternoon session is over. Little by little the intestine becomes accustomed to this bad treatment, being fed scarcely digestible food and having its signals ignored. It becomes sluggish and contributes through digesting its contents too slowly to the process of self-poisoning. When the digestive processes get out of balance and this expresses itself in constipation, then the poisons that are normally eliminated from the body remain there too long and are partially re-absorbed through the large intestine. Almost everyone has experienced this: ignore the signal for even just a few minutes, and it can be hours or even days before it comes back again. What happens during this time you now know.

Of course it is not always easy to interrupt school lessons or business transactions with the words: "Would you excuse me a moment...?" But the alternative is self-poisoning. Pay no attention to the sidelong glances and do your health a favour.

The opposite extreme, a person who is meticulously attentive to 'regularity' and regulates his watch by his trips to the toilet, is of course equally mistaken. Often there are good reasons for the 'unpunctuality' of the bowels. Every person has his own rhythm – the goal should be to get to know it and try to do it justice.

2. A Brief Look at Herbal Lore

Take your time to think about the lines that follow, make a mental note of what is said, and return to it again and again in the coming days. At first sight the information contained there seems incredible, but it has been substantiated by direct experience in every human generation. It is our hope that through your own efforts you will discover what it actually signifies.

Nature always allows a quite specific diversity of herbs to grow around a house – provided that the soil is still in its natural state and not artificially fertilised or sprayed. Which herbs these are depends on who is living in the house and which plants its inhabitants need for their well-being, and for the prevention, relief and healing of any illnesses that may arise. If one of the inhabitants has a physical weak point or gets a particular illness, the corresponding herb will appear in the vicinity, simultaneously, or sometimes even a short while beforehand – as if out of the blue. When these occupants leave and another family moves in, then the nature and composition of the herbs in the immediate surroundings will change and adapt to the health requirements of the new inhabitants.

What is the significance of this information for you? Why do so many people always come back to the idea that nature has to be 'mastered', when all the time it deals so wisely and generously with us? Did you know that many of our 'weeds' – from stinging nettles through gout-weed through daisies to dandelions – possess immense healing powers for a great many ailments? Why is it that the sight of them causes so many people to eradicate them without mercy instead of availing themselves of their great usefulness? What is it that prevents us from acting upon what we all know in our hearts, namely that we are only leaves on the tree of nature?

Perhaps you now see the multicoloured manifold world of medicinal and seasoning herbs, those miniature powerhouses, in a different light. There is hardly a physical ailment, hardly an illness, that cannot be relieved or healed by means of the leaves, fruit or roots of a naturally occurring plant. Anyone who works lovingly and wisely with herbs in the kitchen not only conjures up tasty dishes on the table but also health for all the people that sit around it. Many of our kitchen herbs are plants with preventive and curative effects on many illnesses – from parsley and chives through rosemary and sage to lovage and mugwort. Unfortunately in many cases they are now only considered to be taste enhancers – a property that is completely insignificant once one knows what profound value they can have for a healthy life.

With the table of comparative vitamin C content on page 207 we are not trying to prove the great value of numerous wild herbs, but merely to place before you just what we are depriving ourselves of in favour of feeble and tasteless vegetables from guaranteed chemically sprayed greenhouse cultivation. Similar tables can be drawn up for all the other vitamins, as well as for protein and mineral content: in every case herbs and wild vegetables come out far better than cultivated vegetables.

Vitamin C content in mg/100 g of edible portion (averages)

Cultivated vegetables		Wild vegetables	
endive salad	10	daisies	87
chicory	10	coltsfoot	104
lettuce	13	chickweed	115
green beans	20	dandelions	115
asparagus	21	common sorrel	117
green peas	25	gallant soldier	125
leeks	30	lesser celandine	131
lamb's lettuce	35	goosefoot	157
Chinese cabbage	36	wild mallows	178
Swiss chard	39	cow parsley	179
Savoy cabbage	45	Good King Henry	184
white cabbage	46	gout-weed	201
red cabbage	46	Fat hen	236
fresh spinach	52	hogweed	291
garden cress	39	watercress	314
cauliflower	73	stinging nettle	333
curly cale	95	hairy willow herb	351
broccoli	114	great burnet	360
Brussels sprouts	114	silverweed	402
average value	47		209

Source

Cultivated vegetables: Souci et al. 1986–7   Wild vegetables: Franke & Kensbock 1981, Schneider 1984

The main reasons for the decline in herbal knowledge in the last century are not only to be sought in the rise of the pharmaceutical industry, but also above all in the fact that two of its 'secrets' have almost slid into oblivion. Their rediscovery is what concerns us here.

The Secrets Lore of Medicinal Herbs

Many readers have perhaps already heard reports or even had personal experiences with cranky preachers of herbalism or gnarled old mountain farmers who by applying a few dried plants or strange-smelling elixirs were able to heal even severe illnesses and wounds. To be sure, we do not know every secret and successful formula of these people; however, we shall be revealing the most important of them on the following pages. In this section, as in all the others in this book, we trust that you prefer personal experience to all forms of theory. For this reason we shall not involve ourselves in the disputes that rage between the adherents of various trends of belief, and we leave it to you to form your own judgement.

One secret of all successful medicinal herbalists is contained in the insight that each plant that has a healing effect can only unfold its complete power as a *totality* – that when the active agents it contains are isolated in a chemically pure form, they do not have nearly the same effect and never will – despite all the assurances of science to the contrary.

A multiplicity of active agents is contained in every herb, often gathered together in a single plant, and new agents are still being discovered today, even in plants that have been known for a long time. After numerous shifts in medical outlook the recognition is slowly gaining acceptance once more that the whole is always more than the sum of its parts, that the pure active agents of a medicinal herb, even when in high, barely tolerable doses are still weaker in the long run than the plant or part of a plant taken as an entity in itself. Someone who strips a plant down to its component parts in order to release its active agents is like a person who takes a bird apart to fathom the secret of its song – or who reads the notes of a Mozart serenade and thinks to himself: "What a lot of wasted paper between the notes!"

Using the active agents in their pure form is often just the same nonsense as was dreamed up by nutritional science at the turn of the century when it declared that the roughage in food was superfluous. Of course plants contain materials which seem to be useless or ineffective when they are extracted and used experimentally on mice and men with the limited methods of science. Many of these seemingly superfluous materials even possess, depending on the dose, a more or less faint toxic effect. What is overlooked here is the fact that nature in its wisdom has also built such toxins into the plant so that they can act as a protection and antidote against an overdose of the healing agents in the plant. In fact each 'good' agent when in its pure form and taken in large doses sometimes possesses a poisonous effect equal to that of the slightly poisonous components of the plant.

To tear apart the interplay and harmony between all the components of a plant makes no sense at all. Nature does not work in such a roundabout way that it forces us first with great effort and expense to extract the 'goodness' in plants before we can make use of it.

The fact that a medicinal herb can only work in its totality is part of age-old folk-wisdom, and it can never be driven into oblivion through the efforts of the pharmaceutical industry and health ministries – through expert opinion which is financed by these agencies (and is thus of course quite unbiased). Just as a hundred years ago recognised medicine thought differently than it does today, in a hundred years' time it will look back pityingly on the current state of medical knowledge. However, there is no need for the reader to wait another hundred years, until the hands with which he is gathering nettles receive the blessing of scientific research. No one is dictating to us yet that we have to believe that sage only displays its effectiveness when it has been grown in large plantations, sprayed with pesticides and reaches us packed in tubes, tea bags and pills.

So do not be afraid: always use the totality of a medicinal herb or of one of its parts – fruit, root, leaf or flower or all of them together. Which parts of a plant promise the greatest effect is written in any good herbal book.

Which of these herbs do you think is more effective?

A sage seed seeks out for itself a particular place to open up, grow and ripen. In its 'correct' place it sprouts up, encounters sun, wind and rain, struggles to assert itself, puts down deep roots in order to get to vital moisture and minerals, grows in the neighbourhood of numerous other plants, adapts to the climate of radiation and all the negative influences in the environment in order to survive. This wild sage is plucked by skilled hands at just the right moment, lovingly and carefully dried or stored, prepared into an infusion for liver or gall-bladder complaints and drunk at the right moment by a sick person living in the same surroundings under the same climatic conditions as the plant itself. In other words: the sage grew *for* this suffering person.

Another sage seed grows up on a distant plantation, sown at any old time, perhaps ripening in a greenhouse, nursed, watered and tended, treated with pesticides, rescued from weeds, putting down feeble and shallow roots, gathered at any old time and sold to a pharmaceutical firm. There some time or other it is further processed and extracted, the active agents are isolated and processed into a preparation to combat liver and gall-bladder complaints; this turns up at a wholesalers and eventually reaches the pharmacies of another country and is prescribed by a doctor for a sick person. In other words, *what did this sage grow for?*

This example contains the second secret of all medicinal herb experts: the effectiveness of a plant is determined by correct timing when gathering, processing and using it, as well as the location in which it grows.

If you follow all three stimuli – the correct moment of gathering, processing and application – then the beneficial effects of the medicinal herb will be greatly increased and will be able to relieve and heal even protracted and chronic illnesses that are not amenable to conventional therapeutic methods. If the plant originates from near you its curative power will be additionally enhanced.

Perhaps you now see our advice that you should use local vegetables, fruit and other foods in a somewhat clearer light. If you yourself are in a position to observe the correct timing when dealing with herbs, you will now find out all the rules connected with this.

Correct Timing in Herbal Knowledge

First of all a word regarding the gathering of wild herbs: respect for nature and consideration for one's neighbours dictate that with all herbs (including 'weeds') you only gather as much as you need for your current purposes or for your anticipated winter requirements. Always stick to herbs that you know well and can identify with certainty. Always leave a few plants behind and only pick what will be required for use. That is usually less than you think. You should proceed with especial care when digging up roots, because otherwise the plant could be exterminated, at least on the site where you found it.

Rare herbs that are protected by law should only be bought in herbal shops, even though you then have no control over origin and timing. The spirit of the plant is still alive and can be of service to you if you use it at the right time, particularly if you have confidence in your own powers of self-healing.

The power of a wild herb is not evenly distributed over the whole plant. Many gathering times are very unfavourable because the active agent is located in the root, but it is the flowers that you need to use. It can also happen that you are gathering flowers or leaves when in fact the curative power is currently concentrated in the fruit. In choosing the correct time for gathering your personal feeling and observation of the state of the weather should always take precedence. Certainly the flower days (Gemini, Libra and Aquarius) are in general very suitable for picking flowers, but if the sky is overcast and the weather is cold, then the fact that it's a favourable moment will not help much. One should always be alert to what is appropriate and feasible *today*. The advice concerning the correct time for gathering herbs is very valuable, but if good, dry weather conditions are not forthcoming then it's pointless to collect herbs.

The Best Season

A plant has the greatest curative power when it is still young. The effort that it had to make in order to germinate and sprout also increases the power that it is able to deliver to us. With young plants the ingredients are released more easily, with older plants often not at all (for instance silicic acid). For this reason the spring is almost always the most favourable season for gathering herbs, but with many herbs enough young plants (or at least young leaves) can still be found at other times of the year to cover your needs.

The Best Time of Day

The best times to dig up *roots* are at night, early in the morning and in the evening. Late morning, when the dew has dried, is the best gathering time for *leaves*. *Flowers* should be fully unfolded and picked in sunshine. Their healing power is greatly reduced shortly before they fade. *Seeds and fruit* may be gathered at any time of day. They are less sensitive than other parts of the plant; however, one should avoid the heat of midday.

Phase and Position of the Moon in the Zodiac

The current phase of the moon and its position in the zodiac have a significant bearing on gathering and also on using medicinal herbs. A herb that is gathered for the healing or strengthening of those parts of the body that are governed by the zodiac sign of the gathering day is especially effective. For example, herbs gathered on Taurus days are particularly helpful with throat complaints. An excellent tea for bladder inflammations can be made from white dead nettles gathered on Libra days. The various stimuli are once again summarised in the following table:

Sign	Gather herbs for...
Aries	headaches, eye complaints
Taurus	sore throat, ear complaints
Gemini	tensions in the shoulders, lung complaints (for inhalation)
Cancer	bronchitis; stomach, liver and gall-bladder complaints
Leo	heart and circulation complaints
Virgo	disorders of the digestive organs and pancreas, nervous complaints
Libra	hip complaints, diseases of the kidneys and gall-bladder
Scorpio	diseases of the sexual and eliminating organs; good gathering day for all herbs
Sagittarius	vein diseases
Capricorn	bone and joint complaints, skin diseases
Aquarius	vein diseases
Pisces	foot complaints

However, do not forget that when you are gathering herbs the weather must be dry. It may well be that one has to wait a little longer for good conditions, but on the other hand there are many prolonged and chronic sicknesses that frequently can be successfully treated with herbs collected during the correct sign of the zodiac.

Full Moon and Scorpio

The full moon and the moon in Scorpio are ideal gathering times
for all herbs and areas of use. At full moon the entire plant is active
in all its parts – no doubt one reason why in former times practitioners of herbal medicine were greeted with mistrust: they were
(and still are) often out and about at night, because the curative
power is then at its height and the light of the full moon assists the
search.

The Individual Parts of the Plant

* The correct moment to dig up *roots* is the early spring, when the
plant is not yet in full growth, or the autumn, when the herb has
withdrawn into itself again; the curative forces have then descended
into the roots. You should always dig up roots when the moon is
full, waning or new – particularly those that serve to cure serious
illnesses. New moon is a good moment because the powers of the
plant have gone down into the roots. Under no circumstances
should the roots be exposed to sunlight. The night hours before
sunrise or the late evening are therefore the best times.

The root days of Taurus, Capricorn and Virgo are suitable as
gathering days (or better still, gathering nights); however, Taurus
is not quite so good as the other two signs.

* Almost the whole year is suitable for gathering *leaves*, provided
that the plants are young. After the plant has already been producing sap for a some time, or is already in bloom or has not been
mown, it is no longer so suitable for curative purposes. It is not
necessary that picking should take place when the sun is shining,
but the morning dew should have evaporated, so late morning is
the best time. Leaves should be gathered when the moon is waxing, between new and full moon and on leaf days (Cancer, Scorpio
and Pisces). As we have already mentioned, herbs gathered during
Scorpio possess a special curative power. In addition they are outstandingly suitable for drying, preserving and storing. On the other

hand, herbs gathered during Cancer and Pisces are better used straight away.

A special exception to this is the *stinging nettle*. This outstanding blood-purifying remedy should be gathered exclusively when the moon is on the wane, and nettle tea should also only be drunk during that period (for precise details about a cure using stinging nettles see page 146).

* For *flowers* the most favourable gathering times are spring and summer, when the plants are in full bloom, particularly at midday. The weather should be warm, the sun should be shining, so that the flowers are open and the healing force has travelled to the blooms; faded plants are unsuitable. You should gather the flowers when the moon is waxing or full, preferably on flower days (Gemini, Libra or Aquarius) – or simply during the day at full moon, regardless of the zodiac sign.

* Fruits and seeds should be ripe when gathered, neither green nor squashy. Thus only summer or autumn are likely gathering times. More important than the time of day is that the weather should be dry; however, you should avoid the greatest midday heat. Fruits and seeds gathered when the moon is waxing are more suited for immediate use, because they do not dry well and absorb too much juice. Good gathering days are the fruit days (Aries, Leo and Sagittarius) when the moon is waning: these guarantee good keeping properties. The most unfavourable days for collecting fruit are Capricorn, Pisces, Cancer and Virgo.

Stocking up Medicinal Herbs

Herbs that are not intended for immediate use but rather as winter supplies should be gathered either shortly before full moon, during full moon or when the moon is on the wane. Admittedly a plant gathered when the moon is waning does not contain the greatest possible curative power, but then what is the use of gathering a plant for storage during the waxing moon – a plant that will not dry properly and will start to go mouldy and rot after a short time?

In addition plants have different drying times. You should therefore take particular care to extend the drying time of plants that were gathered when the moon was waxing into the waning phases of the moon. Carry out the 'rustle test' before packing or storing in containers: dried herbs that do not rustle or crackle, when the waning phase and new moon are already past, are unsuitable for lengthy storage and should be used straight away.

Care is the highest precept when preserving, drying, storing and keeping herbs. If a mistake were to cause the destruction of a large quantity of these valuable gifts of nature, that would indeed be regrettable. When drying the plants take them to a shady spot and turn them often. A natural material that is pervious to air, perhaps a wooden duckboard or paper, is a suitable base; but under no circumstances use any kind of metal or plastic sheets.

The correct time for storing and filling in jars or cardboard boxes is always when the moon is on the wane, regardless of the date the herbs were gathered. Never put them into containers when the moon is waxing, otherwise there is a danger they might rot. Dark jars, cardboard boxes and paper bags are the most suitable containers. The plants will remain dry and protected from the light, and both aroma and medicinal power will be retained.

Incidentally, in the case of many medicinal and kitchen herbs (such as marjoram, thyme, lovage and parsley) it is sufficient to hang several plants upside down like a bunch of flowers in an airy place until they have dried. This method saves space, looks good, and the aroma creates a pleasant atmosphere in a room. Quick-drying herbs are most suited for this as there is then no danger of rotting. Kitchen herbs that are constantly used should simply be hung up and pulled off when needed.

After reading these tips you are perhaps coming round to thinking that herbs bought from a pharmacy, health food store or herbal store are worthless, since in their preparation attention has almost never been paid to the art of correct timing. However, you should not underestimate the power of these plants. They have their value and can help very well, above all when they are used with the correct mental attitude. Inwardly express an invitation to the plant to unite with your own powers of self-healing: then sometimes when a cold is coming on it will help to chew a few stalks of chives. It is only in chronic, stubborn illnesses that the correct moment of gathering is of quite particular importance and should be adhered to absolutely. The successes of herbal practitioners speak for themselves.

Preparation and Use

Medicinal herbs often have the best effect when eaten raw as a salad (watercress, young dandelion), as a vegetable (sage, elderberry) or as a spinach (stinging nettles, wood garlic). In addition to that there are many other equally effective methods of preparation and use, about which numerous herbals give valuable advice, such as which method of use promises most success in dealing with a specific problem. We should like to discuss a few of these methods here:

* *Teas and infusions*: For the preparation of teas young herbs containing essential, rapidly volatile oils are especially suitable. Prolonged boiling would reduce their curative effect.

Put as much of the dried or fresh herb as you can hold in three fingers into a cup and pour boiling water over. Cover and leave to draw for three to ten minutes and then strain (don't use a metal strainer). A valid rule of thumb is that the tea is ready when the herbs have sunk to the bottom; however, some herbs that contain a lot of oil will not sink even after several hours: in such cases ten to fifteen minutes is enough. The tea should be drunk at once because the medicinal ingredients are evaporating all the time.

* *Boiling* (extraction): Boiling is suitable for plants containing curative ingredients that are not readily soluble (silicic acid, bitters, tannic acid), and especially for wood, roots or stems. Put the plants in an enamel pot full of cold water and bring slowly to the boil. The boiling time is a matter of instinct; as a rule fifteen minutes is enough, sometimes a little longer. Where possible avoid using pots made of steel, iron, copper or brass.

* *Cold extraction*: With cold extraction one puts sensitive herbs in a pot and leaves them standing overnight. In addition to this it is sometimes a good idea next day to strain the herbs and bring them to the boil in some fresh water (not the liquid produced by cold extraction) and in this way to gain the remaining medicinal ingredients. Extracts containing oils produce mild embrocations.

* *Raw juices*: Many herbs are good for crushing. However, the juices do not keep well and should be used at once (depending on the herb, as a drink or perhaps as a compress).

* *Tinctures*: Tinctures are thin extracts which are mostly obtained from diluted ethyl alcohol. Place a handful of herbs in dark bottles and fill them up for example with fruit brandy, until the herbs are covered. Store for about two weeks in a warm place and the tincture will be ready for use.

* *Ointments and plaster mixtures*: Plants and plant extracts can be ground or boiled down with soft fats and made into ointments or mixtures for plasters. If it is possible for you to buy meat from a farmer who still raises his stock in a natural way, then ask him for fat from a pig that was slaughtered at full moon (perhaps he will actually know that the meat is then much more succulent and keeps better). The fat should be rendered down at a low heat and when the moon is waning; but not on a Virgo day, otherwise it will easily go mouldy and not keep so well.

Fat like this is very valuable both as the basis of an ointment and also for poultices. Put fresh herbs (for example marigolds) into the warmed pork fat and allow it to fry for a short time – about as long as for an escalope. Two handfuls of herbs to a jam-jar of fat are sufficient. Stand the mixture in a cool place overnight and warm it gently the following day until it becomes fluid once more. Strain it through a fine sieve into clean jars and store it in the dark. Such an ointment is an outstanding remedy for various illnesses, for instance as a chest embrocation for coughs and bronchitis or for varicose veins.

Patience and love are needed for this work: it cannot produce good results under pressure. It is only in this way that the right feel can be developed for the preparation and relative amounts of herbs and fat, which is left to your instinct. When producing ointments you should also always use enamel pots and wooden spoons for stirring.

A good time for the production of ointments is when the moon is waxing, possibly a flower day (Gemini, Libra, Aquarius) and full moon. Plants possess great curative powers at full moon, and then after the overnight cooling period the jars are filled when the moon is on the wane – which guarantees the ointment will keep. Bottling in general should take place when the moon is waning; however, not on Cancer or Virgo days. It is perfectly all right to leave ready-heated pots of ointment and flowers in a cellar or refrigerator until the moon has started to wane and only then sieve and bottle them.

* *Herb pillows*: Herbs for herb pillows should be picked when the moon is waxing, and when the moon is on the wane they should be put into pillows of a thick, natural material (e.g. linen) and then sewn up. If they are gathered on flower days (Gemini, Libra, Aquarius), their fragrance will give pleasure for a long time. Even herbs that have been bought should be processed when the moon is waning. Air them and loosen the pillows when the weather is dry, in order to prevent the herbs from rotting.

Herb pillows used for rheumatism, allergies, nervousness, disordered sleep and many other situations, can bring about considerable relief. Let yourself be guided by a chemist as to which herbs to use in a particular case.

Choosing the Right Plant

How then do you select the right plant? Which herb, which mixture of herbs promises to be most successful?

This final section attempts to give some assistance in finding an answer to this question. Numerous herbals provide information about the various effects of the plants described in them, and whether the plant should be used in its totality or only one of its parts. It is not our intention to replace these books, but the table on pages 221–223 may possibly make your decision easier. In it herbs are given in order of their efficacy. In our experience those named first work the best.

You should not forget, however, that lists of herbs giving their effects are ultimately almost a side issue. What is much more important is your attitude towards their application and your own instinct in the choice of the correct plant. Almost every plant is helpful (either using parts of it or in its entirety) in numerous disorders and illnesses; conversely in a specific illness there are a multitude of herbs that can act as a relieving or healing remedy. On top of that not every plant helps every person equally. In the same complaint a medicinal herb might not agree with one person at all, while for another person it can bring a rapid cure to a lengthy illness. At one time a particular herb may do you a lot of good – a camomile tea, for instance, while on another occasion it is no use at all for the very same complaint. There is no patent formula or panacea – nothing that helps every time.

You should therefore choose according to instinct and feeling: if the name of a medicinal herb 'grabs' you, regardless of its order in the table, if you discover a well-known herb in your surroundings that somehow appeals to you, or if you have the feeling that right now this is 'your' plant, then give it a try in all confidence.

Effect	Plants
elimination	senna leaves, alder bark, buckthorn, fumitory, dandelion roots, yarrow
strengthening connective tissue	field horsetail, common knotgrass, ribwort plantain, comfrey, heather, french bean, common agrimony, stinging nettle, marjoram, cucumber, spinach, onion, Iceland moss, millet, barley
	Many of these plants contain silicic acid. This has an anti-inflammatory effect, both externally and internally, and cures metabolic disorders in the connective tissues. Only use young plants, as hardly any silicic acid is released from the older ones. Since this silicic acid is to be absorbed by the body, teas, compresses and poultices prepared from these herbs are more effective when the moon is waxing
improving the blood picture	stinging nettle, yarrow, sage, marigold, rhubarb, celery, lovage, parsley, field horsetail, blackcurrant, elder, carrot, bedstraw, St John's wort, radish, thyme, onion, crane's bill, cress, garlic
lowering blood pressure	mistletoe, garlic, wood garlic, onion, field horsetail
purifying the blood	stinging nettle, dandelion, pansy, fennel, yarrow
staunching bleeding	shepherd's purse, yarrow, mistletoe, dandelion
lowering blood sugar level	valerian, stinging nettle, elder leaves, dandelion, bilberry leaves, onion, watercress
anti-inflammatory	comfrey, ribwort plantain, coltsfoot, agrimony, common knotgrass, great plantain, camomile
activating the gall bladder	dandelion, camomile, gentian, lesser bindweed, buck-bean, radish, St John's wort, greater celandine, peppermint, garlic, agrimony
checking goitre	lettuce, oat, carrot, spinach, apple, watercress, garlic
relieving pain and cramp	valerian, peppermint, camomile, yarrow, St John's wort, heather, savory, birch leaves, field horsetail, common knotgrass, silverweed, balm, rosemary, sage, apple peel (infusion: drink as hot as possible)

Effect	Plants
tightening up (skin-care)	marjoram, ribwort plantain, centaury, dandelion, rose, speedwell, lady's mantle, coltsfoot, agrimony, walnut, St John's wort
flatulence	caraway, anise, fennel, sage, peppermint, balm, yarrow, camomile
bladder complaints	white dead nettles, yarrow, camomile, dandelion, stinging nettle, field horsetail, rhubarb, crane's bill
gynaecological disorders	lady's mantle, yarrow, stinging nettles, crane's bill, sage, shepherd's purse

painful menstruation:
    yarrow, St John's wort, camomile, valerian, mugwort, balm, peppermint

excessive menstruation:
    shepherd's purse, lady's mantle, field horsetail, stinging nettle, white dead nettle, yarrow, bloodwort, snakeweed

missed period:
    St John's wort, marigold, wormwood, parsley, fennel, balm, wild angelica root

improving milk secretion:
    caraway, borage, marjoram, fenugreek, hemp agrimony, burnet saxifrage, coriander, anise, fennel

reducing milk secretion:
    walnut leaves, hop seeds, sage

Effect	Plants
skin problems	plantain, yarrow, onion, sage, field horsetail, lady's mantle, coltsfoot, St John's wort, elderflower, lime blossom, marigold, parsley, rhubarb, walnut leaves, pansy, burdock root
rheumatism and gout	field horsetail, stinging nettle, elderflower, birch leaves, heather, arnica, rose-hip, parsley root, cowslip root, shepherd's purse, juniper berries, coltsfoot, yarrow, horse chestnut bark, hops
complaints of the lower abdomen	lady's mantle, yarrow, beetroot, marigold, crane's bill, white dead nettle, rhubarb, mistletoe, field horsetail, stinging nettle, shepherd's purse, wild angelica, sage, valerian

Effect	Plants
small and large intestines	beetroot, dandelion, yarrow, lady's mantle, stinging nettle, comfrey, camomile, garlic, marigold, onion, shepherd's purse, rhubarb, field horsetail, fennel
bones/joints	comfrey, marigold, sage, yarrow, sesame, sunflower, onion, lentil, rhubarb, stinging nettle, cabbage, plantain, radish
liver/gall-bladder	dandelion, sage, yarrow, greater celandine, common clubmoss, field horsetail, camomile, caraway, St John's wort, stinging nettle, beetroot
lungs	plantain, sage, ground ivy, watercress, field horsetail, onion, marjoram, mullein, beetroot, yarrow
lymph glands	crane's bill, beetroot, radish, bedstraw, garlic/wood garlic, burnet saxifrage, field horsetail, onion, plantain
stomach	centaury, yarrow, white dead nettle, marigold, St John's wort, field horsetail, mistletoe, beetroot, sage, carrot, chive, radish
spleen/pancreas	dandelion, rhubarb, sage, yarrow, beetroot, onion, lentil, mistletoe, sweet woodruff, field horsetail
kidneys	camomile, St John's wort, marigold, beetroot, sage, white dead nettle, rhubarb, bedstraw, golden rod, lady's mantle, plantain, crane's bill, stinging nettle
prostate and testicles	pumpkin seeds, field horsetail, garlic, hairy willow herb, crane's bill, sage, birch, yarrow, plantain, marigold, camomile
thyroid gland	bedstraw, marigold, beetroot, yarrow, crane's bill, stinging nettle, field horsetail, valerian, rhubarb, watercress

III. The Pulse of Life

Man is adequately equipped for all his true needs
if he trusts his senses
and develops them in such a way
that they remain worthy of that trust.

Goethe

Whether we concede the fact with good grace or obstinately resist it, whether our investigative spirit tries to experience it or whether we ignore it to our own detriment: atoms and stones, plants and animals – and with them human beings, who carry each of these forms of energy within them – all are subject to rhythms, cycles and transforming movement, in creation as well as in destruction. From breath to heartbeat, from the circulation of the bodily fluids to the cycle of birth, death and rebirth, everywhere our life is touched and moved by an up and down, by a fading and renewal, by the augmentation and diminution of manifold forces – not merely those indicated by the moon's place up high. Life itself is a circling, an oscillating, a vibrating, a swinging to and fro – in a word: it is a dance. 'Continuous growth', on the other hand, an idol of our times, is against all nature, an artificial invention of our deranged, eccentric, short-sighted epoch, in which it passes for normal to have to brace oneself at almost any price against downwards movement and recession.

In order to awaken and keep awake your pleasure in the dance of life, we should like in this part of the book to introduce you to two types of rhythm that no one can ever dodge – *biorhythms* and the *daily rhythms of the organs*.

1. In the Force Field of the Biorhythms

How often it happens that for a few hours or days we are not 'on top of things', not 'with it'; for no recognisable reason we feel irritable, lacking self-control, unable to concentrate. Then again at other times we experience a physical or mental high: we face the day with elation, nothing can ruffle us – clearly also for no particular reason.

In this chapter we should like to acquaint you with one possible reason for these strange fluctuations and inconsistencies: the three human biorhythms. We shall try to show you how they work, what value a knowledge of them can have for you, and also of course how they are calculated.

The Three Rhythms of Life

The forces of human biorhythms affect body, mind and emotions from the day of our birth. They colour much of what we do, feel and think. Making oneself aware of this interplay of colours can be of great advantage in many spheres of life, both professional and private; the reason for this is principally that the effects are in many respects predictable. Already in ancient Greece doctors took their patients' 'good' and 'bad' days into account. Forgotten and blotted out of our awareness for many a long year in the west, these forces have been rediscovered in our century and allocated the exotic-sounding name of *biorhythm*. Translated into common parlance, this simply means 'rhythm of life' or 'pulse of life'.

From the day we are born there are three rhythms that accompany us in the tempo of an extremely slow inner clock with a regularity that is somewhat rare in nature, almost stubborn:

* the *physical rhythm*, with a length of 23 days
* the *emotional rhythm* of 28 days
* the *intellectual rhythm*, which lasts exactly 33 days

Each of these rhythms gives us for up to half its duration a *high-phase* that slowly rises to a peak. Immediately this peak is reached it rapidly falls back sharply, almost vertically to its starting point, and then passes over into a descending low-phase until the lowest point has been reached. From there it returns, rising in a sharp vertical to its starting point, where the high-low pulse starts all over again.

The illustration opposite, which plots the rather remarkable course of one such curve, is intended to help you to visualise this rhythm. We have chosen as our example the 28 day emotional rhythm. If you are already acquainted to some extent with bio-rhythms you will perhaps be surprised by this diagram. Be patient: an explanation awaits you on page 238.

In the illustration you can see how the curve starts by reaching upwards, then on the 14th day – the first transition day (A) – it sinks sharply away to the 'zero line', after which it travels for 14 days down to the low-point. On the second transition day, after 28 days (B) one cycle has been completed and the rhythm begins again.

The physical rhythm follows exactly the same course, however, the high phase ends after only 11.5 days, and the entire cycle is over in 23 days. It therefore has a steeper curve.

The intellectual rhythm ends its high-phase after 16.5 days, at which point it changes; the ensuing low-phase arrives at the start-ing point of a new cycle after a total of 33 days. Thus of the three rhythm its curve has the gentlest rise and fall.

The transition days are of particular importance for all the rhythms. They mark a period that is almost always critical, and which can last for hours, sometimes even a whole day or more.

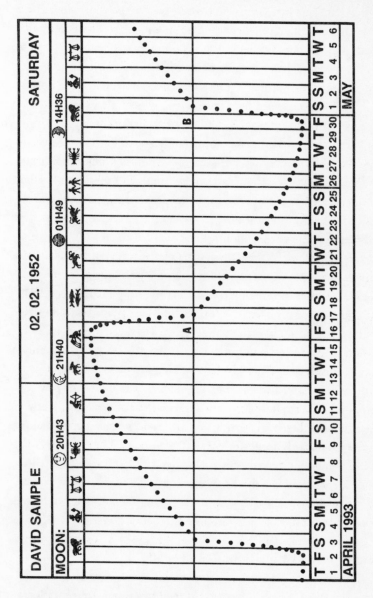

Biorhythm curve (emotional biorhythm)
A: first transition day – B: second transition day and start of new cycle

Their effect on body, mind and emotions can be compared with a miniature climatic change, similar to the change of forces that occurs at full moon. The transition from low to high is often felt to be less decisive than the change from the high to the low phase. The reason for this is probably that the transition from low to high has already been preceded by a few days in which in any case one has not been on top form physically, emotionally or intellectually.

These three rhythms incessantly influence us all, whoever we are. In addition they interpenetrate one another, augmenting and diminishing each other and interacting with numerous other influences, such as state of health, age, environment, stress etc.

The following illustration shows what the three rhythms can look like in the course of a month. You will be able to tell from this diagram that the physical and emotional rhythms of the person in the example are reaching a low point on April 30, whilst the intellectual rhythm is in the high-phase. In this way the three rhythms can colour one another and contribute to the amplification or the dampening of their various influences. The intimate interplay of body, intellect and emotions means that the effects of the three rhythms cannot be determined unambiguously and in the same way for every person. They are very individual: an intellectual low can have an indirect effect on one's physical state of health; conversely an emotional high can in certain circumstances cause a physical low to be temporarily forgotten.

So, what does it mean when you are passing through an intellectual high? How do the high and low phases of the individual rhythms make themselves felt in everyday life? What should we look out for on transition days?

The Physical Biorhythm (23 Days)
The knowledge of one's own physical biorhythm is especially interesting for people who are engaged in some form of physical activity, whether in sport or professionally, for instance as a

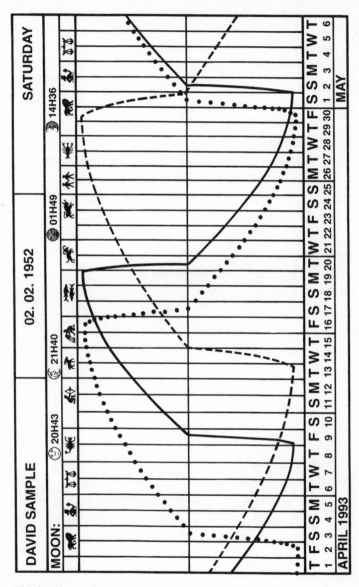

The three human biorhythms
—— physical (23 days)
.... emotional (28 days)
------ intellectual (33 days)

masseur, dancer, builder etc. They sense the influence of the physical biorhythm more clearly than other people.

As a rule during the *high-phase* we feel we have more vitality and staying power; physical tasks are accomplished with greater ease, everything goes more smoothly; in sport we are more efficient. There is also an influence on enterprise and dynamism, self confidence and courage.

Generally *transition days* in the physical biorhythm are a critical time: as far as health is concerned one is somewhat more vulnerable than on other days; tasks that normally could be handled without any problem require greater concentration at this time; in the physical interplay of nerves, muscles and joints there can be something gumming up the works.

Many midwives know all about physical biorhythms: they know that the 11th day (the transition day in the physical biorhythm) marks a critical moment for the new-born child. Vomiting, or other bodily symptoms that give cause for concern, can occur more frequently at this time. "After a month babies are over the worst" – this insight of midwives and paediatricians is based, among other things, on the fact that after 33 days the little ones have for the first time lived through all three rhythms with their high and low phases and transition days.

The *low-phase* is characterised by a gradual falling away of strength and reduced resilience; strenuous efforts necessitate longer periods of recovery. A trip in the mountains in the low days before the second transition day, is more demanding than, say, during the high-phase. The last days of the low-phase are especially suited to recovery and rest, in order to gather new strength.

The Emotional Biorhythm (28 Days)

This rhythm influences our inward and outward powers of perception and sensation, our emotions in general, our intuition and creativity. It is of especial importance for professions in which one has to deal with people – for educators, doctors, nurses, pastoral workers and the like.

In the high-phase one is emotionally more mobile, and it is easier to recognise the positive sides of life. One has no difficulty adopting and maintaining an optimistic outlook on life. Anyone who works in a service profession – whether as a waiter, a teacher or a pastoral worker, will now build up to top form and will be able to do a lot of good through the power of positive thoughts.

At 14 day intervals, always on the day of the week on which you were born, the emotional rhythm presents you with a transition day, a short and sometimes rather confused period of time. Emotional chaos, mental conflicts, taking offence over trifles: the transition days provide just the right climate for this sort of thing. Perhaps we can find in this a reason why people born on a Sunday really are favoured by fate: always on a Sunday, at intervals of 14 days they experience a critical day; and people can generally get through Sundays without any problems, since as a rule there are no heavy demands placed on them (except in the case of an overloaded private life – the origin of the concept of 'Sunday stress').

During the low-phase we are not so good at dealing with bad news; it is easier to slide into a basic mood of pessimism, despondency and anxiety. The senselessness of many things in life is experienced more acutely at this time. Someone who is inclined to let himself be ruled by a guilty conscience is a more willing victim than usual. In these days, especially at the end of the low-phase, increased self-discipline is necessary in order not to give too much scope to pessimism. It is pointless giving children a severe talking to when they are just going through their emotional low: it simply goes in one ear and out of the other.

The Intellectual Biorhythm (33 Days)

This relates above all to the capacity to work and plan in one's head. The affected spheres of life are logic, reason, the ability to learn, thinking predictively, powers of deduction and a sense of direction that is both inward and outward – in the truest sense of the word, presence of mind. Teachers in all fields, politicians, experts, journalists and writers all experience the ups and downs of this rhythm with particular force.

No doubt you can imagine the effect that the high-phase has in the intellectual rhythm: all activities that depend on understanding receive a boost; one can absorb intellectual study materials and information more easily and can process and interpret them with the utmost ease. It is easier to concentrate: a seminar for further education that one attends in the high-phase is bound to be more profitable than the same thing during the 16.5 days of the low-phase.

The transition days in the intellectual rhythm inhibit intellectual resilience. The capacity to react is under par. Everyone involved with road traffic should behave with greater care than usual and have the courage to face the fact that even they are more likely to make a mistake. At this time the absorption of new learning material is often blocked. Avoiding complex exercises or else increasing one's concentration are the best methods here for adapting to the change of mental climate.

The same applies to the period between day 20 and day 33 in the intellectual rhythm. In the low-phase one gradually becomes more and more intellectually immobile and more prone to mental exhaustion, if the tasks are too tricky. Pleasure in learning and making decisions begins to flag; and anxieties become as tangible as if they were already reality.

Biorhythms in Daily Life

Anyone who keeps track of his own biorhythms will rapidly discover for himself how useful this knowledge is. Especially when dealing with children in schools of all sorts it could be of great advantage. When a school child's biorhythms are in the low-phase it is often totally senseless to try and drum in new material. Parents who have the welfare of their children at heart can keep an eye on their biorhythms and avoid burdening them with extra demands at least during these days.

Teachers in the low-phase might well discover that during such days they are scarcely capable of communicating their subject matter in a clear and comprehensible manner. They could watch out for their own low periods and draw up lists of the low periods of their charges; at the very least they should watch out for transition days. Experience has shown that coaches who take into account the biorhythms of their young clients achieve great success even with pupils and problem children who previously were chronically weak. We can well imagine coaches or a team of school teachers getting together and setting up a project that would turn 'biorhythmic scheduling' into a successful trademark.

It would not be difficult in state schools, given the large number of classes in the same year, to group the children according to their biorhythmic profile and arrange the syllabus to reflect it. Smaller village schools could achieve excellent results if at the very least there was an insight into the importance of these rhythms. In the past working in accordance with biorhythms has shown itself to be a real blessing especially in the care of children with dyslexia or general learning difficulties. Of course this sounds like pie in the sky; but it would only take a good programmer a couple days to configure one of the many biorhythm programs in such a way that once the birth dates of all the pupils had been entered it would print out the allocation into classes in a matter of minutes – including the *collective* low-phases that the class would go through.

There is many a tricky undertaking that would promise much more chance of success if you set the date for it on a biorhythmically favourable day: tests of all kinds (especially driving tests), interviews, applications, conversations with subordinates and superiors, difficult phases of work. With sportsmen at the same level of performance one should make allowances before a major contest for those whose biorhythms are in the high-phase.

Current literature on biorhythms sometimes describes the possible effects of spouses or professional colleagues having different biorhythms. Some authors even go so far as to consider strongly divergent rhythms to be a negative element in a marriage or business partnership. To be sure that is not entirely false, but it would be totally erroneous to derive a universally valid rule from it. There are basic advantages when the high and low phases of two people coincide to a reasonable extent. One will thus be on the same wave-length as one's partner much more often. However, it is easy to see what can happen if one also shares the low-phases with one's partner. Good will and the capacity to pull one another out of the quagmire are rare commodities in these highly insured times.

Conversely, if the rhythms are exactly contrary it may be more difficult when one is in a high-phase to sweep along or inspire a partner who is currently in a low-phase; but on the other hand it is much easier, given some good will, to help one another through the low-phases. Seen in the long term an average degree of agreement is definitely more favourable than either of the two extremes – very high agreement or none at all.

Experience has shown one thing: a great deal has already been gained in a relationship between partners if one is aware of the 'dodgy' day in the emotional curve of one's comrade – that day which regularly every fortnight on the day of the week he was born gives him a few uneasy hours. As everywhere else insight and empathy are of central importance here: if you know that your bad mood, lack of concentration or listlessness – or that of your opposite number – is connected with the current biorhythms, then it is much easier to deal with the situation. It isn't a matter of putting up with all sorts of nastiness or shifting the blame on to one's biorhythms, but rather of learning how to understand.

If you know that it is nature itself that imposes all those temperamental, unfocused, forgetful moments on your partner, then you will find it easier to accept him for what he is. Conversely this form of acceptance gives one the chance to practice *genuine* acceptance, without making the inner excuse: "Oh well, he/she just can't help it..." – an acceptance and love given without any question as to reasons or conditions. And only that is worthy of the name love.

To sum up you can derive the greatest profit from the knowledge of biorhythms if you observe the following rules and advice:

* It only makes sense to get to know your own biorhythms if you explore and discover the rhythm little by little, all by yourself with no help at all from outside, and then finally accept it. Above all you should not use it as a fig leaf – as an excuse in your everyday life. Just as with the lunar rhythms, there are no 'good' and 'bad' days in human biorhythms. It always depends on your ability to make use of your knowledge of the biorhythms at a given moment.

* Whenever you are able to decide for yourself the timing of important tasks and projects – in which you wish or have to be physically, intellectually or emotionally on top form – you should pay attention to your biorhythms and then fix a favourable day for the project in question.

* Experiencing one's own biorhythms is always a fundamentally personal matter. It can never be generalised. The knowledge you have is only applicable to yourself. You can never deduce from it any recommendations as to how another person ought to handle his own biorhythms. Sometimes perhaps one can experience an intellectual or physical high as more of a strain than the low-phase. In extreme cases, when all the curves are low one can in certain circumstances gain completely new insights in a flash, because the strength is lacking to bolster up one's own prejudices and fixed ideas, one's own mental defence mechanisms against the truth.

The resultant high in the midst of the biorythmic low, the relief at not having to chase after ideals at all costs: that is something we would wish for everyone.

Teething Troubles of an Ancient Knowledge

The ancient knowledge concerning human biorhythms is still a long way from regaining the importance that it deserves. Altogether there are three reasons for this:

Firstly: in the modern, unnaturally organised world it is difficult for an individual to pay attention to his biorhythms. There is not a company boss in the land that would accept them as a reason for someone not turning up to work, or at least not being entrusted with awkward tasks. Even our school timetables come into being in offices that are remote from nature, thought out by people who are themselves remote from nature, and have anything but the welfare of the children on their minds. So as a defence of their inertia there prevails in many circles a scarcely concealed motive to ignore or even suppress knowledge about biorhythms. And all that despite the fact that countless hours of coaching could be dispensed with, countless failures could be avoided, if biorhythms were once more to be taken into account. In all spheres of industry and commerce there would be much less of what today is called 'human error'.

Such ignorance, however does nothing to alter the reality of biorhythms, and their power to speed or retard matters. The fact that there are other and better ways of going about things is sufficiently borne out by examples: the pilots of *Swissair*, for instance are not allowed to fly on biorhythmically critical days. Human error as a cause of accident is virtually unknown in this airline. In China, India and especially Japan biorhythms play a large part in important political and economic decisions. In particular the economic giant, Japan, in its industry and commerce pays close attention to the biorhythms of its workers, salaried staff and managers. It is scarcely

credible that Japan would allow itself the luxury of paying attention to something that did not exist or was of trivial importance.

How to put matters right? That is something we leave to your spirit
of inventiveness, for we wrote this book only for you, not for institutions of whatever description. As is so often the case, you cannot
expect any help from above. Here, too, it is valid to say that where
there's an insight a will can ripen. Where there's a will there's a way.

A second important reason for the hesitant revival of knowledge
about biorhythms may be found in the fact that all literature on the
subject and even computer programs represent them in a manner
that is pictorially inappropriate. One thus gains a false impression
of their true course.

The following illustration (using the example of the emotional
rhythm) shows how biorhythms are mostly depicted.

Why biorhythms should have been represented up till now as a
smooth sine wave, we do not know. The re-discoverers and
contemporary authors writing on the subject were perhaps unable
to imagine a rhythm in nature that followed such a remarkable
course: gently ascending, falling back sharply to the starting point,
gently sinking then climbing steeply to the starting point – like a
valve that slowly opens and then shuts with lightning speed.

The presumed shape of a sine wave, on the other hand, creates
the impression that the high and low phases are felt most intensely
exactly in their middle. However, this does not correspond to the
experience of any person who is acquainted with biorhythms, has
sensed them exactly and knows that high and low phases affect us
most intensely at the end, shortly before the transition days. With
the sine-wave representation the question also remains unanswered
as to why precisely the transition days, shown as gentle transits
through the zero point, should mark a critical period. It is much
easier to imagine from the actual course of the biorhythm curve
why these transition days are critical: the change takes place rapidly,
in a matter of a few hours.

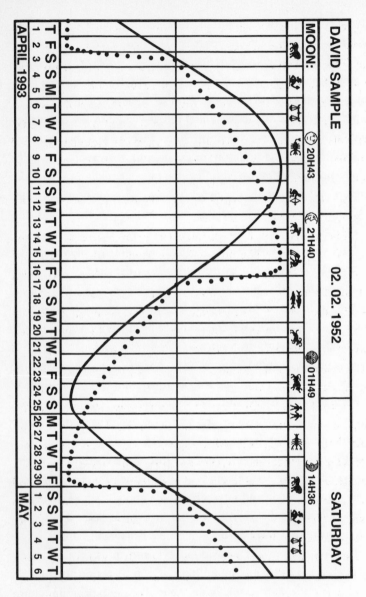

The emotional biorhythm
.... actual course
—— mistakenly assumed course

Because in modern times we are often compelled to ignore, or even suppress the actual course and repercussions of the biorhythms, someone who is not in the know has at first no other option than to accept the pictorial representation of a sine wave, if he is interested in the subject. And yet, as with all false information, in the course of time he will not feel altogether comfortable with his 'knowledge'. Something within him will kick against it and say, perhaps unconsciously: "That doesn't tally with what I feel." And that is how it can happen that through a simple error of draughtsmanship the acceptance of a valid piece of ancient knowledge can be delayed for decades.

Let us remind you: we have indicated again and again, that you possess deep within you an infallible instinct for the truth. If this natural force is made accessible to someone who has never heard anything about biorhythms, then he will be able really to accept it and translate it into his everyday life, provided he can sense it as it really is. Try to track down your personal biorhythms and experience their effects. Then you will grasp their existence and their usefulness, and nothing and no one will ever again be able to persuade you otherwise.

The third and perhaps the most important reason for the relatively slight acquaintance with biorhythms is this: *one has to feel them*. And that is the biggest problem. If like so many other people, our life is directed towards feeling and experiencing and sensing reality as little as possible, if we are afraid of the negative experiences and set-backs of life and we try to damp them down, then we will no longer experience so strongly the high and low phases and the mild chaos of the transition days.

Someone who strives after a life without low phases, who tries to fill in life's valley bottoms, often does not notice that he does this at the expense of the wonderful view from the mountain peaks. Someone who always wants to be on a high, because this is required of him, or simply because he always wants to feel good, is overlooking the fact that he is thereby totally over-taxing himself and ultimately conjuring up all kinds of illness and depression, since it simply is not possible to be on a continuous high.

The fact is that anyone who anaesthetises or stimulates himself during the low-phase is anaesthetising his total capacity for sensation and perception, i.e. also his perception of the beneficial forces of the high-phase. The result is a lukewarm life: admittedly without apparent low phases, but also without the intense experience of the heights that every life has to offer – a life packed in cotton-wool, without movement. Such a life passes without any preparation for the essential depths, which every life has in store, and without which a genuine inner development is not possible. Even the loss of a beloved domestic pet then becomes a blow of fate, to say nothing of the death of a beloved human being. The meaning of life does not lie in making things 'better and better' for everyone, but also in un-learning the habit of holding tight. Anyone that holds a butterfly tight will kill it. Everything that we hold tight dies.

Getting to know and accepting biorhythms can prove to be a real blessing, because it gently prepares us for the long-wave rhythms of the high and low phases of an entire life. It is especially advantageous to combine one's own biorhythms with the lunar rhythms, for instance using a calendar that contains both sets of information – your personal biorhythms, the phase of the moon and the position of the moon in the zodiac.

Calculating Biorhythms

So how do you find out the make-up of your biorhythms on a given day? How are they calculated?

There are two possibilities for you if you wish to carry out the calculation by hand; and there is a third possibility that we have created especially for you.

For the first calculation method you will need an ordinary pocket calculator. If you keep the result in a diary you will only have to work it out *once*, or at most you will only need to go over it later as a check. Let's go through it step by step:

1. First calculate the number of days that have elapsed from your date of birth up to the date of the calculation.

For this you must first multiply your age by 365, then add the days since your last birthday, and finally add the days for leap years, when February has an extra day. (Basically leap years are all years that are divisible by 4. There is an exception to this: years that are also divisible by 100 but not by 400 are *not* leap years. 1900 was not a leap year but 2000 will be.)

NB: if your year of birth is a leap year, you must only add an extra day if your birthday falls *before* February 29.

If the year of the calculation is a leap year, you must only add an extra day if the day for which you are calculating comes *after* February 29.

Example calculation:

Date of Birth 2.2.1952
Date of Calculation 27.4.1993
Age (41) multiplied by 365 14965
Number of days since last birthday 84
Additional days from leap years 11
Total number of days elapsed 15060

Note down the total number of days and go on to the next step.

2. **In the second stage divide your total number of days:**
   - **first by 23 (for the physical rhythm)**
   - **then by 28 (for the emotional rhythm)**
   - **and finally by 33 (for the intellectual rhythm).**

Working with a pocket calculator you thus have three numbers, each with a few places before the decimal point and a lot of places after the decimal point. The part of the number before the decimal point is of no further interest; it only tells us how many times you have lived through the rhythm in question.

The part of the number after the decimal point (the first three places are enough) tells us what fraction of the rhythm in question is already behind you on the day of the calculation – in other words in what phase of the physical, emotional or intellectual rhythms you are currently located. And that of course is what you wanted to find out.

Let's take as an example the number obtained in step 1:
Total number of days elapsed: 15060
divided by 23 (physical rhythm): 654.782
divided by 28 (emotional rhythm): 537.857
divided by 33 (intellectual rhythm): 456.363

To obtain the *physical rhythm* multiply the portion of the number after the decimal point (in this example 0.782) by 23, which will give you the number of days that have elapsed since the beginning of the cycle, since the starting point of the high-phase. In the above example you get the figure 17.9.

'17.9' means that almost 18 days have passed since the beginning of the physical cycle. Thus the transition day that comes halfway through the period is long past. The person in this example is already six and a half days into the low-phase, in the downwards curve of the physical rhythm (see illustration on page 231).

The two other rhythms are calculated in the same way:

For the *emotional rhythm* take the portion of the number after the decimal point (in this example 0.857) and multiply it by 28. This gives 23.9, which rounds up to 24. And so the person in the example is in the 24th day of the emotional rhythm, and is also a long way past the middle transition day, and has already been experiencing the downwards phase of the emotional rhythm for about ten days.

For the *intellectual rhythm* take the portion of the number after the decimal point (in this example 0.363) and multiply it by 33. This gives 11.9. Thus the person is living in the 12th day of his intellectual rhythm, in the middle of the high-phase and about four and a half days before the transition to the low-phase.

If you now write in *on the calculation day* in your diary the number 18 for the physical rhythm, the number 24 for the emotional rhythm and the number 12 for the intellectual rhythm, and continue through the following days increasing each of the numbers by one, then you will be able to keep track and make use of the rhythms for months or even years ahead, without needing to repeat the calculation. Only you must always remember to start again at number 1 after 23 days (physical), after 28 days (emotional) and after 33 days (intellectual). The illustration on page 247 shows how April and May 1993 might have looked in the diary of the sample person. Straight away you can see that over the week-end of 1-2 May the subject would not exactly be on top form: all three rhythms come up together with critical transition days.

You can tell whether you have calculated correctly if the transition days of the emotional rhythm are always on the day of the week that you were born. If for instance you were born on a Wednesday then numbers 14 and 28 must always fall on a Wednesday, otherwise your number games do not add up and you'll have to repeat your calculation (the person in the example was born on a Saturday). As a check on your book-keeping we would recommend that when changing diaries or when especially important appointments come up you should carry out the calculations once more.

The second method of biorhythm calculation is reserved for those who like working with their brains: mental arithmetic without a pocket calculator.

Carry out exactly the same steps as with the pocket calculator method, only with a pencil and paper, just as you learned to do in primary school. There is one difference, though, that you should note: when you divide the total number of days that have elapsed in your life by the length of a particular rhythm, you do not finish up with some numbers after a decimal point but with a *remainder*.

Just settle for the remainder: there's no need to go on with the division. This remainder is in fact the exact number of days that have passed since the start of the particular rhythm – the number which, as described above, you can enter in your diary and from which you can count forward.

The third way to calculate personal biorhythms is the simplest of all.

There are numerous biorhythm programs on the market for all operating systems (however, without a lunar calendar). Almost all of them still use the incorrect sine wave form to display the various rhythms and some give additional help with interpretation. If you already own such a program you only have to bear in mind that in reality the rhythms run their course as we have depicted in our illustrations and that the interpretations do not always fit you personally. There are also a number of pocket calculators and even wristwatches which can indicate the current biorhythms once the date of birth has been registered.

1993 APRIL					1993 MAY			
		Phys	*Emot*	*Intellet*			*Phys*	*Emot*	*Intellet*

1993 APRIL					1993 MAY				
		Phys	*Emot*	*Intellet*			*Phys*	*Emot*	*Intellet*
1	Thu				1	Sat	22	(28)	(16)
2	Fri				2	Sun	(23)	1	17
3	Sat				3	Mon	1	2	18
4	Sun				4	Tue	2	3	19
5	Mon				5	Wed	3	4	20
6	Tue				6	Thu	4	5	21
7	Wed				7	Fri	5	6	22
8	Thu				8	Sat	6	7	23
9	Fri				9	Sun	7	8	24
10	Sat				10	Mon	8	9	25
11	Sun				11	Tue	9	10	26
12	Mon				12	Wed	10	11	27
13	Tue				13	Thu	(11)	12	28
14	Wed				14	Fri	12	13	29
15	Thu				15	Sat	13	(14)	30
16	Fri				16	Sun	14	15	31
17	Sat				17	Mon	15	16	32
18	Sun				18	Tue	16	17	(33)
19	Mon				19	Wed	17	18	1
20	Tue				20	Thu	18	19	2
21	Wed				21	Fri	19	20	3
22	Thu				22	Sat	20	21	4
23	Fri				23	Sun	21	22	5
24	Sat				24	Mon	22	23	6
25	Sun				25	Tue	(23)	24	7
26	Mon	*Phys*	*Emot*	*Intellet*	26	Wed	1	25	8
27	Tue	18	24	12	27	Thu	2	26	9
28	Wed	19	25	13	28	Fri	3	27	10
29	Thu	20	26	14	29	Sat	4	(28)	11
30	Fri	21	27	15	30	Sun	5	1	12
					31	Mon	6	2	13

Entering biorhythms in a diary

2. The Daily Rhythm of the Organs

Why is the sleep between one and three o'clock in the morning so important for the whole body? Why is it easier to get children to go to bed before seven in the evening than after? What makes forty winks in the office between one and three in the afternoon so refreshing and healthy? Perhaps the following pages will give a plausible answer to these questions that puzzle many of us.

In the same way that the physical biorhythm affects the whole body, each individual organ in the body is subject to a rhythm of its own which in the course of each 24 hours produces in it a high-phase immediately followed by a low-phase. At specific, unchanging times the organs work particularly effectively for two hours and then immediately afterwards they treat themselves to a recovery phase in which for about two hours they rest and regenerate themselves.

This knowledge, too, is not yet widespread; and yet, as you will see, many people in all parts of the world are consciously or unconsciously guided by the possibilities and requirements implicit in it.

The rhythms of the organs behave in the manner shown in the table on page 250.

If little by little you become familiar with the rhythms of your organs, you will be able to take numerous measures that serve your well-being and health, at the right moment throughout the day, regardless of the position of the moon, thus enhancing their effectiveness even more – for example taking medicines or flushing out poisons. And it is just as we found in the case of biorhythms: a great many enigmatic pieces of behaviour that we all recognise within ourselves can be plausibly explained by the rhythms of our organs. If for example you know that tiredness between one and two in the afternoon is a healthy signal caused by the body, then there is no need for you to work up a guilty conscience for yourself (or others) simply because you happen to be overcome by a fit of lethargy. Particularly parents and teachers can draw great benefit from the information that follows, since it will make it easier for them to understand better many of the 'abnormal' behaviour patterns of their charges.

Let's set off together through a typical day, starting, as most people do: the alarm clock rings – breakfast time!

Organ	High-phase	Low-phase
stomach	7 a.m. – 9 a.m.	9 a.m. – 11 a.m.
spleen and pancreas	9 a.m. – 11a.m.	11 a.m. – 1 p.m.
heart	11 a.m. – 1p.m.	1 p.m. – 3 p.m.
small intestine	1 p.m. – 3 p.m.	2 p.m. – 5 p.m.
bladder	3 p.m. – 5 p.m.	5 p.m. – 7 p.m.
kidneys	5 p.m. – 7 p.m.	7 p.m. – 9 p.m.
circulation	7 p.m. – 9 p.m.	9 p.m. – 11 p.m.
general energy accumulation	9 p.m. – 11 p.m.	11 p.m. – 1 a.m.
gall-bladder	11 p.m. – 1 a.m.	1 a.m. – 3 a.m.
liver	1 a.m. – 3 a.m.	3 a.m. – 5 a.m.
lungs	3 a.m. – 5 a.m.	5 a.m. – 7 a.m.
large intestine	5 a.m. – 7 a.m.	7 a.m. – 9 a.m.

From Seven to Nine in the Morning –
Stomach

The large intestine is taking a short rest after doing its work, the stomach is working at full speed and is ready for a fresh supply of energy. But what kind of energy? What do you start your day with? With rings under your eyes, a cigarette, a cup of coffee and the morning newspaper? Or a well-balanced muesli breakfast with high nutritional value and some herbal tea?

As you will have discovered in part II, that question is ultimately less important than whether you start your day in such a way that you launch into it with drive and optimism. And it is not the composition of your breakfast that determines that, but the feelings and thoughts with which you get out of bed.

Sometimes one might gain the impression that there are basically only two kinds of people: those that worry and those that don't. Those laden with worries, for whom past and future are more important than the present, drag themselves out of bed in the morning and say to themselves: "I wonder how many things are going to go wrong today. What expectations am I going to have to satisfy yet again?" They always have the feeling that nothing is going to succeed, they always look on the dark side and reckon on being let down – which is precisely what happens, *because* that's what they are reckoning on. On the other hand, someone who does not worry will hop out of bed in the morning, pull back the curtains, laugh in the face of the grey weather and declare that it's going to be a wonderful day. In the eyes of such people nothing ever seems to go wrong; they learn from every mistake, they do not confuse the essential with the inessential; they are great problem solvers and always land on their feet.

It is unimportant which group you happen to belong to at the moment (probably sometimes the one, sometimes the other). But what is important is the fact that you always have the *choice* which one you want to belong to.

The agony of choice is perhaps made easier by the insight that getting up in the morning, and the first minutes afterwards, very often determine how the rest of the day will unfold – in the same way that your favourite song, which you have just heard on the radio, continues to echo for a long time in your memory and colours the experiences that follow. Of course coffee and morning cigarettes are unhealthy, but if that's what you *need* in order to start the day in good spirits and an optimistic frame of mind, then don't let anyone persuade you otherwise.

The early hours of the morning afford an especially good opportunity for you to get to know your own instinct and to act according to it, for example devising your breakfast just as you see fit (this presupposes that you can already trust your instinct: two glasses of whisky for breakfast do not exactly testify to a highly developed sense of what is appropriate...). It is really sad what people in recent decades have been trying to palm off on us as a 'healthy breakfast'. Of course raw fruit and vegetables and organically grown and raised foodstuffs are healthy, but they do not suit everyone. If you like coffee better than tea, why not? If a morning cigarette keeps your stool regular, why not? If crisp morning rolls baked from white flour and with plenty of butter on them taste better to you than wholemeal rolls, there's no need always to deny yourself.

So what is particularly important in the morning is a relaxed, stress-free atmosphere. But how do many people organise their start to the day? The alarm clock rings at a time that just about leaves enough leeway to deal in a hectic, stressful rush with getting washed and dressed, having breakfast and looking after children etc. – almost as if we should feel guilty if we don't let rip straight away and go hell for leather – as if we had to prove something. For many the newspaper serves as a protective shield to ward off the chatter of a partner, mental stress and the prattling of children, and in order to enjoy some peace and quiet for at least a few seconds. Even that does not always work: if possible one also has to believe that the newspaper is actually mirroring reality and talking about real life.

What a waste of energy!

You always have the choice as to what mental and physical nourishment you offer or load into your waiting stomach and mind. You should get up in good time in order to be able to proceed at a leisurely tempo. Take your time over your shower (just how important that is you can read in part IV), eat and drink in comfort whatever tastes good to you and satisfies you. Go without the newspaper if its contents regularly depress you or sour your mood. And if indeed you want your behaviour to prove something, the best person to prove it to is yourself: "Let's see what I have to offer this day and what this day has to offer me..."

No one is born a morning cross-patch. It is something we grow into or are made into – through bad sleeping places (see page 305), bad news, bad thoughts – or whatever. How do you want your mornings to be? What do you want to digest every morning? What is preventing you from getting up happy in the morning? Find the answer and go into action.

From Nine to Eleven in the Morning – Spleen/Pancreas

The spleen and pancreas are now going full steam ahead, and the stomach is resting. Because of this a heavy breakfast taken after nine in the morning has an even more bloating and fatiguing effect.

The pancreas controls the blood-sugar level; if one tries to still slight feelings of hunger with something sweet during these two hours, the blood-sugar level rises and the pancreas has to work hard to bring it down. For this reason eating or drinking things with a high sugar content is only a temporary expedient, and after short while brings about a further dropping off in performance, which is often artificially overcome by means of coffee – truly a vicious circle. Try to do without anything sweet, even if you find it difficult, at least for these two hours.

Children especially clamour for sweet things between nine and eleven in the morning: after even a short time they become bad-tempered, excitable, impatient and bored. This bad mood can then often continue far into the day, particularly if one tries to divert the children with further sweets, or babies with totally superfluous bottle-feeds.

But this effect also occurs with adults, the only difference being that they are better at controlling themselves. However, self-discipline does not alter the effect of sweets at all, it only uses up energy. One remarkable additional fact is that during these two hours one reacts more sensitively to unkindness and criticism. If the effect of sweet things is added to this then something can quickly brew up that is no longer so easily managed even with a great deal of self-control.

Infections heal faster in the morning than in the afternoon, because the spleen continually produces white corpuscles, important helpers for our powers of self-healing. The fact that the spleen is working at top speed in the morning has an interesting side effect: blood tests usually take place in the morning. Almost always one has to take them with an empty stomach, and it is therefore only human not to want to wait until the afternoon before appeasing a growling stomach. And yet it should be borne in mind that the results of blood tests will always turn out somewhat differently if, instead of between 9 and 11, they are taken between 11 and 1 (i.e. during the recovery phase of the spleen). Thus for instance the erythrocyte sedimentation rate will be higher. As a rule the differences are not crucial, but in some illnesses they can have a strong influence on the subsequent therapy, which can be a disadvantage in serious cases.

It is part of standard practice in hospitals to do blood tests by the dozen during the spleen's high-phase, without paying any attention to this connection. It would therefore be useful in cases where an empty stomach is not important to postpone the test until the afternoon in order to obtain a more meaningful result and thus be able to adapt the therapy better.

From Eleven in the Morning to One in the Afternoon – Heart

During the high-phase of the heart's activity you should avoid overburdening our trusty pump by eating till bursting point and should only eat enough to still your hunger. In any case the feeling of fullness usually doesn't set in until five minutes after eating. Unfortunately it is not always possible to have a refreshing rest period after a meal; but at the very least you could postpone a stressful shopping spree until another time of the day.

Someone who does no physical work might do well to miss out on lunch in the canteen altogether. Why is it that part-time staff are often as productive as a full-time worker? The answer follows shortly.

From One to Three in the Afternoon – Small Intestine

Almost everyone will have noticed that around one o'clock there is a sudden feeling of fatigue and a falling off of performance, especially after a substantial lunch. Heart activity and circulation sink, and the small intestine, which bears the main burden in many digestive processes, tries to come into its own. It works especially well at this time and wants the rest of the body to take a break. Its activity is controlled by the vegetative nervous system, which is not *normally* susceptible to conscious influence and which can be disrupted and blocked by any form of stress or nervousness. The tranquil siesta of southern climes is thus an extremely sensible institution. The fact that it has not established itself in most of the temperate regions is to be explained by the chaotic, short-sighted work-ethic prevailing in these parts, which confuses essential leisure with laziness. The fact that the practice of working to fixed starting and finishing times was only introduced in this present century has generally been forgotten. At the very least longer breaks at midday could drastically reduce the number of absences due to sickness and the associated costs for our firms and institutions.

From Three to Five in the Afternoon – Bladder

The bladder, an important detoxifying organ, works particularly well between three and five in the afternoon.

If at this time on a fine day you gather a bunch of white dead-nettles and keep them in a vase, you will be able to pluck the flowers for many days (regardless of the weather) and produce an excellent tea from them that acts as a preventive against bladder infections. Picking them when the waxing moon is in Scorpio (i.e. from May onwards) will yield the best curative tea. You may also usefully take teas for the bladder until 7 p.m., when the high-phase for the kidneys takes over from that of the bladder.

All teas for purifying the blood work best between 3 p.m. and 7 p.m. when the moon is on the wane. It is generally a good idea to drink a lot during these four hours (see page 146).

From Five in the Afternoon to Seven in the Evening – Kidneys

During these two hours a central detoxifying organ – the kidneys – is working at its best. We have already frequently mentioned the importance for the body of properly functioning detoxification. If for instance you are able to fix an appointment after 5 p.m. for reflex-zone massage you should seize the opportunity: particularly for over-taxed kidneys, and hence for the whole body, a treatment at this time can be extremely effective (if also a little painful sometimes – a sign that the treatment is beginning to work).

After 7 p.m. one should not drink so much any more if possible – particularly just before going to bed. Cocoa and milk put an especial strain on the kidneys, since milk is no longer processed very well at this time. Warm milk at bedtime, which is always generously offered or even recommended, actually does more harm than good. Do not be surprised if you have a troubled sleep and bad dreams. Milk is a food, not a drink.

From Seven to Nine in the Evening – Circulation

Many parents have this experience every evening: if they manage to get their children to bed before seven o'clock, they often go to sleep without any problem. After that time putting them to bed often develops into a grim struggle which the children usually win one way or another, because nobody can be forced to sleep. It is not without good reason that they resist: between seven and nine in the evening the circulation is working at its best. At this time body and mind have quite other plans than going to sleep.

Indeed there are many children that only really wake up at this time. How many squabbles and quarrels could be avoided if only we could accept this rhythm, at least with older children, and not force them to go to bed. For many children this would even be the best time for them to do their homework; for some it is only at this late hour that they discover any taste for learning at all. If your children should happen to belong to this group, then we can only advise you to give up your daily struggle. The discord that it causes in the long run goes far deeper than the short-term peace that a few hours gained without the children might bring.

From Nine to Eleven in the Evening – General Accumulation of Energy

These two hours of 'general accumulation of energy' are called by the Chinese, after one of the body meridians, 'the time of the three-fold warmer'. Anyone who is susceptible to cold during this time, or who can only go to sleep in a warmed room, ought not to over-look this signal. Some kind of physical or mental equilibrium has been upset and requires attention.

For many people these two hours also number among the hours of power, during which their energy really gets going. This is particularly clearly noticeable among young people, who at this time are more likely to think of going to a disco than having a good rest in readiness for a new day. Perhaps many older people would have conserved this instinct if they had not had the nonsense drummed into them: "You've got to go to bed, otherwise you won't get enough sleep for tomorrow." Were you ever physically tired after a really pleasant evening, or after making merry through the night?

Even after ten hours of sleep, a lukewarm life makes one tired during the day as well. Fortunately young people often listen well enough to their natural instinct. They should not let themselves be deprived of it; though it can happen nowadays that one meets a young person who creates a more old-fashioned impression than his parents – who is more anxious about his pension than they are.

From Eleven in the Evening to One in the Morning – Gall-bladder

The gall-bladder, the organ whose secretions help with the processing of food in the small intestine, and the liver, the major organ of detoxification, have their most active time between eleven at night and three in the morning. Anyone who regularly wakes up at this time has reason to watch out for the functioning of his gall-bladder and liver. In general you should avoid fatty meals in the evening. Evening meals that are rich in fats will tax these organs even further and hinder their optimal functioning.

A person who has problems with his gall-bladder can benefit from warm and moist compresses between eleven and one. In addition you should drink hot tea in large gulps, and never cold drinks. Radish juice is a good supporting remedy. The intestine should be completely relieved, if necessary with an enema, and the body must be kept warm.

In the event of gall-bladder or liver problems, night-shift work is pure poison, since neither organ is able to recover.

From One to Three in the Morning – Liver

The fact that rest is good for the liver, indeed that sleeping cures are even prescribed for it, is doubtless attributable to the fact that it is *only during sleep* that the liver can regenerate itself and perform its vital work of detoxification. Thus, if the liver is heavily taxed between one and three in the morning then that is especially detrimental. In the recovery from this no small role is played by a thorough warming through of the body (which of course generally occurs in bed).

Taken together, nicotine and alcoholic drinks put a far greater strain on the organism between one and five in the morning than at other times – a fact that explains a grim statistic: women suffer much less from damage to the liver than men, because the drinkers among them mostly tend to indulge their craving in secret and during the day.

From Three to Five in the Morning – Lungs

Mountaineers and hikers know that a 3 a.m. start gets them going much better than 'sleeping in' until five in the morning. The high-phase for the lungs lasts in fact from 3 to 5 a.m. A good start makes it much easier for them to bridge over the drop in strength after five o'clock – by then they will have got into their stride. Smokers are well-acquainted with the tickling in the throat every morning: during the night the lungs have been working overtime trying to shovel out what does not belong there with the cilia on their inner surface.

Incidentally, anyone who regularly wakes up at the same time during the night has good reason to suspect that something is not right with whatever organ is currently going through its high-phase.

From Five to Seven in the Morning – Large Intestine

Food remains for about two hours in the small intestine and about twenty hours in the large intestine. Diarrhoea is an indicator of digestion problems in the small intestine, whilst constipation indicates that the solidifying process in the large intestine has gone on for too long. Especially between five and seven in the morning it is possible to assist the detoxifying work of the large intestine by drinking a glass of *lukewarm* water or eating some dried fruit.

By means of this little journey through the course of a day you have made the acquaintance of yet another inner clock, which you can now profitably observe. To be sure, its ticking does not harmonise in every respect with the pattern of behaviour that people try to drum into us around here, as being normal, appropriate or even healthy. However, with the knowledge of these rhythms you will now find it easier to trust your instinct, and to eliminate many internal and external points of friction between normality and reality.

One of the most destructive ideas that our epoch has brought into the world is the conviction that a person's physical age has any bearing at all on mental or physical condition, efficiency, capacity for sexual love, mobility and the like. If you believe that, then assuredly things will turn out the way that science and statistics would have you expect. But if you do not wish to regard ageing as a biological strait-jacket, if your body is to keep step with the youthfulness that you can feel inwardly every second of your life, then it would be as well not only to crush these convictions like so many fleas, but also to keep track of your inner clocks and adapt a little to their ebb and flow. If it were really so, would there be people – for example artists such as Goethe, Picasso, Arthur Rubinstein – who can still produce masterpieces at the age of eighty (while many young people of thirty sit around waiting resignedly for their pension)? Of course not!

Everyday living leads us to feel every day that happiness has nothing to do with age, wealth and ultimately even health, but rather with inner peace and contentedness with oneself and the world, quite regardless of the external state of that world and of the condition of one's own body. To be sure, your thoughts obviously can only slowly change the state of the external world, and sometimes not at all. But you can change *your* world, the inner world, in fractions of a second, without thereby having to close your eyes to the outer world. It is sufficient to know that no one has ever whined his way back to health, that no problem was ever solved by complaining.

So, make a decision, without waiting for anyone else's approval, and neither go to bed (not even after 11 p.m.) nor into retirement, as long as your own feeling tells you otherwise.

After this journey through the day many readers will be exercised by the question of how travel across time zones affects things. For example, what if a plane journey carries you in a few hours to a country where the sun is still high in the sky while your inner clocks are signalling that it's time for a night-cap? Anyone who has undertaken such journeys knows that many bodily functions become confused and that it takes a few days to regain the usual measure of physical well-being and merge in with the rhythm of the new environment.

Unfortunately it is not possible to offer any comprehensive advice on the subject. Travellers and frequent passengers know the problem and have worked out one or two methods to get through the adjustment quickly. However, many of the problems of adjustment can be reduced to the *mental processes* of the individual: for instance many a case of constipation stems from the fact that when we are in a foreign country we are very cautious at first and unwilling to 'give of ourselves' until we have gained confidence in our own capacity to cope with the new situation. On the other hand there are many people for whom a trip from one side of the planet to the other across all its time zones means almost nothing at all. They have mastered the art of feeling at home wherever they are. Such fortunate individuals certainly manage to adjust their bodily rhythms most rapidly. These are people who travel light in their journey through life – physically as well as in their hearts.

Observe yourself, look, become aware, make notes: your own experience with the organic rhythms (and everything else contained in this book) is more important that any external information.

Admittedly information is important, but ultimately it is only a tool. The head and hand that make use of a tool have to depend on experience and practice. However, the heart which guides both head and hand does not depend on anything – with the exception of the memory of itself and its own true home.

IV. Healthy Building and Living

Your house shall be not an anchor but a mast.
You shall not fold your wings that you may pass
through doors, nor bend your heads that they strike
not against a ceiling, nor fear to breathe.
Your house shall not hold your secret
nor shelter your longing.
For that which is boundless in you
abides in the mansion of the sky,
whose door is the morning mist, and
whose windows are the songs and silences of the night.

Kahlil Gibran: The Prophet

Our body is like a dependable sailing ship, a robust vessel in which we plough through the waves of life. In order to withstand unscathed the inevitable storms and doldrums, there is a need, as we have already amply demonstrated, for a certain measure of maintenance and care. In this part of the book we wish to answer the question of how to make our houses and dwellings – the ship's masts that hold the sails for our journey through life, as Kahlil Gibran poetically expresses it – into health-giving and solidly built areas, spaces which give us strength rather than costing us strength.

Of course, from the very beginning it is people themselves who with the good naturedness or the cheerlessness of their thoughts fill their dwellings either with life and happiness or with discord and exhaustion. Whether our houses and flats become slender masts that offer themselves gaily to the wind and waves, or massive anchors that render our short journey on earth tedious and fatiguing – *the choice is ours*.

However, the captain's navigational skill is futile if the mast is rotten: the best will, the healthiest attitude towards body and life can sometimes be of no avail, if the danger comes from outside, if ignorance, negligence, material constraints or the craving for profit, turn houses into zones of disturbance and sources of harmful substances, thus undermining our health.

Poisonous substances and radiation, which are part and parcel of our modern, 'progressive' dwellings and building materials – with which we furnish, paint, varnish, seal, glue, insulate – transform many of our living and sleeping quarters into areas of slowly creeping weakness and fatigue, ranging up to serious damage to health and even death. From the USA comes the concept of 'house sickness syndrome' – a collective expression for a series of grave physical disorders and illnesses which have a common cause: breathing in or coming into contact with exhalations and poisons contained in the walls and internal materials of new buildings. These escape and are breathed in either in gaseous form or as dust. Almost in the same way that miners had to reckon with pneumoconiosis as an occupational disease, many of us either consciously or unconsciously, out of apathy or resignation have actually become accustomed to living with these poisons and their long-term adverse consequences for our health. This process of habituation is facilitated by the authorities through the establishment of official limits concerning the quantity of harmful substances in the air, food and building materials – prescribed according to standards that may well look good in the laboratory but are never valid in individual cases – firstly because one poison almost never appears on its own but rather in conjunction with many other mutually interacting substances, secondly because the tables of limits usually only take into account the short-term damaging effects, and thirdly because only *known* harmful substances are included, not unknown or new substances. We have yet to convince the manufacturers by dint of cogent proof of the harmlessness or toxicity of the latter (i.e. with a great many of cases of illness and death).

If a baby falls ill from the formaldehyde content of the air around chipboard furniture, it is a matter of indifference that many other infants are just about able to tolerate the same air.

The construction of modern apartment blocks only rarely follows the timeless fundamental rules of healthy building that is fit for human habitation (perhaps because most builders and architects do not build for themselves). Political will has fallen asleep, broadbased information is lacking – above all the information that there is absolutely no need for healthy building and living to be more expensive than normal methods of building, especially when one includes re-usability and environmental compatibility in the bill. (How much does it cost to dispose of hazardous waste, such as a sealed parquet floor?)

In particular the art of correctly timing the individual stages of building and development – and above all the art of distinguishing between good and bad places – have almost fallen into oblivion. Cases where there is a genuine will to build in a humane fashion often end in despair after many years because these two arts are unknown and a great deal of effort comes to nothing. It is our especial concern to revive these arts, for ignoring them can not only seriously delay and in many areas block the development of ecologically sound building, but it can also undermine your personal efforts to be healthy. However, if you take to heart the few important basic rules, then you will have taken a major step towards making your living area a health-giving and invigorating environment.

Undoubtedly environmentalists have already done a lot to reduce this creeping self-poisoning and in many areas even to bring it to a halt. Asbestos, formaldehyde, dioxin – names of poisonous substances that are keywords reminding us of the resolute efforts of these people on behalf of a natural, worthwhile environment. However, many pioneers and rediscoverers of ecologically sound methods of building and living are not really doing themselves and the rest of us a service if they fight too fanatically for the good cause, or if in view of the general situation they come close to despair. Such bitterness is understandable, but it should never be allowed to lead to a situation in which one wears oneself out in trench warfare against commerce, politics and industry, thus destroying a lot of the good that such work could produce. Without self confidence and confidence in the future everything will stay as it is.

Moreover, many well-intentioned people are consciously or unconsciously dependent on the results of their activity and want their life's work to bear *visible* fruit, and they seek confirmation in their environment. Admittedly that is an understandable wish, but it would be better to abandon it altogether. The danger of becoming dependent on people who graciously dispense applause is too great. The journey towards humane, healthy building and living is accomplished in small, scarcely perceptible steps. To expect admiration in an epoch in which greed and fear hold sway is the surest way to fail in one's good intentions. It will be some time yet before we have a solar power system on each roof and make use of the earth's heat, before we use rainwater to flush our toilets, before manufacturers do not think first and foremost of their wallets but rather the welfare of their customers – before we have befriended nature in all spheres of life and linked ourselves back into its cycles.

The signs of a change for the better are increasing: many consumers, many builders and decorators, joiners, painters, paperhangers and handymen have started the process of rethinking and are increasingly paying attention to such terms as 'environmentally friendly', 'non-toxic', 'bio-degradable' and the like. In spite of this it transpires again and again that such expressions are made prematurely or inaccurately, and that they are often no more than commercially effective eye-wash. And we shall probably go on for some time being offered products in shops and DIY supermarkets whose harmfulness and poisonous effects only come to light over a long period of time (even if they bear an environmentally friendly seal).

* As long as politics and commerce work hand in hand to keep us dependent and immature;

* as long as we have to serve as guinea pigs for well-known and ever-new chemicals and radiations – in the air we breathe, building materials, clothing, food, medicines, electrical equipment, etc.;

* as long as legal limits merely establish the time within which it is permissible to damage our health, and as long as babies and old people are not taken into account when these limits are set;

* as long as we almost always have to wait first for scientific proof, before indolent policy-makers or irresponsible manufacturers decide to 'do something';

* as long as the fact that a radiation or a substance turns out after many years to be detrimental to health does not result in prosecution for bodily harm or manslaughter;

– as long as this is the situation we shall have to take things into our own hands – we shall have to wake up and stay awake. And even if everything does change for the better, this will only happen because we have woken up, because we have no longer surrendered responsibility for our lives. We, the 'individuals'.

It is only rarely possible to expect from above the precise help and information that you need in your own personal case. The people 'up there', paid for out of our pockets and the servants of us all, are all too often far-removed from reality and from the true needs of their employers – and that is *us*. And yet the desire for governments to pass laws that prescribe humane and healthy workplaces and habitations is quite understandable, if one has no solutions of one's own in view, if the necessary information is lacking concerning what contribution one could personally make. On the other hand, given adequate information – we would like to emphasise that – there is almost nothing that one cannot take in hand for oneself, whether as a builder, householder or tenant. Only insights that have been gained through one's own initiative can last, can introduce a genuine change in thinking and calm action which will finally bring that genuine satisfaction and fulfilment which no rote-learnt or blindly received formulae and laws could ever produce. Then the fear that as an individual one can do nothing about it does not even arise. Go ahead and realise for yourself the laws you aspire to *before* they are enacted – by means of your own purchasing decisions.

It is only in this way that genuine inner security can grow. Every confidence, if only promised, – ("Vote for our party. We will do everything for environmental protection!") – holds people in dependence and thus in helplessness and fear.

If starting from today you no longer shove the responsibility for your actions and their consequences on to other people, to say nothing of politicians, experts or manufacturing companies, then there is no longer any occasion for bitterness or despair. Of course to a certain extent we are compelled to exercise trust when we try out and purchase a product. But blind trust is out of place here, as it is everywhere else in life. In plain English blind trust simply means: "You take over the responsibility. I'm right if everything goes well; it's your fault if something goes wrong."

Examine things with your own instinct and common sense, do not let yourself be lulled to sleep by advertising slogans, and every time you decide for or against a particular product or measure remember four fundamental truths:

* Through your decision you determine what is produced or imported and who earns your money. Whether we are talking about vegetables, wood, paints or heating systems, you are and you remain King Customer. Every single one of your decisions is a thousand times more earth-shaking than the vote you cast in the election or a three-hour political speech.

* 'Fast-working' is not always a euphemism for 'poisonous', but almost always. 'Slow-working' is often the characteristic of a good product – but not always.

* Hard-wearing, resistant, indestructible, durable, long-lasting – each of these effective marketing qualities begs the question: is it possible without great expenditure to return the product to the cycle of nature? Or will archaeologists in a thousand years be able to measure our foolishness from the composition of our rubbish tips and the poison-content of our bones?

* Someone who shows off must have a need to do so: the manufacturer of a good, humane product never needs to convince people – it is quite sufficient for him unobtrusively to make it available to them. Companies which genuinely have the health of their users at heart often tread the boards very softly.

Have confidence in your own judgement, examine things carefully, weigh them up and then come to your own decision – without any pressure or compulsion. This lack of compulsion transforms your decision into a very strong force – much stronger than you perhaps imagine at the moment. Even in 1960 shirts and blouses of pure cotton were almost nowhere to be found. Now it is getting quite difficult to buy outer clothing made from 100% synthetic material (except in developing countries where we palm off our rubbish, and in regions where there has not yet been any change from below). You should keep in mind that it was not a law but exclusively the consciousness and instinct of the individual concerning the harmfulness of synthetic clothing that brought about this change – in other words: *your* instinct. Your instinct is also the only means to put a stop *from the outset* to products that are unnecessary, harmful to health and hostile to nature.

On the following pages we shall be acquainting you with information and alternatives enabling you to make healthier living a reality in your own home, without any additional expenditure of time and money. We shall confront the vested interest in keeping us in the dark with the only means we have at our disposal: information. Your contribution to the success of your intentions is easy to formulate: never try, in any sphere of life, to shift the responsibility for an improvement in the situation on to anyone else.

1. Building, Extending, Renovating – Correct Timing

To build and live in tune with natural and lunar rhythms is easier and pleasanter to achieve, is cheaper in both the short- and long-term, and brings you an important step closer to the aim of living a healthy life and not exploiting nature. Numerous problems in house-building and interior development can be avoided if one carries out the work according to the position of the moon and using wood felled at the correct time – our most precious raw material.

The fact that in general people no longer pay attention to lunar rhythms in the domain of building, maintenance and home improvement is hardly surprising. It would seem that freedom and self-realisation are basic rights that take priority over our obligations towards ourselves, our neighbours and nature: at least that is the message that has been constantly fed to us every day for a long time.

Insisting on our basic rights has led us to forget that every basic *right* is accompanied by ten basic *duties*.

We have gradually lulled ourselves to sleep with the conviction that paint vapours transform themselves instantly into healthy air, that protective agents for timber must be harmless if they come in green tins, that a caustic cleansing fluid turns into clear drinking water the moment it reaches the waste-pipe, and that we can really only learn how to live by watching television. And above all: that we have a right to the rapid fulfilment of our wishes – with immediate effect. Planned today, ready tomorrow!

Naturally in the course of time many constraints arise from this one-sided emphasis on freedom and basic rights, and the field of house-building and renovation is no exception: stress-laden two-income families are compelled to make rapid decisions, to rely on the advice of experts and to trust advertising leaflets. Assisted by industry and advertising, work on and in the house has degenerated into a necessary evil or a peripheral hobby; every promise of work made easier was joyfully received without any concern for such effects as massively increasing power consumption (of which a high percentage appears on the bill not of industry but of private households), or atmospheric and environmental pollution. In all these labour-saving measures and devices we overlook how short-term the savings really are and how much we pay in terms of over-exploitation of ourselves and of nature for this rapid efficiency and 'comfort'. Did you know that in order to produce a battery fifty times more energy has to be used than the battery will ever yield? Or that in order to produce one car the energy consumed would be enough to supply a normal household with electricity for ten years? Anyone who perceives such connections will no longer be so keen to pay the price of this exploitation.

It is not for nothing that the old proverb is current among initiates of the building trade that "in the first year an enemy, in the second year a friend, in the third year the builder" should move into a new house. This saying is based on the fact that it is usually several years before a new building has got over its teething troubles, for example the residual dampness of inadequately dried brick walls, which have been the cause of many a rheumatic illness. Nowadays on top of that there are serious gas emissions from building materials, paints and impregnating substances, which make breathing difficult for the first occupants.

We could easily pack this proverb away in the box of curios of the past, if only we paid attention to correct timing in building, interior development and renovation. Residual dampness in poorly drying walls and ceilings, and many other problems which are often accepted almost fatalistically, would never arise in the first place.

In order to apply the rules for healthy living, the information and helpful tips contained in this chapter, as well as all the other parts of this book, only a single investment is required: *patience*. One has personally to take in hand many things that would otherwise be left to the architect and the builders: from the choice of building materials, the type of heat insulation for the heating system, the paints and varnishes, to the setting up of a timetable based on the rules of correct timing for each phase of the building work. All of this demands patience and information.

Perhaps it will help you in coming to your decisions to ask yourself the following questions:

* If you build for yourself, how often will you do it in your lifetime?

* If you build for others would you yourself want to live in the atmosphere of such a house?

* And how important to you is the nice feeling that you have done everything in your power and knowledge for the health of its inhabitants?

Nature has a lot of patience with us human beings. We should have patience with her, too. For she works slowly in her own deliberate way. Apple blossom sometimes blooms overnight; however, the buds already started to form during the previous autumn.

From Ground Inspection to Path Building

According to information from an architect known to us who has been building ecologically sound houses for 15 years, enthusiasm for environmentally friendly building and home improvement has fallen off somewhat in recent times.

The reason for this lies probably in the fact that every builder who sets about building such a house may well be mindful of natural building materials and environmentally friendly heating systems, but in the course of time he has a number of bad experiences. If the roof truss warps into curves after a few years or splits the wood, then even with the best will in the world he can be driven to despair. One can also often observe how natural wood and natural materials, left untreated for the best of reasons, perhaps on the facade of a house, after some years nonetheless have to be treated at considerable expense, with waterproofing material for instance. The good intention was there, but watching wood getting wetter and wetter and threatening to rot makes many a builder throw up his hands. For such people it can amount to a revelation to start following the lunar rhythms.

However, this can have serious consequences for the building industry, the building materials industry and the timber industry: their products – furniture, heating insulation, buildings, building timber of all kinds, and much more – would become much more durable, which in addition would render superfluous the very great expenditure on maintenance, renovation, and measures to protect wood. All of which makes these things seem less interesting in a throw-away society. Nonetheless, many people have already grasped the point: such a society does not have any future. Everyone is happy to enjoy the beneficial applications of science, technology and progress without thinking too much about the disadvantages. But if the possibility exists of solving the problem of waste, if it is possible to release fewer poisons into our bodies and surroundings, if the durability of wood that is cut at the right time permits moderate reforestation, then everyone ought to know about such possibilities and be able to take advantage of them. Under certain circumstances today ecological building materials, heating insulation, natural paints and products made from wood cut at the right time still work out somewhat more expensive, perhaps because it is only small business that can afford to pay more attention to correct timing, or simply because experience in dealing with these materials is lacking. On the other hand the future will bring us back to the small, local business which, working in close association with processing craftsmen, will market its products directly.

We know from experience how quickly word can get around when foresters, sawmill-owners, architects, bricklayers, foremen, painters, joiners, carpenters and interior decorators carry out their work according to the rules of correct timing and use the right wood. They are already to be found in many places, their clientele is massive, and the result of their work speaks for itself: environmental compatibility, value for health, and quality are becoming the decisive factors for an increasing number of people. In times like today, when ecological house-building is no longer an alien term, sufficient customers can be found who know how to appreciate the work of such people.

Inspecting the Ground

Just what an inestimable benefit for your health can be gained by inspecting the ground before starting to build is something you will discover in the next chapter (see page 305). Perhaps your interest will then be awakened in having the building site investigated for so-called *zones of disturbance*, in order to determine the exact layout of the house. It can be well worth your while to call in a specialist for this task, for many zones of disturbance run in such a way that shifting the position of the house by a yard would be sufficient to avoid strong, health-threatening disruptive radiations, which could possibly run through several rooms.

But a ground inspection is still a good idea even if the site is too small to permit an alternative position for the house. After measuring up, the subsequent division of the rooms can be carried out in such a way that bedrooms and work rooms are kept clear of disruptive radiations from the very start. Masters of this craft can examine a site at any time, but to be on the safe side the following rule applies:

Inspection of the ground by an expert for the purpose of surveying zones of disturbance should take place when the moon is waxing – the closer to full moon the better. Earth radiations become stronger the more the moon waxes.

Digging out the Cellar

The moment chosen for all excavation work determines to a large extent the behaviour of ground water both at the time and above all subsequently. The waxing moon and water days (Cancer, Scorpio and Pisces) are unfavourable times, because seeping ground water will pour into the excavation and it is easier for it subsequently to force its way through the foundations and the cellar wall.

The movement of earth and the excavation of cellars should take place when the moon is waning. Although not essential, earth days (Taurus, Virgo and Capricorn) are the most favourable.

Foundations

The base plate or foundation can generally be poured at any time. Anyone wanting to be on the safe side should avoid the watery signs (Cancer, Scorpio and Pisces), because otherwise the foundation will stay moist for a longer time and will not dry out evenly.

Cellar

When building the cellar walls it would in fact be something of a disadvantage to disregard the correct moment. Work carried out during a watery sign (Cancer, Scorpio and Pisces) will not allow the walls to dry properly, will lead to greater humidity in the air and as a result the drying out process will take place very slowly. The result could be a cellar that is a breeding ground for mould. The rule is:

The favourable moment for erecting cellar walls is during the light and warmth signs (Gemini, Libra, Aquarius and Aries, Leo, Sagittarius); if this causes scheduling difficulties, then choose the earth signs (Taurus, Virgo and Capricorn).

Ceilings

With all ceilings including that of the cellar a slow drying-out is desirable in order to avoid cracks. In the case of concrete ceilings people usually find sprinkling water over them serves this purpose (spray the ceiling every 2–3 hours or so with a hose). Working at the correct time can significantly improve the result.

Ceilings can be poured at any time with the exception of Leo days (in order to avoid drying too quickly). If there is no alternative, then keep the ceiling continually moist throughout the Leo days.

Building the Walls

The time for building load-bearing walls may be freely chosen; though here, too, if it is possible at no greater cost to take correct timing into account, then the waning moon would be slightly more favourable because the shell of the building will dry out more quickly. One comment, perhaps: concrete as a building material for walls, especially if steel-reinforced, makes people ill and tired. Almost any other natural building material, providing it 'breathes' (does not inhibit evaporation), would be more suitable.

The Roof Truss

A roof truss made from wood cut at the right time (see page 288) and likewise erected at the right time is a real blessing. Many builders can tell you a thing or two about the trouble a roof truss can cause, often after only a short time: warping or rotting wood, displaced or broken tiles, water damage, etc.

Wood that is erected when the moon is waxing will warp and

cause the tiles to move; if it is erected in Cancer it will warp severely and rot easily. Having the patience to wait for the correct moment is especially worthwhile here.

Roof trusses should be erected when the moon is on the wane, preferably during the sign of Capricorn. Taurus is also a suitable time. You should always steer clear of the zodiac sign Cancer.

Covering the Roof

The roof over one's head can also profit from being laid down at the correct time. If this is done when the moon is waxing then the tiles will sometimes fail to hold together well: they will get displaced and can break. One should avoid watery days (Cancer, Scorpio and Pisces) because otherwise the roof will pick up dirt more easily and will encourage moss to grow.

Covering the roof should take place when the moon is waning. The light and warmth days are ideal (Gemini, Libra, Aquarius and Aries, Leo, Sagittarius).

Exterior Rendering and Interior Plaster, External Cladding

Even in new buildings it is possible to observe cracks in the rendering or plaster-work; sometimes after a very short time whole chunks of it fall out of the wall. External cladding of timber or wooden shingles (see the information about wood on page 295) can become twisted and distorted. The reason for this is often not the quality of the building materials used, or weather conditions or sharp changes in temperature, but rather incorrect timing of the work. It is possible for you to side-step such undesirable consequences:

Rendering and plastering, as well as external cladding should be carried out when the moon is waning. The sign Cancer should always be avoided, because plaster and rendering do not stick well and wood stays damp. Leo when the moon is waxing is unfavourable for rendering, because the drying process is too rapid.

Partition Walls, Concrete and Stone Stairs, Electrical Installation

Partition walls, stone stairs and all work connected with electricity supply and distribution can be carried out at any time – which will be a comfort for those who are beginning to get the feeling that every single building phase has to be worked out exactly, and who are wondering how they are going to sell the idea to the foreman. You should use spare time for such work.

Wooden Stairs

Wood that warps and twists and splits, wooden staircases that creak and crack, particularly spiral staircases, in which the joints can even work loose: these are a problem in many houses. Quite apart from the fact that the wood itself may possibly have been cut at the wrong time, to a great extent the time of installation plays a decisive role in producing these undesirable effects.

Wooden staircases should be installed while the moon is on the wane. The ideal time is during Capricorn days. Always avoid Cancer days.

Plumbing

At last we have some work about the house for which the watery signs can be of some use. The effect that is achieved by watching out for the correct time is based entirely on experience and cannot be explained: drinking water stays fresher, corrosion in all pipes and also appliances occurs much more slowly or is absent altogether. If you want to enjoy these benefits for yourself pay attention to the rule:

All plumbing work in the house should take place on water days (Cancer, Scorpio and Pisces) regardless of the moon's phase.

Wooden Windows and Doors

Wooden windows and doors that are installed when the moon is waxing or is in a watery sign (Cancer, Scorpio and Pisces) can become distorted and then not close properly and begin to rot prematurely as a result of penetrating damp. If you wish to play safe, and especially when you do not know whether the wood for the windows and doors was cut at the right time, then you should follow this rule:

Wooden windows and doors should be installed when the moon is waning and under no circumstances on watery days (Cancer, Scorpio and Pisces). The ideal time is during Capricorn days with the moon on the wane.

Incidentally, the time you select to replace removable winter windows has a bearing on whether they continually steam or mist up throughout the winter. Anyone who could do without that, and who prefers a clear view to a film of mist should pay attention to correct timing: winter or outer windows should be fitted during the air signs Aquarius or Gemini.

Heating for the First Time

The first time that a new house is heated it is worthwhile paying attention to correct timing: the chimney will draw better and the house will quickly get a good warming through, the last dampness will be driven from the walls, and the subsequent build-up of soot will be much slighter.

The first heating of new buildings should take place when the moon is waning, during Aries, Leo or Sagittarius.

This rule also applies to the first heating in autumn before the winter heating period.

Floor Coverings

Floor coverings of all sorts (fitted carpets, linoleum, cork etc.) also benefit from being laid down at the correct time: the covering adjusts well and doesn't buckle up when there are sharp changes of temperature or humidity. The rule is simple:

The laying of floor coverings of all types ought to take place when the moon is waning.

Wooden Floors

Fitted carpets have become an established feature not merely because tastes have changed in questions of how we live. Wood that has been cut and installed at the wrong time, parquet floors that have been sealed with pure poison (hazardous waste!) have soured our pleasure in a genuine wooden floor. And yet there is nothing more beautiful and environmentally friendly than a floor made out of untreated wood, which ultimately costs as much as one of the better fitted carpets but will last a hundred years longer. However, it would be extremely helpful here to obtain timber that has been felled at the right time.

The rules that apply for wooden floors are similar to those for wooden staircases. If it is laid when the moon is on the wane, the floor stays quiet and firm (unless you happen to have a goblin in the house). Even frequent moist cleaning and wiping will do it no harm. Floors that are laid down during Cancer days generally creak constantly, develop cracks and gradually rot, particularly if the moon was waxing at the time the work was done.

The best time to lay wooden floors is when the moon is waning, ideally during the Capricorn days. Do not lay a floor during the Cancer days.

Wooden Ceilings and Panelling

The same rules apply here as with wooden floors; however, the consequences of carrying out the work at an unfavourable time are not quite so evident. If they are fitted when the moon is waxing, wooden ceilings and panelling sometimes creak, the wood warps more and can develop cracks, particularly when the weather changes or the temperature and humidity fluctuate.

Wooden ceilings and panelling are best fitted when the moon is on the wane and under no circumstances during Cancer days.

Paint-work, Varnishing, Waterproofing, Gluing

Many dyes, emulsion paints, varnishes and glues that are harmful to health and to the environment were only able to gain acceptance at the expense of gentler lime wash paints and natural products, because they literally overran the subtle influences of the natural rhythms and apparently rendered the observation of correct timing superfluous.

The use of natural products would certainly be easier in this area if people were to abide by the rules of correct timing. In terms of effortless preparation, effectiveness and durability they are scarcely inferior to or just as good as today's fast-working poison brews. When worked with at the right time, paint and undercoat dry well, form beautiful surfaces and last longer. Products combine well: the brush glides along almost by itself. Lime wash paints allow the undercoat to breathe and yet they inhibit damp.

Of course we realise that a switch to natural products cannot take place from one day to the next. However, observing the rules of correct timing even with poisonous products makes extremely good sense.

When processed during the waning moon poisonous vapours and dusts remain more firmly bound in the products and cause less pollution to the air we breathe. That is to say the product and the object treated remain as poisonous as before, only the emission of harmful substances is slighter.

On the other hand, when the moon is waxing, paints, varnishes and glues that are applied with a brush release their solvents and poisons more intensely and for longer periods of time. If for instance one is trying to remove coats of poisonous paint from furniture and the like (by sanding or stripping with chemicals) it is essential to do such work when the moon is waning. First of all the work will be far easier, secondly the body will not absorb the poisons so readily (you have already seen the reason for this in the first part of the book). At the same time the moon should not be in Cancer or Gemini (danger of damage to the lungs) – or in Leo (damage to the heart or circulation).

Harmful vapours generally pass over to the body and all the other objects in the room; for this reason it is often practically useless to remove poisonous coatings (of wood preservative, for instance) that have been there for decades. That is also the reason why legal proceedings against the irresponsible manufacturers of such poisons have until now only rarely been successful: it is difficult to prove the cause of the illness, because the substances have already been absorbed, the toxic effect often does not appear for years, while the product itself no longer has any harmful effect, or may even no longer be on the market. As long as the burden of proof lies with the injured party, you don't have much of a chance against these poison brewers. Thus, for the sake of your health and the environment, or – if you are using natural products – for reasons of ease of processing, durability and beauty, you should always keep to the following rules:

Whether the product is natural or not, painting, varnishing, impregnating and gluing ought always to be done during the period of the waning moon.

Do not do this work during Leo or Cancer days. On Cancer

days one would breathe too much poison in, and moisture can remain between the paint and the wood. In Leo the paint dries too quickly, and it can become brittle and flake off.

In general drying does not proceed so well during water days (Cancer, Scorpio and Pisces) and a subsequent attack of fungus cannot be ruled out.

Fences, Posts

Sometimes when walking in the country or the town one walks past untreated wooden fence posts which have been standing rock-solid in the ground for forty years or more, whilst perhaps on the other side of the road there are totally rotten, pressure impregnated wooden fences that have scarcely clocked up more than ten years. The reason for this difference is certainly not to be sought merely in the quality of the wood, but also in the time at which the fence was erected. If the timing is right, posts driven into the ground automatically remain firm, and nails stay put in the wood. The rule for erecting posts of all sorts is as follows:

The most suitable time for erecting or renewing fences is when the moon is on the wane, particularly the earth days (Taurus, Virgo, Capricorn) or directly on the day of the new moon. Cancer days are unfavourable, because the posts will loosen by themselves and rot more quickly.

Paving Stones, Verandas, Paths

A great many architects, builders and handymen must have already learnt through experience that paving stones laid out of doors sometimes become wobbly after a short time (especially if they have been laid directly on the soil), that verandas or paths covered with gravel become uneven, that after only a short time paths become eroded or develop pot-holes – despite all their care and expertise. On other occasions everything is as firm as if it were set in concrete, and even on bare earth improvements to paths are a lasting success. Here, too, the timing of the work is of decisive importance:

Paving stones in the garden or on paths should be laid when the moon is waning. One should always avoid Cancer days, because the slabs will work loose and never become fixed. Paths and country tracks should also be laid or filled with gravel when the moon is on the wane. Capricorn days are especially suitable for this. Cancer days should be avoided because everything will quickly become eroded.

Gardens

Of course a beautiful, well-kept garden can contribute a lot to improving the health and well-being of its owners, not merely on account of its flowers and cosy nooks, but also because of the opportunity it gives to grow healthy vegetables, herbs and fruit. Just what a great benefit can be derived from a knowledge of the rules of correct timing, is something that the almost a million readers of our first book, *Vom richtigen Zeitpunkt*, have discovered. To repeat it all here would exceed the confines of this present book.*

If you have gained confidence in these rules you are perhaps now asking yourself: How am I going to persuade a firm of builders or a foreman to fall in with my projected schedule for the various building phases?

First of all: you are the customer; you are the boss. Your own health and wallet are on the line. Be forearmed with patience and forbearance, but don't stand for any talk of "Impossible! Can't be done!" Print out the table on page 300 for your contractor, or give

---

* Published in German, November 1992. To date it has been translated into eight other languages, and will shortly be published in the English language by The C.W. Daniel Company Ltd, Saffron Walden, England. It is concerned mainly with the influence of natural and lunar rhythms in gardening, agriculture and forestry, but also touches on domestic and health matters.

him a copy of the whole book, so that he can find out about the consequences of working at the wrong times. Perhaps it will be a revelation for him to discover just why certain things in the past simply didn't come off and perhaps even led to extra work or claims for compensation.

We recommend that you compile a schedule folder. Make copies of a moon calendar – as many as you need – for each building phase, using a complete page for each type of work. Then write in the ideal times in the lunar cycle for each type of work in green ink, favourable times in blue ink and unfavourable times in red ink – similar to the example in the illustration, in which the colours are indicated by lines points and dashes. Finally put the individual pages and possibly the big table at the end of the chapter in their own folder.

Armed with such a folder you will have a good overview of each individual activity in the house-building or renovating process, and the pressure of the schedule will not seem so great, because there will be plenty of alternatives. You will thus make the work of planning easier for you and your team, and even if despite everything certain dates cannot be postponed (perhaps because the weather also has a say in the matter) at the very least you will be able to steer clear of the most unfavourable days.

Timed Timber: Building Material No. 1

Especially in alpine countries foresters in former times meticulously followed the rules concerning the correct time to fell trees. It was obligatory to draw up detailed plans for the year in accordance with the lunar calendar, because what are currently the best times always vary from year to year. Formerly no one had to suffer the effects of poisonous wood preservatives: the choice of the correct time to fell timber alone was enough to ensure the required quality and load-

1993

Extract from a calendar showing the favourable times for individual building phases and types of work in the house (in this example a roof truss)

April	May	June
T 1 Scorpio	S 1 Leo	T 1 Libra
F 2 Leo	S 2 Virgo	W 2 Scorpio
S 3 Leo	M 3 Virgo	T 3 Scorpio
S 4 Virgo	T 4 Libra	F 4 Sagittarius ○ 14.03
M 5 Virgo	W 5 Libra	S 5 Sagittarius
T 6 Libra ○ 19.44	T 6 Scorpio ○ 04.35	S 6 Capricorn
W 7 Libra	F 7 Scorpio	M 7 Capricorn
T 8 Scorpio	S 8 Sagittarius	T 8 Capricorn
F 9 Scorpio Good Friday	S 9 Sagittarius	W 9 Aquarius
S 10 Sagittarius	M10 Capricorn	T 10 Aquarius
S 11 Sagittarius	T 11 Capricorn	F 11 Pisces
M12 Capricorn Easter Monday	W12 Aquarius	S 12 Pisces ☾
T 13 Capricorn ☾	T 13 Aquarius ☾	S 13 Aries
W14 Capricorn	F 14 Aquarius	M14 Aries
T 15 Aquarius	S 15 Pisces	T 15 Aries
F 16 Aquarius	S 16 Pisces	W16 Taurus
S 17 Pisces	M17 Aries	T 17 Taurus
S 18 Pisces	T 18 Aries	F 18 Gemini
M19 Pisces	W19 Aries	S 19 Gemini
T 20 Aries	T 20 Taurus	S 20 Gemini ● 02.53
W21 Aries	F 21 Taurus ● 15.07	M21 Cancer
T 22 Taurus ● 00.50	S 22 Gemini	T 22 Cancer
F 23 Taurus	S 23 Gemini	W23 Leo
S 24 Taurus	M24 Cancer	T 24 Leo
S 25 Gemini	T 25 Cancer	F 25 Virgo
M26 Gemini	W26 Cancer	S 26 Virgo)
T 27 Cancer	T 27 Leo	S 27 Libra
W28 Cancer	F 28 Leo)	M28 Libra
T 29 Leo)	S 29 Virgo	T 29 Scorpio
F 30 Leo	S 30 Virgo	W30 Scorpio
	M31 Libra Whit Monday	

	= ideal		Aries		Libra
⋮ = favourable		Taurus		Scorpio
¦ = unfavourable		Gemini		Sagittarius
‖ = very unfavourable		Cancer		Capricorn
○ Full moon ● New moon		Leo		Aquarious
☾ Waning) Waxing		Virgo		Pisces

bearing capacity of timber. Observance of these rules, which have been valid for thousands of years, can also make an important contribution to healthy living and a natural environment. Do not forget: wood that has been treated with preservatives and sealed (parquet, panelling, etc.) is *toxic waste*. It is not even fit to burn, since numerous poisons would be released.

Anyone who insists on it will find any number of examples which prove the validity of these ancient rules, from Alaska to Siberia, Sweden to South Africa: churches that in part are more than a thousand years old, farmhouses and barns, wooden chimneys and balconies which have endured wind and weather, ice and even fire without any protective coating, speak to us in the clearest terms. People are astonished to see ancient threshing floors which were laid down without any glue and which have warped or shrunk so little that one still cannot get a razor-blade between the boards. We can see garden furniture or sheds made of planed, untreated wood, exposed year in year out to the weather, without a single crack or gap, without any unevenness and as hard as rock. We grope our way cautiously over brand new wooden bridges that are already so slippery and rotten after only a few years that one has to think about pulling them down. And then on the other hand we stride across plenty of hard-wearing wooden bridges that are many decades old, without needing to look nervously for the handrail out of the corner of our eye.

The secret that can explain all these remarkable experiences is this: the work was done at the right moment; the wood was cut down, processed and used at the right time. In many regions even today people keep to the correct days for felling timber.

Basically there are no good and bad days for the production of timber. The decisive factor is the purpose of the wood in question. It makes a big difference whether wood is intended for floors, barrels, bridges, roof trusses, musical instruments or carving. Wood is a fundamentally living substance; even after it has been felled it continues to 'work': depending on the type of wood, age, size, season, time of felling, it will dry rapidly or slowly, remain soft or become hard, remain heavy or become light, develop cracks or remain unchanged, twist or remain straight, fall prey to rot and woodworm or remain protected against decay and pests.

Almost everyone who has anything to do with felling and working with timber knows that winter is in general the best time for obtaining timber, in particular the period between December 21 and January 6. (For readers in the southern hemisphere, see page 24.) At that time the sap has gone down, and the timber will warp less after it has been felled. However, in addition to that there are a large number of special dates which have a clearly discernible bearing on the characteristics of wood – all of them connected with the current position of the moon. On the following pages you will also become acquainted with a number of special rhythms: rules and particular dates that are completely independent of the lunar cycle. Only those who apply them will discover their validity.

Just how well our forefathers knew what they were doing can clearly be seen from the comprehensive set of rules from the Austrian Tyrol on the following page. It goes back to very ancient times, though the present text dates from the year 1912. All the rules stated in this old document are as valid as ever.

There now follows a partial translation of these rules insofar as they are applicable to healthy building and living, together with one or two additional tips, organised according to the quality of wood that is desirable for a particular purpose.

Non-rotting, Hard Wood

This quality of wood can be obtained during the last two days in March with the moon on the wane in Pisces. However, it does not happen every year that the zodiac sign Pisces occurs in the waning phase of the moon. Still, there are alternative dates: New Year's

MOON SIGNS FOR WOOD-CUTTING AND WASTING

By Ludwig Weinhold.
Recorded by Michael Ober, master cartwright in St. Johann, Tyrol, copied by Josef Schmutzer, December 25, 1912.

1. Wasting days are April 3, July 30, and St. Achatius Day, even better when the these fall during the waning moon or on a Lady Saint Day. These days are good for weeding and clearing, and also for casting bullets and scrap metal.
2. For timber to remain firm and tight fitting it is good to cut it in the first eight days after new moon in December, on a day with a weak sign. For straight-wood or tool-wood, beech etc. to remain tight fitting and firm, it should be new moon in Scorpio.
3. So that the wood does not rot it should be cut in the last two days of March with the waning moon in Pisces.
4. So that the wood does not burn, there is only one day when it should be cut: March 1st, preferably after sunset.
5. So that the wood does not shrink it should be cut on the third day of autumn. At the start of autumn on September 24, when the moon is three days old and on a Lady Saint Day when it is a Cancer day.
6. Working on firewood so that it grows back well should be done in October during the first quarter of the waxing moon.
7. Timber for sawing should be cut down when the moon is waxing in Pisces; then boards and timber will not be worm-ridden.
8. Timber for bridges and arches should be cut down when the moon is waning in Pisces or Cancer.
9. So that the wood becomes light it should be cut down with the moon in Scorpio and in August. If it is cut down in Taurus, i.e. when the August moon has been waning for one day, then it will remain heavy.
10. So that the wood does not develop cracks or open up it should be cut before new moon in November.
11. So that the wood does not split, it should be cut on June 24 between 11 and 12 o'clock.
12. Straight-wood or tool-wood should be cut down on February 26 when the moon is on the wane – better still on a Cancer day.

These moon signs have all been proven and tested.

Day, January 7, January 25, January 31 to February 2 inclusive. Timber that is cut down on these six days will not rot or get wood-worm. Furthermore, wood that is cut at new year or between January 31 and February 2 will in time become very hard.

Non-inflammable Wood

Yes, you did read correctly: timber that is cut down on March 1st, particularly after sunset, is fire-resistant! Possibly this can be explained by an eventual change in the resins contained in the wood. A joiner and woodwork teacher of our acquaintance had wood that was obtained in this way duly tested by a wood research state institute. It received the German fire-prevention grade 'F 60', which means that it can be used for internal building work without any fire-protection treatment.

Alternative days are the new moon in Libra (only once or twice a year; wood of this sort does not shrink and can be used when freshly cut – without needing to be stored for drying), the last day before new moon in December and the last 48 hours before the new moon in March.

Non-shrinking Wood

In many spheres of use wood must not shrink: in other words: circumference, extension and volume must not decrease. Such wood is best cut on St. Thomas Day (December 21) between 11 and 12 o'clock. This day is considered to be the best wood-cutting day of all. After this time timber should, with certain exceptions, only be cut down in winter when the moon is waning. Other periods suitable for non-shrinking wood are: February evenings after sunset when the moon is on the wane, September 27, every month the three days after new moon, on Lady Saints' Days (among others, August 15 and September 8) when these fall on Cancer days, or the new moon in the sign of Libra. Timber that is felled in February after sunset will become rock-hard.

Wood for Tools and Furniture

Wood that is cut in the first eight days after the December new moon in Aquarius or Pisces is suited to this purpose. Likewise the new moon in Scorpio (usually in November) and February 26 when the moon is waning, particularly when it is also in Cancer. However, wood that is cut in Scorpio should have its bark removed immediately, because otherwise it will quickly fall prey to bark beetle! Someone who is in other respects observing the correct timing for wood-cutting (for instance the period between December 21 and January 6) does not necessarily have to strip the bark at once, since there is little or no likelihood of attack from beetles (even when there are felled trunks stored nearby). In fact removing the bark can have the disadvantage that if the wood is exposed to sunlight for a lengthy period it develops fine cracks which render it unusable for certain purposes.

Firewood

When cutting firewood it is desirable that everything should grow back well afterwards. The most suitable time for this is the first seven days of the waxing moon in October. In general, however, firewood should be cut after the winter solstice when the moon is on the wane (do not remove the tree top straight away and leave the timber pointing downhill for some time).

Timber for Planks, Sawing and Building

The most suitable time for timber for planks and sawing is the waxing phase of the moon in Pisces, because the wood will not then be attacked by pests. The zodiac sign Pisces only appears in the waxing moon from September to March.

Timber for Floors and Tools

The best time is during the Scorpio days in August (strip the bark at once). If in addition the wood is to remain heavy (for instance for a floor that will take a lot of strain), then one should choose the first day after full moon in Taurus (does not occur every year).

Non-splitting Wood

Wood of this sort – for instance for furniture and carving – is best felled in the days prior to the new moon in November. Equally acceptable alternatives are March 25, June 29 and December 31. Wood that is cut down on these three days does not break or split. Here, too, the top of the tree should point down the valley and the tree should be left to lie for some time so that residual sap can be drawn to the top.

Wood that is to be used quickly, for instance when rebuilding after a fire, must under no circumstances split later. The best felling time is June 24 between 11 and 12 midday (between 12 and 1 p.m. summer time). Formerly that was a special day. Timber labourers would turn out in swarms and for a whole hour would saw for all they were worth.

Shingles and Wooden Gutters

Regardless of species, trees grow straight up, spiralling to the right or spiralling to the left (as can be seen from the bark). The difference is not difficult to recognise: a rightwards spiralling tree screws upwards like a corkscrew held upright. Joiners take this direction of rotation into account when using a particular piece of wood, because, among other things, wood that spirals to the left warps more than wood that spirals to the right or straight wood.

Roof shingles, for example, should either be straight-grained or slightly spiralling to the left. In wet weather the shingle stretches; in sunshine, on the other hand it twists slightly, thus allowing drying air under the surface.

With wooden *gutters* the converse is true: the grain of the wood should run straight or spiral slightly to the right, because right-spiralling wood 'stays put' after it has been felled – that is to say the rotation does not continue. Left-spiralling wood will cause the gutter to twist little by little and the water will run over the edge.

Incidentally lightning usually strikes trees that spiral to the left. If you are caught in a thunderstorm in the forest you should only stand under a straight or rightwards-spiralling tree, and certainly never under trees that already show lightning scars (see page 314).

After reading this list of rules your first question will probably be: how can one be sure that one obtains wood which has been felled at the most favourable time for the purpose in mind?

In many cases nowadays that is unfortunately not possible, but never fear: by sticking to the correct times for processing and installing you can put right a lot of the harm caused by an unfavourable felling time. However, if you do get the chance to find out the felling time from the timber merchant, or even to arrange it with the forester, then seize it with both hands.

Take a look in the yellow pages and ring up some timber merchants or have an association of timber merchants send you their list of members. Enquire from these companies whether they can let you know the felling time of the wood you want. There are many timber merchants will greet your enquiry with a knowing wink and lead you to a particular stack of timber, if you insist on your special requirements.

Of course for many firms today correct timing is a matter of indifference, because no importance is attached to this or because the company has grown too large. Large firms are unable (or unwilling) any longer to pay attention to quality, because mass production rules out the possibility of catering for the unique needs of the individual customer and because durability does not pay. Small companies on the other hand do have the possibility of discovering the pleasure of taking responsibility for themselves – of building close contacts with their customers, and, most importantly, of learning what satisfaction can be derived from thinking and acting in natural contexts. Working in collaboration with other small businesses, they can keep everything under one roof, from the personal selection of appropriate trees in a good location, through felling at the correct time, to counselling of the customer concerning the correct care, for instance, of a wooden floor. They can monitor the micro-climate of the locality in which they reside much better than large companies, which earn more from over-exploitation than from protecting the environment. Long transportation distances and the associated environmental pollution can thus be avoided.

On the other hand, in many companies the good will is there, but the knowledge is still lacking, or else a certain reticence is to be observed. Following the rules of correct timing appears at first sight alien, complicated and expensive, but it is nothing of the sort. The work has to be done in any case, and a plan for the year is quickly drawn up.

Simply keep looking until you find you are dealing with a timber company that knows what you are talking about. They are in the majority, even if a lot of them will not admit it straight off. Perhaps they will try to ignore your wishes and fob you off with some such phrase as: "Wood is wood." Ridiculous! What would you think of a greengrocer who flung the comment in your face: "Vegetables are vegetables", at the same time as filling the bag with irradiated, lifeless, chemically sprayed peppers from Holland, instead of the local, organically grown tomatoes you asked for. Every timber merchant, every joiner knows that, depending on the time of felling, two spruce firs growing *side by side* can display totally different characteristics – quite apart from the differences arising from types of wood and countries of origin. And so you should not accept any apologies or excuses.

At this point let us enunciate a clear recommendation: whenever possible you should use *local* wood. The reason for this can be found in the second part of this book, in which we discussed the importance and value for health of local foodstuffs. Local timber possesses all the qualities necessary to transform your home into an invigorating force field, whereas for example many tropical woods (particularly mahogany) produce a radiation that is debilitating for the organism.

There is an immense contribution to be made towards the task of healthy living through the rediscovery and observance of the old rules of forestry and tree felling. So you should stick to your guns and not let yourself be fobbed off. The customer is king.

Tips for Healthy House Maintenance

Finally here are a few hints in the general field of house-building and living, which directly or indirectly have a bearing on health and the environment, whether it is because you need fewer resources because the work is performed so effortlessly, or simply because it's more fun that way.

Cleaning Wooden and Parquet Floors

Wooden floors should only be thoroughly scrubbed when the moon is waning. A solution of *wood ash suds* is best suited for such work. When the moon is waxing you should simply sweep the floor, or else mop it during a light sign (Gemini, Libra, Aquarius). If you mop the floor during a water sign (Cancer, Scorpio, Pisces) while the moon is waxing, moisture can get in the cracks, and eventually the wood may warp or even rot.

The recipe for ash suds: put about two fingers of wood ash in a bucket (about the same proportion water to ashes as you would put water to tea), fill the bucket with boiling water and keep it covered. Stir frequently and then pour the resultant suds into a mop bucket. Use the suds as you would a normal soapy solution for washing the floor, and after scrubbing wipe it off with clear water.

A general rule for all washing and cleaning tasks: when the moon is waning everything works better, more easily and more thoroughly.

Cleaning Windows and Glass

Often streaks and smears are left behind after windows have been cleaned. However if you watch out for a light or warmth day (Gemini, Libra, Aquarius and Aries, Leo, Sagittarius) when the moon is waning, water with a shot of ethyl alcohol and some newspaper will be enough to give a clear view. Strong or concentrated substances are unnecessary. Incidentally, when cleaning extremely dirty window frames you would achieve even better results on a watery day (Cancer, Scorpio, Pisces). It is well worth the wait.

Cleaning Gutters

"Large streams from little fountains flow." Many a gutter blocked with leaves has brought about serious water damage to house facades and interiors. The extraordinary thing is the almost magnetic attraction that some gutters seem to have for such rubbish. It would be of great benefit in such cases to pay heed to correct timing:

Gutters do not get blocked so easily if they are cleaned when the moon is on the wane.

Mould

Tightly shutting windows and badly insulated walls can lead to the formation of mould if the humidity is high. When the moon is waning it is much easier to remove this effectively and on a long-term basis. At that time mild remedies, for instance vinegar and water, applied with a scrubbing brush, would serve the purpose very well.

Activity	Ideal time	Favourable	Advantages of correct timing
Site inspection by a dowser	—	waxing moon	enhanced feeling for radiation
Earth-moving/ excavation	waning moon in Taurus, Virgo	waning moon	ground water does not rise so much
Foundations	—	—	—
Cellar	Gemini, Libra Aquarius or Aries Leo, Saggitarius	possibly Taurus Virgo, Capricorn	moisture disperses from the walls quicker; the cellar stays dry
Cellar ceiling	—	—	—
Building walls	—	waning moon	shell of building dries quicker and walls last longer
Ceilings	—	—	—
Roof truss	waning moon in Capricorn or Taurus	waning moon, but not Cancer days	great durability and strength, beams do not split or rise
Roof covering	waning moon in Gemini, Libra Aquarius or Aries Leo, Saggitarius	waning moon	tiles dry quicker, no moss gathers – or very little
Rendering and plastering, outer cladding	—	waning moon, but not Cancer days	firm and long-lasting
Dividing walls	—	—	—
Wooden stairs	waning moon in Capricorn	waning moon, but not Cancer days	longer lasting, no creaking
Stone stairs	—	—	—
Electrical wiring	—	—	—
Plumbing	Cancer, Scorpio Pisces	Cancer, Scorpio, Pisces	(less important than before) reduced corrosion, fresher water

Unfavourable	Very unfavourable	Disadvantages of incorrect timing
—	—	—
waxing moon	waxing moon in Cancer, Scorpio,	ground water stays longer in the excavation
Cancer, Scorpio, Pisces	—	foundation plate stays moist for a long time
Cancer, Scorpio, Pisces	—	moisture remains longer or even permanently in the walls; increased danger of permanent mould
—	Leo	cracks more easily – dries too quickly
—	—	—
—	Leo	ceiling often dries too fast, danger of cracks forming
waxing moon	waxing moon in Cancer	wood warps unevenly; danger of whole roof truss distorting
waxing moon	waxing moon in Cancer, Scorpio, Pisces	roof remains damp too long, giving rise to a large amount of dirt and the growth of moss
waxing moon	waxing moon in Cancer	danger of cracks forming and coming loose; wood warps more severely
—	—	—
waxing moon	waxing moon in Cancer	joints come loose more easily; severe warping and creaking
—	—	—
—	—	—
Taurus, Virgo Capricorn		furring up or external blockages, heavier corrosion

Activity	Ideal time	Favourable	Advantages of correct timing
Wooden windows/doors	waning moon in Capricorn, Aquarius Gemini	waning moon, but not in Cancer, Scorpio, Pisces	remain firm, close well and dry quickly after storms
First heating	waning moon in Aries, Leo Saggitarius	—	chimney draws well, heat spreads more quickly
Floor covering		waning moon	lies even, no buckling
Wooden floors	waning moon in Capricorn	waning moon, but not in Cancer	great strength and durability; wood does not rot and stays attractive
Wooden ceilings and panelling	—	waning moon, but not in Cancer	no gaps, no displacement
Paint-work, varnishing, waterproofing, gluing	—	waning moon, but not in Leo or Cancer	great durability, no flaking, easy to work with, low consumption of materials, even penetration
Erecting posts	new moon	waning moon, Taurus, Virgo, Capricorn	ever greater firmness over time, greater durability, less rotting
Paving stones/ verandas	waning moon in Taurus, Virgo, Capricorn	waning moon	paving stones embed themselves firmly and evenly on natural earth
Paths/country tracks	waning moon in Capricorn	waning moon	no erosion after rain; ground becomes ever harder; repairs last

Unfavourable	Very unfavourable	Disadvantages of incorrect timing
waxing moon	waxing moon in Cancer, Scorpio Pisces	windows and doors easily become distorted; moisture stays in the wood; the wood rots
—	waxing moon in Cancer, Scorpio, Pisces	smoke comes back into room; heavy build-up of soot in the chimney
waxing moon		sometimes rucks up; textile or synthetic coverings develop creases
waxing moon	waxing moon in Cancer	after some years floor becomes rotten and uneven, danger of fissures developing
waxing moon	waxing moon in Cancer	forming of gaps, loud cracking when the weather changes
waxing moon in Cancer, Scorpio Pisces, Leo	waxing moon in Leo or Cancer	in Leo flaking paint and strain on the circulation through fumes; on Cancer days straining on the lungs through poisonous fumes, frequent moisture between paint and wood (danger of rot and flaking)
waxing moon	waxing moon in Cancer	posts come out of the ground, do not hold, and rot quickly
waxing moon	waxing moon in Cancer	paving stones wobble and come loose; they continually rise up from the earth; slugs gather underneath
waxing moon	waxing moon in Cancer	erosion of gravel; repairs are only effective for a short time

Correct Ventilation

As a rule we let too little air in, particularly in winter. Especially in new buildings this is often the only way to change the bad air inside. Regular ventilation is essential and always better than no ventilation at all.

Ventilate generously on light and warmth days (Gemini, Libra, Aquarius and Aries, Leo, Sagittarius); only ventilate briefly and quickly on earth and water days (Taurus, Virgo, Capricorn and Cancer, Scorpio, Pisces).

By means of the table on page 300 you will be able to see at a glance what are the favourable and unfavourable times for all house-building and renovating tasks.

2. The Science of Place

Healthy building and living: for those who have the feeling that they want to or ought to do something in this area, we should like in the following pages to guide them in a direction that at first glance – or even second glance – can nowadays cause surprise or even hostility and rejection. We are familiar with every imaginable reaction – from calm interest to ironic wisecracks. However, we do not regard it as any part of our duty to demolish doubt and scepticism, but rather to make our direct experience and knowledge available to you.

Briefly, the theme of our present chapter is this:

In the countryside, in our cities and villages, in every house and apartment – everywhere there are good and bad places for human beings, regardless of what is actually in these places – whether it is a field, tree, wall, table, office chair, bed, toilet, kitchen cupboard or carpet. Staying for any length of time in bad places almost always has a bad effect – even to the point of damaging our health. They weaken our bodies, our powers of self-healing and our immune system. The possibility exists of recognising such places and staying away from them.

There is hardly a subject in this book that so thoroughly eludes modern patterns of thinking and conventional scientific reasoning; and yet at the same time there is hardly a theme that is as important for us all and of such far-reaching consequence for human health.

A single example: a builder has built a house – according to all the rules of natural, ecologically sound building and in a beautiful rural area. If he then moves in and sleeps with the head end of his bed over a bad spot, then it will all have been in vain. The possible consequences that ensue may range from uncomfortable, troubled sleep, to frequent migraine attacks, to tumours and even suicide (serious suicidal intentions generally only develop in people who sleep over a bad place).

What are the influences, what are the forces that can transform a particular location into a good or bad place? In order to answer this question, let us range a little further afield.

The Work of the Dragon-rider

Many thousands of years ago, when our forefathers abandoned the life of wandering nomads and settled down, they saw themselves confronted by a difficulty of a very particular kind. In addition to the problems of animal husbandry and the development of agricultural plants – sowing, cultivation, harvesting and storage – they discovered that they could not simply settle indiscriminately and at random in particular areas, and that there were 'places of power' and 'good places', but also certain places that could weaken the human organism and its immune system.

In many parts of the world, but especially in ancient China, there gradually developed the art of 'being in the right place at the right time'. The first book on the subject of investigating ground radiations, now almost 4000 years old, originates from Emperor Yu (in one picture he is actually represented as a dowser). *Feng-Shui*, 'wind and water' is the name the Chinese gave to this skill, and masters of the art were called 'those who ride dragons'. The expertise of these people, who worked all over the world under the most varied names, consisted in being sensitive to the flow of energy in nature, detecting the fields of force and lines of energy that encompass and penetrate the earth like a tightly-woven, almost grid-like net. Their activity consisted in finding for people and their fixed abodes those places in which they would be *strengthened* by the force fields in the environment. In their eyes, setting up a fixed dwelling on some arbitrary spot on the landscape was tantamount to saying: "This field has been flooded every spring for hundreds of years; but I'm going to build my house here, anyway, because maybe this year it won't rain so much."

The Chinese called energy streams that were favourable and positive for human beings 'the blue dragon', and negative energy 'the white tiger'. These streams criss-cross invisible to the eye all over the world, like so many roads, paths, ways and transmission

'Those who ride dragons': ancient Chinese diviners survey the radiation conditions on a building site.

lines. At certain points these lines of force amplify or cross one another and interact with the living creatures in the area – with plants, animals and human beings. This effect can be either positive or negative for us humans, either invigorating or debilitating.

The short-term memory of our culture has made us forget that not only in distant China but also nearly everywhere in the world dowsers and diviners (as the 'dragon-riders' were often called) used to look for water and investigate good and bad places, and that in Europe right up to World War II it was very common, at least in the country, to consult with a dowser before building a house. His task was to work out the most favourable spot – both for the site of the building and subsequently for sleeping and working areas and accommodation for animals.

We have probably forgotten this because we often tend to be convinced that nobody lived on the earth before we did, and that science always advances along a path from what was worse to what is better. How many more Chernobyls and toxic catastrophes will we need before we open our eyes?

A Radiant World

What exactly are they examining – these dragon-riders, dowsers and radiesthetists, as they are also called – when they survey a particular place? Anyone who asks a competent present-day dowser about this will in most cases get to hear such expressions as telluric radiations, water veins, ground radiation, Curry lines, disturbance zones, Hartmann lines, and so on – a lot of words, but for our purposes only one collective meaning: there are energies, for the most part unknown to science, which determine whether a particular spot is beneficial or otherwise for human beings.

We, too, are in the same situation: if we search for a concept to describe the extraordinary influence that makes good places good and bad positions bad, we can for the time being see no alternative but to give them the general name of radiation or earth ray. Perhaps 'blue dragon' and 'white tiger' have a more poetic and vivid ring about them, but in order to present this subject to you in a plausible manner we shall have to use other words.

So why 'radiation'?

Modern physics now knows that the entire universe consists of radiations, for every object radiates, and does so with especial strength when it finds itself in a process of rapid transformation or decay. This is true of every physical object, whether it is a star, sun, stone or living creature. Minerals are 'solid' radiation, plants are transformed sunlight, herbivorous animals are doubly transformed light; we humans feed on these transformed rays and light and transmit rays of our own – heat (infra-red light), thought waves, static electricity, magnetic forces, etc.

Our current opportunities for scientific discovery have led physicists to the knowledge that in the universe and on our planet there are numerous natural sources of radiation. These emit heat and light rays, neutron rays, proton rays and X-rays, which constantly affect us more or less strongly. In addition to this naturally occurring radiation (to which our bodies are well-adapted) we have through our own activities in the space of a few decades artificially increased the grand total of radiations on the earth – by means of nuclear tests, electrical apparatus, VDU screens, radio waves, microwave ovens, satellites, transmission lines, etc. These artificial waves are added to the quantity of radiation from natural sources.

We also know that some of these radiations and vibrations can heal; some are neutral in their effect on human beings, and some are harmful and even deadly. But which rays can heal? Which do harm?

A light bulb radiates – light and warmth. Uranium radiates with a specific force that is not visible to the eye. Human beings are 'radiant', for they radiate warmth, kindness, coldness, calmness or 'attractiveness'. Each human thought radiates into the world, transforms itself into forms of reality and returns to its originator. Power-points, VDU screens, quartz crystals, radio telephones, radio alarm clocks, glow-worms, an electrically-charged polyester pullover, plastic building blocks, recycled paper, transmission towers, good places, bad places – all of these things emit radiations; all produce an effect in the visible world, sometimes immediately, but in most cases only after a period of time, sometimes measured in decades.

You should bear this in mind: only a tiny fraction of this incredible diversity of radiations is known to science; and again only a fraction of the known radiations is known from the standpoint of its *biological effect* on the human organism.

As far as the effects on us human beings are concerned, the overwhelming remainder of unknown radiations – whether earth rays, thought waves, neutron rays or other forms of radiation – are swept under the carpet of science, in keeping with the motto: anything that cannot be measured (yet) does not exist; and we're the ones that decide how things are measured. Science is in the situation of the colour-blind person who set out to describe a rainbow. When he got home he reported that it ranged 'from dark grey to light grey'. However, since 'light grey' sometimes constitutes insufficient information for certain essential purposes, and since our forefathers were not so foolish as to wait for scientific explanations, they experienced a portion of these unknown radiations through other means than the currently accepted narrow method of gaining knowledge. It is this experience that we wish to pass on.

The transition from known to unknown radiation is fluid. People have always known that fires and heaters radiate, and have exploited this effect. It is only recently that people have found out that uranium radiates and they still believe that they can control its effects (which will never be the case). People know that transmission lines emit radiation, but they still won't admit that living in their immediate vicinity weakens the immune system and undermines health (even though the fact that vines growing beneath such cables lean away to one side states the case in the clearest language).

It is known that radio telephones emit radiation (in the form of magnetic fields), but not yet known what effects such radiation has on the body *in the long-term*. Numerous guinea pigs are currently engaged in investigating this effect; their findings may be expected in a few years. We may be certain of one thing: there will be no massive compensation payments as a result, but rather – as we have already seen with computer screens – advertising slogans for new radio telephones, such as: 'Brand new! Now: low radiation!' Are we going to stand for that? At least where earth radiation is concerned, there is no need to do so.

Earth rays are not visible and not measurable using conventional methods. Today, just as in the past, their presence and effect can only be established through experience. Perhaps that is why science has so much trouble accepting the existence of good and bad places, because even now it is still too proud to recognise that this will *never* be fully ascertainable by means of measuring instruments (electromagnetic and radioactive radiation are exceptions). This is a fact that unfortunately not even those who are earnestly de-liberating on the subject have yet taken on board.

We wish to affirm: only a human being, as the most sensitive measuring instrument in the universe, is capable of determining *exactly* the quality of a sleeping or working area. Ultimately only his inner instinct can decide. On the other hand there also seems to be little inclination on the part of empirical science to make a thorough investigation of phenomena that, given a modicum of good will, can be demonstrated with the greatest of ease. As long as we have a situation where any scientist instantly looses his reputation the moment he turns his attention to this subject, things will stay like this for some time to come.

However, no one should be compelled to wait for proof before being able to evade the debilitating force of a bad place. Anyone who only finds out twenty years from now that science has discovered something 'new' concerning earth rays, may not have much more time among us in order to enjoy the fruits of this belated recognition.

The knowledge of earth rays is not new, any more than the knowledge of lunar rhythms, bloodletting, biorhythms and all the other things that you have encountered in this book. At most what is new is the degree of arrogance with which so many experts today believe that they can dispense with the old, the tried and tested. Fortunately they are still among us, these dragon-riders and dowsers. Their knowledge has still not died out.

The Masters of the Right Place

What is a dowser, and how does he work nowadays?

Many people grow up with the capacity to feel bad and good places *directly*; many dowsers do not discover it until they are advanced in years.* The fact is that not everyone is born with this capacity, just as not everyone has what it takes to be a good pianist. It develops by way of a calling.

Here, as in all arts, there are beginners, advanced practitioners and masters. Their art is among other things the visible consequence of the capacity to call a temporary halt to self-interest, desires, expectations and thoughts, and bring oneself into a state of inner equilibrium and then leave the decision to one's instinct, one's inner antennae. It goes without saying that as a rule such a faculty is slow to develop.

When dowsers investigate good and bad places in dwellings, their

* Only a few people are fortunate enough to know a good dowser or diviner in their neighbourhood. For those who would therefore like to try out and develop *their own* abilities as a 'dragon-rider' and dowser, we recommend the books by Sig Lonegren on dowsing and the use of the pendulum. (e.g: Sig Lonegren: *The Pendulum Kit*, Eddison Sadd Editions, London) and *The Pendulum Book* by Jack Chandu published by The C.W. Daniel Co. Ltd, Saffron Walden, Essex, England.

instinct creates a connection between the total situation of a person's own radiations and the radiation climate of the place in question. It makes no difference whether the radiation stems from electrical equipment, transmission lines, earth rays, water veins or plastic toys. The ability to answer the question of which type of radiation is dominant in a given place – whether artificial or natural in origin – is developed to widely varying degrees among dowsers; but as far as the ultimate result is concerned – whether a place is 'good' or 'bad' – it is of trivial interest.

For example, many dowsers restrict themselves exclusively to looking for springs and water-bearing strata – perhaps as a consequence of the fact that generally in former times both church and state viewed such people's highly developed faculties with suspicion and even persecuted them (although long after this prohibition they themselves continued to have churches and official buildings surveyed for radiations). The success rate of many modern water diviners is about 85 percent, whereas companies in developing countries, for instance, using the latest scientific search methods come across water in at most 20 percent of their bore-holes.

In the investigation of good and bad spots in interior rooms the survey results of good dowsers can sometimes be very individual: for example, when someone moves into an apartment that had been surveyed previously, a new inspection should be undertaken, because every person is surrounded by a different climate of radiation. Similarly, when there have been major structural alterations in the immediate vicinity – for instance, the excavation of an underground garage – the radiation situation can change and suddenly transform good places into bad or vice versa.

Dowsers are in every respect as varied as other people are. Some of them make use of particular tools to translate their capacity into valid advice – wooden or metal rods, pendulums etc. Some of them observe signs from the animal and plant world which already served our forefathers as a means to investigate the qualities of a place.

For among them there are 'ray-seekers' – animals or plants that thrive in places that are bad for people – and 'ray-fleers' – living creatures which like human beings do not feel well in spots of negative radiation.

In open country plants in any case only put down roots in places that are favourable for them. *Ray-fleers* in the garden are pomiferous trees (apple, pear, etc.), currant bushes and lilac; in the forest, limes and beeches (lightning only strikes disturbed zones and points where rays intersect; for this reason these trees have been immortalised in proverbs as places to take shelter in a thunderstorm). Indoor ray-fleers are: begonias, azaleas and African hemp.

Ray-seekers in the plant world, on the other hand, thrive in spots that are bad for us. In this group, among others, are: stone-fruit trees (cherry, plum, peach, etc.), ivy and mistletoe (probably the reason for the success of mistletoe preparations in cases of cancer. Mistletoe binds rays in the same way as a cat's skin, and cats are noted ray-seekers). In the forest oaks, spruce, fir and larch are among the ray-seekers. These trees grow over water veins and are thus prone to attract lightning, as is attested in folklore. Trees and flowers that people plant on unfavourable places either grow crookedly, leaning away from the spot, or else they become stunted and sick (cancerous growths) and die.

Many animals are noted signallers of the quality of a place. Storks and swallows are widely held to bring good luck, perhaps because they only nest where the surrounding radiation is positive. Dogs that are not over-bred (and also wild birds, horses, cows, pigs, sheep and hens) belong to the ray-fleeing group. Wherever they settle is also a good spot for us.

In former times people used to drive sheep to a building site and observe their behaviour. Wherever the flock lay down to sleep was the best place to build the house. In the open air animals always seek out the best place for them; however, indoors in pens and stalls they are at a disadvantage. Ray-fleeing animals can become infertile

or sick if they are forced into places with negative radiation – something that is known to many farmers. A dog kennel that is placed in the wrong spot will be shunned by the dog.

Cats, insects, bacteria and intestinal worms, on the other hand, are ray-seekers – they prefer and thrive in spots that are unfavourable for people. Ants and bees always build their nests at the intersection of two lines of force, i.e. on very bad spots. Cats often lie on an intersection, or at any rate on a place with very strong negative radiation. They are able to absorb radiations that are harmful for humans and discharge them again in the open air. If cats are unable to run around outside they cannot decontaminate themselves – one of the main reasons why such animals display behavioural disorders in the course of time. Since earth radiation increases as the moon waxes and reaches a climax at full moon, it is bordering on cruelty not to let cats out at full moon (sleepwalking takes place mostly when the moon is full – likewise a sign that the increased radiation is driving the sleeper out of bed). For rheumatic complaints it is beneficial to lay a cat's skin over the affected part, not merely because the warmth does good but because it helps the body to discharge radiation – an important therapeutic procedure in many cases of rheumatic disorder.

However, observing the animal and plant world and using rods and pendulums are merely ancillary tools: beyond all their methods of measurement the most capable dowsers are well aware that *they themselves* are the tool that endows their judgement with value and validity; that they are the instrument of a force, a higher power that goes beyond the individual. The masters among them are even able simply through the sensitivity of the palms of their hands to examine a piece of paper on which is drawn the points of the compass and the position of a bed in a room – without ever having been physically present in the room. Of course, they often do actually come into the house, but that is merely because very few people know about and have sufficient confidence in this means of knowledge. Such master diviners often work simultaneously as long-distance healers – as people who are able to empathise with people and situations in far-off places and re-establish a healing equilibrium there by means of their mental and spiritual powers. Incredible as it may seem, this tallies with our experience. How much credence would someone living in the 15th century have given to a report about the benefits and function of radio?

What are the effects and symptoms that enable you yourself to recognise whether you are suffering from an extended stay in a bad place?

The Scene of the Crime: 'Bad Spot'

To describe dowsers as 'sensitive to radiation' is too vague. Everyone without exception is susceptible to radiations of all sorts. Each of us comes to realise it, sooner or later, if we are exposed to harmful radiations when we regularly and over a long period of time sleep or work in a bad place. The effect of strong solar radiation is familiar to everybody. However, the theme of the present section is the fact that negative earth radiation can have an equally harmful effect.

In thinking about physical disorders and illnesses, we have forgotten to consider sleeping and working in a bad place. Since no one has informed us of this, we automatically seek, along with academic medicine and science, for causes that fit into the contemporary mental pigeon-hole. Anyone who has decided to assume that the cause of a chronic illness is *exclusively* to be found in the body or the mind will only look for causes in the body or the mental outlook of the subject. In which case the possibility that a bad spot might trigger off an illness no longer fits into his scheme of things.

But perhaps one or two experiences will come to your assistance and make it easier for you to accept the existence of good and bad places.

Many parents will have noticed this: some babies twist and turn in bed, cry a lot, and often end up in the morning lying in a corner of the cot. Infants and even sensitive children of school-age often cannot stand being in their own bed at night: they fall out and carry on sleeping, or else they slip into bed with their parents or a brother or sister – without there being any recognisable psychological reason for this. School children who move up to a new class and sit at a new desk may become sleepy or restless there or without any apparent reason start to lag behind in their work, whereas up to that point everything was going well. Sometimes parents set up a very expensive and tasteful children's room with a desk in it, only to find that the child still comes to the kitchen to do his homework. In all such cases when searching for causes one should think first of all about sleeping or sitting in a bad place before taking any other steps.

In the adult world, too, there are many things that elude explanation even after a closer look. Perhaps you have noticed how some housewives stand at an angle or at a distance from their kitchen table, or that there are chairs in the living room that inexplicably remain empty, or that there are certain places in your apartment where you regularly become tired or restless.

Many an able and popular teacher one day takes a 'bad' class with which he simply cannot get along. Sometimes he unconsciously copes with the situation by walking up and down or continually sitting on the desk instead of behind it.

Formerly it was known that in certain farms, no milkmaid could stick it longer than a couple of months, that the farmer or the farmer's wife always died young there, or that the cattle fell ill much more frequently, almost as if there was a curse weighing down on the house.

Many doctors and nurses know that in certain beds complications arise much more frequently for patients, that doses of medicine produce stronger side-effects, that healing phases are more protracted.

In most of the cases we have mentioned sleeping or working in the wrong place is definitely the trigger factor. As a rule you have good reason to assume that you are sleeping or working on a bad spot if you observe the following symptoms in yourself or your child:

Troubled sleep that does not provide any genuine rest, taking a long time to get up to speed in the morning, frequent lapses of concentration, chronic tiredness, feelings of pressure in the head or heart, frequent headaches or backache or spinal complaints, moods of depression.

To sit or sleep regularly in a bad place generally weakens the immune system and thus prepares the way for the outbreak of a great many disorders and illnesses. As a result it can be responsible or at least partially responsible for protracted chronic illnesses, chronic headaches, attacks of migraine and the like. Anyone who finds that he suffers from a *constantly recurring* disturbance of his well-being ought to take a look at the radiation situation in the place where he sleeps or works as a contributory cause of the complaint.

Individual reactions to a bad place vary. Some people with a strongly-developed immune system can spend years in a bed that is located over a radiation intersection without ever becoming seriously ill; whilst others become restless and nervous after sitting on a bad spot for only a few minutes. Some people have become so accustomed to the negative energies of bad spots that they are actually attracted to them – like addicts who cannot manage without their fix. Their feelings concerning a particular place are thus not always a sure sign of its quality.

Even so, as a rule the effects on health of a bad spot are long-lasting. Especially in the case of the following illnesses moving to a good place can have a preventive, relieving or curative effect: arthritis; asthma; chronic bed-wetting; high blood pressure; epilepsy, gout; heart disease; multiple sclerosis; neurodermatitis; Parkinson's disease; rheumatoid arthritis; pseudo croup; rheumatism; and all diseases characterised by the word 'morbus' or 'syndrome' (e.g. Bekhterev's disease, Crohn's disease).

At this point we would like to draw special attention to one or two disorders, illnesses and hitherto unexplained events which in our experience are almost always or exclusively triggered off by sleeping in the wrong place.

Suicides: Investigations by competent dowsers have shown that most suicides slept with their heads over a radiation intersection. Before it gets to that point, frequent depressions are a signal for a bad spot.

Cot deaths: These sudden deaths that can overtake children up to the age of two are a complete enigma for science. The only common factor that has so far been discerned is heavy perspiration prior to death.

> *Cot deaths are due to the fact that the child and its bed were located over a severe zone of disturbance. Another child should never have to sleep over a spot where a cot death has occurred.*

Infertility: Very frequently infertility is a symptom of sleeping over a radiation intersection in the region of the sex organs. This is also the reason why in such cases unexpected pregnancies often occur on holiday, and these in turn frequently end in a miscarriage if the same bad place is resumed on returning home. Doctors often recommend a holiday journey in cases of infertility, because they know from experience that there is a connection between a change of scene and pregnancy. Now you, too, know the reason for this.

Cancer: Cancer is purely a disease of radiation, triggered off by a variety of natural or artificial radiations in conjunction with other harmful effects. This subject is of such importance that we have devoted an entire section to it.

Cancer: A Radiation Disease from the Outset

An experienced healer, doctor and dowser of our acquaintance has come to the unambiguous conclusion after decades of investigations that cancer is almost always the result of a *diversity* of causal factors working together -- it is never a question of just a single cause. The combination involved can vary immensely: from asbestos fibres, falls from a bike, removal of tissue at the wrong time, radiations of all kinds, too much exposure to sunlight – to psychological traumas that sometimes go a long way back. When the package of harmful effects has reached critical mass, often a minimal impetus is all that is needed to set the cancerous growth in motion – perhaps a minor operation, a fall, a bruise, a few asbestos fibres, a sunburn. A powerful trigger and an extremely debilitating influence in all this, he discovered, is the presence of radiations of all kinds. Alongside artificially created radiations the decisive role is played here by earth rays. His conclusion is as follows:

> *In every pathological growth in the human body, whether it is a cyst, tumour or cancer, harmful radiations weakening the immune system play a part, and included in these are earth radiations. Influences that weaken the immune system always lead, in the absence of harmful radiations, to other disorders and illnesses, but not to pathological growths.*

In his eyes and in the light of his practical experience as an orthodox physician, the methods that are customary today for the treatment of cancer – chemotherapy and radiation – are, with very few exceptions, nothing other than death by instalments. We share his view and also his experience – together with many other medical practitioners. Medical research is simply too proud to admit that at a cost of billions it has become lost in a deep impasse – quite apart from the fact that research is in any case more interested in research than it is in healing. The doctors, who know better, are for their part probably of the opinion that they cannot afford the public loss of face, either financially or morally. Doubtless they would prefer to leave it to coming generations of physicians to iron out the mistake, and meanwhile appeal to the courts actually to prescribe this 'method of treatment' to their patients – as happened recently. In Germany in 1993 the parents of a girl suffering from leukaemia refused to go on subjecting her to the torture of 'scientifically recognised' poisoning and radiation therapy. Whereupon the cancer specialists tried to have the child legally removed from the parent's care so that they could go through with the therapy.

What madness! Just imagine: that doctors who a hundred years ago were resisting washing their hands between patients during childbirth should win the case in a court of law because "...it has been proven scientifically that they are doing everything correctly".

Fortunately today there are courageous pioneers among researchers and doctors who are actively exposing this error, which has long been recognised as such among 'initiates', and pointing to the new direction for science. Anyone who insists on proof of the correlation between frequency of cancer and the amount of radiation merely has to look at the simultaneous steep climb of both factors in the west during the past four decades – as a result of nuclear accidents (not only in Chernobyl), depletion of the ozone layer, irradiated foodstuffs, electrification (from kitchen mixers to radio alarm clocks), textiles, toys, waste paper, and, not least, the arbitrary choice of where to work and sleep. Opponents of this information like to argue that cancer used to be just as common as it is today, only that people did not recognise it as such. That is sheer sleight of hand.

Scientists acknowledge that the frequency of cancer in China and Japan is far lower than the global average; however, they ignore the reason why this is so: this is not to be sought in variations in dietary habits, but rather in the fact that in those countries few people would think of erecting a dwelling without seeking the advice of a dragon-rider or dowser.

Perhaps after all of this you will not be surprised by our own experience: in the past numerous colleagues sought out this doctor acquaintance of ours, had themselves and their children treated and healed by him and had him investigate bad spots and radiations in the surroundings. In almost all cases they came to him at night, in order if possible to avoid being seen. Scarcely any of them ever let their own patients have the benefit of this knowledge. He shares experiences of this sort with many other healers.

As for modern methods of cancer treatment: we know that there is hardly a cancer specialist who would think of subjecting himself or a member of his family to chemotherapy or radiation. Every cancer specialist knows very well just how effective these methods are, but unfortunately he often still lacks the courage to speak the truth. He knows that irradiating cancer is just like "using Beelzebub to drive out the devil". It is impossible to get rid of a poison by means of larger quantities of an even worse one. He also knows that the side effects of chemotherapy almost always place an additional burden on an already weakened body, instead of detoxifying it and strengthening its immune system, and that these effects often render life scarcely worth living or, by that token, worth extending. Above all he knows that these much played-down 'side-effects' almost always lead to the breakdown of the powers of self-healing and thus to mycosis, inflammation of the lungs, cardiac insufficiency etc. – often the eventual cause of death.

He knows that the curative successes that are allegedly demonstrated after irradiation and chemotherapy, often depend on the fact that incurable patients are frequently sent home before they finally die, so that they do not appear in the statistics. He knows, too, that numerous forms of cancer whose outcome is almost always lethal are lumped together with curable, cancer-like forms, again in order to whitewash the statistics – as is the case for instance with leukaemia, which appears in a great variety of forms.

A great many doctors also know that many cancers are actually triggered off by a precautionary examination or by removing a tissue sample (biopsy). You should recall:

Everything that puts a special burden or strain on those parts of the body and organs ruled by the sign through which the moon is currently moving is doubly unfavourable or even harmful. Surgical operations in these areas should be avoided during these days if at all possible.

A biopsy *is* a surgical operation. So do not allow any tissue to be removed from the breast when the moon is in the sign of Cancer. No biopsy of the stomach should be performed when the moon is in Virgo. No biopsy in the region of the sex organs with the moon is in Scorpio (see the organ classification table on page 32).

In addition you should take care only to allow precautionary examinations or biopsies to be carried out when the moon is on the wane.

Hidden deep beneath this inability of scientists and doctors to look these facts in the face, there is an underlying reason.

Underneath the layer of pride, the scientific blind alleys, the agonising and pointless methods of treatment, there lurks the fear of impotence and death. The fear of calmly encountering death and even welcoming it, since in reality it is the friend of all living creatures. The laudable duty of the doctor to prolong life is sometimes transformed into the alien ideology of prolonging death – against all nature, all reason, all sense. It is difficult to accept death as a friend and adviser, because we have been robbed of the memory of and confidence in the fact that with death there begins a new chapter in the life of the soul. Regaining this confidence is a fundamental pillar of the quest for health through one's own initiative.

With all of this we have absolutely no wish to create the impression that cancers are a frequent, let alone inevitable consequence of sleeping or working in bad places. As we have said, numerous factors have to combine before it comes to this – among others, attitude to life, dietary habits, environmental influences, psychological traumas etc. On the other hand we do state quite openly:

No one with cancer sleeps on a good place at home.

It is almost verging on unconscious suicide to come home after a cancer operation, or simply after a long stay in hospital because of a chronic illness of one sort or another – and then sleep in the same bed in the same position. Of course one will not in this case inevitably stay ill or fall ill again, but the debilitating force continues to work.

Ways to the Right Place: The Capable Dowser

Calling in the dowser is still the best way to tell a good place from
a bad one. Happy the area, the village or town whose inhabitants
today – still, or once again at last – can call on their own capable
dowsers for advice, knowing the enormous benefit that the work
of these competent persons can bring them.

Unfortunately the situation here is the same as in other fields in
which during the last few decades we have neglected our instinct:
the honest and capable expert does not live on every street corner;
he isn't in the yellow pages. Thus numerous would-be dowsers,
charlatans and the like invade the countryside and help to give the
art a bad name. On top of that many of the numerous books on
the subject of earth rays and dowsing have done more harm than
good, especially those that look for scientifically acceptable proof.

So how does one recognise a capable dowser?

For may reasons we cannot give a clear answer to this. These
people are outwardly too different in their manner and background,
their methods are too diverse for there to be any generally valid
signs by which to recognise them. However, there are one or two
things that can be stated, hints that you can bear in mind. Perhaps
after receiving this information you will find it easier to encounter
a good dowser.

* The very first difficulty with finding a good dowser is really the
crux of the matter: he will never advertise his work, his art. He is
conscious that he is fulfilling a divine task, he carries it out, and
that is that. If he really does prove to be capable, the word will
quickly get around. In an extremely short time he will in any case
have massive clientele – without any propaganda at all.

* He takes very little money for his work. In many cases he does
not ask for anything. If sums of money come into question with a
capable dowser, then this is generally because his clients do not
want to impose on him and have him spend a lot of time with them

performing a really important service for no recompense. People often can and wish to show their gratitude.

* A good dowser is able to distinguish different types of radiation, including electromagnetic, water and earth rays. This is important because, for example, water veins on their own have no harmful effects. It is only when there is an intersection point with lines of force consisting of earth rays and other water veins that they become fields of disturbance.

* When a dowser comes to you, he first of all measures up the field surrounding the house, without knowing where the working and sleeping areas are located in the house. From the way the lines run he is able to deduce severely debilitating intersection points.

* A capable dowser knows that there is only one remedy for earth rays: move to a good place. He would never try to talk you into expensive and in the long run useless 'shielding equipment' or the like.

* In his conversations with you a capable dowser will seldom express himself in such a way that you are disturbed or frightened. "If you carry on sleeping here you'll soon get cancer" – any dowser who says things like that should be shown the door immediately. However, if you ask him directly: "What is likely to happen if I carry on sleeping on this spot?", then he will not leave you in any doubt as to the possible consequences.

* Even a responsibly thinking beginner in the art of the right place would never get involved in a public display of his ability, let alone one intended to furnish scientific proof of his art. The reason for this is not any excessive modesty in these people, but rather the fact that the presence of even one person who doubts in this art is capable of falsifying the results of the survey, through the power of expectant or sceptical thoughts. Consequently in fact the only dowsers that offer their services to science and the media are those who, to put it mildly, overrate their own capacities somewhat.

Ways to the Right Place: By Your Own Efforts

But what if you do not know a dowser that you can trust, or if your search for such a person comes to nothing? What can you yourself do in order to determine the quality of a place? What action is possible to improve matters?

Unfortunately we cannot offer you a patent formula, because in with the personal, intellectual assessment of whether a working or sleeping area is good or bad is mixed one's entire attitude to life – desires, hopes, expectations and of course imagination, too. All these things falsify the inner impartial instinct and thus the sense for good and bad places. Some people sleep in the best places in the house, and yet they still stuff them full of greed, fear and gloom.

On the other hand that is certainly not so in your case, and so on the following pages you will definitely be able to gain one or two useful pieces of advice.

Change of Place

If after reading this far you have begun to suspect and have reason to suppose that you yourself or someone in your family are sleeping or working in a bad place, first of all try out a rearrangement of the furniture: move your desk or bed to another spot. Usually a distance of about two yards is sufficient to give you a clear sense of whether the new place feels better or not.

"Not a chance. My space is limited." – We often hear this said, and our answer is always the same: there's no excuse, and you always have the freedom of choice. How important is your health to you?

After rearranging the furniture leave at least a fortnight before you try out your instinct for the new place. The reason for this is:

A change from a bad place to a good one can lead to with-drawal symptoms (rather like the initial worsening of symptoms after taking a natural remedy): troubled sleep, nervousness, etc.

One of our acquaintances used to sleep for years on a bad spot and during this time had to endure three heart operations. As a rule he slept too long for his age and did not wake up very refreshed. In spite of his sceptical attitude he finally decided to move his bed by about a yard. It took about two weeks for his sleep to become normal, and now he has a shorter, deeper sleep and wakes up fully rested.

Of course this method is based on the principle of trial and error and can be somewhat tedious. However, it is the *best possible* way if there is no dowser to inspect the various places.

Owners of dogs and cats could gain valuable knowledge through observing their house-mates.

Cats

Cats do not belong in bed, among other things because they are carriers of worms. And yet anyone who has made a habit of letting the cat on to the bed at night is *not* able automatically to conclude that he is sleeping on a bad spot, which cats, being ray-seekers prefer by nature. In fact a cat also absorbs negative radiations that come directly from a human being (for instance through illness or a negative attitude to life).

When cats come up on your lap or on to the bed only for a short

time to rub up against a particular part of your body (your shoulder, say) and then disappear again, they are taking up negative radiations from this part of your body. Possibly you have a weak point there, or even an illness.

However, cats can indeed be used as a 'feeler gauge' for bad spots. On its own a cat never stays for any length of time in a particular place if there is not a prevalence there of radiation that is negative for human beings. You can get it to 'judge' a bed or workplace for you: lay a blanket over the bed and observe how the cat behaves. If it likes to stay for a long time on a particular spot on the bed, then not even a pile of books placed there would deter it from continuing to rest on this *bad* spot. If you often have to shoo your cat away from your desk then it's time to look for another workplace. Conversely, places that it always leaves immediately when you put it there are favourable as a rule for human beings.

Dogs

For dogs exactly the opposite is the case: they are ray-fleers. You should therefore not be surprised occasionally to find your dog sitting on your favourite chair. What you like the dog likes, too: a radiation-free, restful place. However, some pedigree breeds, whether of cats or dogs, have lost this natural instinct. Also particularly dependent animals lie down from time to time in the wrong places, simply in order to be with their master. You have to observe your pet closely before trusting its judgement.

Further Precautionary and Restorative Measures

In order to shut out the amplifying interplay with other sources of radiation you should take some precautionary action. The following points are important to know:

* Electrical equipment, VDUs, radio alarm clocks (next to the bed), live power points, etc. produce radiations and vibrations that are harmful for human beings and create zones of disturbance irrespective of whether they are switched on or off. When switched on a television set radiates about four to seven yards; switched off the range is still about two yards. This situation can be put right by means of a so-called mains free switch, a device which shuts the voltage down to about 12 V when it senses that there is no consumption of current in a given circuit (get information from an ecological builder or specialist electrical shop) – or simply by disconnecting the fuse for the bedroom. Floor heating only has a negative effect when the floor covering is made of synthetic material.

* Numerous objects emit negative radiation, as a rule up to two yards to every side and upwards. As a precaution one should therefore not store objects under cots or beds (clothes, toys, plastic materials, etc.). Plastic toys (especially battery toys) have no place in a child's bed. Mirrors have a disastrous radiation effect. They share the blame for countless cases of sleeplessness and worse and do not belong in the bedroom.

* There is *no* possibility of screening negative earth radiation beneath a bed or workplace by means of some kind of apparatus. Numerous so-called experts, unqualified dowsers and charlatans make a lot of money for themselves with screening equipment and devices, *all of which* are useless in the long run – among other reasons because these objects themselves become heavily charged. The effect of such contraptions only lasts for a short while. After one to eight weeks they act as sources of disturbance themselves.

* Earth rays become amplified as they go upwards to the upper floors of a building. A bad spot on the ground floor has an even more harmful effect on the fifth floor.

* The best direction for sleeping: head to the north, feet to the south; or head to the west, feet to the east. If you sleep with your head to the north there should be no live power cable going through the north wall (possibly fit a mains free switch or switch off at the fuse-box at night).

* If you sleep nearer than fifty yards to a river or stream, then you

should lie at right angles to direction of the water. People that sleep in the direction that the water flows wake up in the morning drained and exhausted; if they sleep in the opposite direction they often wake in the morning with a thick head or a headache because the surge of energy is too great. As a consequence high blood pressure can also set in.

* If you as parents notice that your child's behaviour changes after a change of room at school, and his or her performance suddenly deteriorates, you should insist on a change of desk in the classroom. Of course the ideal situation would be if the teacher or head of school possessed the good sense to introduce what many schools today have already put into practice: place rotation. There at intervals of between two and six weeks every pupil takes up a different place.

Of course this also applies to changes of sleeping place in the home. Observe your child and draw your own conclusions from any changes in his behaviour.

* The materials for a healthy mattress are, in order of quality: straw, natural latex, sheep's wool, horsehair, artificial latex. Foam is also suitable, but for a number of other reasons not recommended for certain people (among other things on account of the danger of static-electric charge). Interior sprung beds are relatively harmless as long as the entire mattress is free of radiation. Otherwise the metal springs distribute the radiation over the entire mattress, even if only one corner of the bed is crossed by a line of force.

Decontamination

Every form of radiation can 'charge up' objects and living beings, just like a strong magnet can magnetise a metal object. When the radiation ceases, decontamination does not ensue immediately.

Thus a successful change of place does not free the body at once from the dose of earth radiation – which has often been absorbed for years. On top of that in our artificial world we are daily bombarded, charged up and kept charged by numerous other negative rays: in department stores, at computer workstations, on synthetic fibre carpets, in proximity to electrical equipment and cables, through severely negative feelings and thoughts (one's own and those of others), and many other situations.

The two most important methods to prevent getting charged up and to effect decontamination are these:

* *Water applications*: Frequent washing of the hands and arms up to the elbows with cold water only and no soap. A lot of radiation gets dammed up in the shoulders, hands and arms (often visible in swollen veins on the back of the hands). Whenever your instinct signals an uncomfortable feeling in this area, perhaps through itching, stinging or a sensation of heaviness, then you should give yourself this treat: cold running water over the hands – until the feeling improves. It is particularly important for children before they go to bed briefly to run water over their hands and arms up to their elbows. Troubled sleep and nightmares then occur much less frequently, because part of the charge of the day has disappeared.

Most people recommend cold showers as invigorating and relaxing, not least because this numbers among the best methods of radiation decontamination. This effect cannot be achieved with standing water in a bathtub. Shower yourself without soap as often as your feel the inclination to do so, particularly when your head feels 'charged' and heavy, and a headache is in the offing – three times a day if you feel like it. And if like us you are a little shy of cold water, at least let the last jets of water run cool to cold over your head and hair.

An interesting point for women and men with long hair: in the course of time long hair can become very highly charged, particularly if in addition you use chemicals and artificial substances in the form of setting lotions, gels and the like. If you often suffer from headaches or migraine, just try having your hair cut shorter, dispensing with all hair-care products that remain in the hair and each morning and evening run some cool water over your head.

Firm brushing with a natural hairbrush is also an effective way to banish radiation.

Finally, anyone who goes swimming every day is taking the best possible action to keep free to a great extent from radiation.

* *Movement in the open air*: Children become charged up more quickly than adults and unconsciously and pleasurably discharge themselves when playing in the open air.

Working in the open air, walking in the great outdoors, to the accompaniment of positive thoughts (especially in the vicinity of trees) number amongst the effective 'methods' to free oneself of radiation. Another helpful factor is the proximity of streams and rivers. To sit, or even to spend the night by flowing water, at right angles to the flow, is a wonderful thing.

Incidentally, there are some plants that have a decontaminating effect. Ferns and cacti, for example, but especially the plant called Baby's tears (*Soleirolia soleirolii*). Frequently during the day, whenever you feel the need, hold your hands over the plant and only water it on watery days (Cancer, Scorpio, Pisces) – it can then stand the treatment better.

Basically people all decontaminate themselves in their own way. You should choose the method with which you feel most comfortable, and follow your own instinct. Some people discharge themselves by doing the ironing, some by driving, some by staying up late into the night, some by reading, some by swimming, hiking or mountaineering.

Gradually your instinct and your experience will bring home to you the perhaps surprising understanding of just what an important role is played by your mental activity in discharging radiation – regardless of the direction from which your thoughts may come. The swelling of the veins on the back of the hands after an awkward phone conversation is often nothing more than the consequence of irradiation by one's own thoughts or those of the person at the end of the line. Sensitive children who bite their nails are thereby attempting to divert to their teeth the contamination in their hands – a consequence of the strain they are under which can find no escape valve. You have already seen in part I of this book just what consequences contamination of the teeth can have via the reflex paths for the whole body. You should therefore bear the following in mind.

If thoughts can make people ill, they can also make them whole. If thoughts can radiate and build up a charge, they can also discharge. Someone who through unrealisable expectations has generated thoughts of anger and irritation with which he subsequently remains 'charged' for a long time, is able to seize hold of these expectations by the scruff of the neck and with thoughts of forgiveness, equanimity and forbearance towards himself trim them down to size and thereby break down the charge. We have the choice.

And with that we close this chapter on the knowledge of the right place. We hope that we have succeeded in conveying to you the far-reaching importance of this information. Whether and how you translate it into practice is something that you must decide. If you wish to take it to heart you should bear in mind one thing: there is never any cause for panic and anxious reactions. If you have really been working or sleeping on a bad place, then generally you will have already been doing so for some time. Necessary changes do not have to take place at the drop of a hat. But one day, all the same.

Grandfather Josef Koller (1879–1968)

*It was his work, his way and his life
to pass on knowledge and experience.
In our book we are placing his knowledge in the hands
of all those who wish to accept it and live by it.*

V. The Power of Thought

The Happiest Man

A man is being chased by a wild tiger.
Just as the tiger is about to reach him
and tear him apart, the man leaps into a chasm.
At the last moment he is able to seize hold
of a root six feet below the edge, but this
begins slowly to break away.
Above him the ravening tiger,
below him the yawning abyss and certain death.
Next to him on a tiny outcrop of rock there is a flower.
The man leans over towards it,
smells it and says: "What a wonderful fragrance!"

In everything that we have been making available to you throughout this book – from the rhythm of the moon and its forces to the erection of a roof truss at the correct time, we have ultimately been guided by two purposes.

First of all we wanted to offer all readers in need of the tools for self-healing and staying healthy something that is practical and tested: valid knowledge and information that has partially slipped into oblivion, knowledge that can be of use in the prevention and curing of illness.

At the same time we wanted to awaken a memory in all readers who wish through their own efforts to stay healthy and become healthy – the memory of the time a long way back when seeing was not yet difficult, when an infallible instinct for what is true guided every inward and outward step we took. The memory of the source of all mental and physical health: the capacity to see, think and act the truth. It is truth alone that makes us healthy, keeps us healthy – makes us whole even if our body is lying in bed racked with fever, or if it is stricken with an incurable disease, or if it is fettered to a wheelchair. For our thoughts are not fettered: nothing can fetter and enslave thought, unless *we ourselves permit it*.

We wanted to remind you that it is your thoughts alone that create your reality, that you are not the victim of circumstances in which you live, that your life is the visible expression and necessary consequence of your thoughts and attitudes – in other words, that you always reap what in your heart and mind you sow.

In this last chapter we should like to remind you once more that your mind and your soul always carry the good seed-corn with them; whether you bring it out and let it come alive, or whether you wish to continue to scatter the lifeless, second-hand, alien seed, is left up to you.

You can savour the smell of each of the sentences that follow, try some of them out, eat what tastes good, spit out what doesn't, digest what seems sensible to you. Every sentence is only valid for you if it awakens something personal in you, something that is your own, if it touches you personally, if in one way or another it moves you – whether to agreement, reflection or rejection. We are not making any claim to universal validity, even if a section is sometimes formulated as if it were true for everyone. Just as there is no medicine that helps all people equally well at all times, there is no accumulation of words that says the same thing to everyone. Your insight is your insight. And there is many an insight into one's own truth that one can share with almost no one in the world.

* * *

Almost all of us grow up nowadays in a force field of dogmas, prejudices and convictions that are diametrically opposed to our direct experience and the perception of our heart. Like the child in the tale of 'The Emperor's New Clothes' we came into the world with a clear, undistorted view of reality – with the all-penetrating gaze that shines from the eyes of every new-born child. Then we did not have to rely on assumptions: we *knew* everything about ourselves and we knew everything about everyone else. We knew what food it was that made us shine – the food that kept us alive a year before our birth and which bears the name of unconditional acceptance, unconditional love. But even after a few weeks of our visit to this world the first veils fall over this powerful light. For many of us the process of growing up and becoming an adult means slowly to be immersed and swallowed up in lies – at first resisting and hesitant, incredulous, effortlessly seeing through every adult falsehood and hypocrisy. However, the lies work like a gigantic vice pressing down on us with imperceptible slowness and squashing us into the mould of the contemporary mentality – that fashion collection of ideologies, moral attitudes and patterns of thought, whose function is to prevent us from ever glimpsing the truth, and to wean us away from love, the one and only genuine food for our soul.

Resistance is pointless, and we do not put up a fight for long. The pain of isolation and solitude as a small, helpless child in the struggle for truth and love, which we carry within us like a treasure, gradually outweighs the pain of becoming accustomed to the lies, making hypocrisy and conformity to this madness seem like the lesser evil. In the beginning we can still recognise that the sweeteners and rewards intended to help deaden the pain of learning to lie are sheer poison, and that they are merely the bribes of the 'normal world', the world of lies. In the beginning we still try to reject them, because our senses and our heart recognise the poison; but then our strength begins to fail. Punishments give us the final impetus to accept falsehood as 'normal', and to content ourselves with the crumbs in the basement of the house of truth.

At first we feel wounded, hesitant and still unconsciously hungering after the essential, then later we actually want at all costs to enter into the false life, to take part in it, to be 'with it' – simply because the solitude of knowing the truth is unbearable, since there is seemingly no one there with whom to share our own awareness, since almost all the older people have forgotten their own past, 'apparelled in celestial light'. Until at last we give up entirely and transform ourselves into well-behaved fully adjusted members of society, playing along with every phoney game.

Small comfort for some, but for many a powerful self-delusion is afforded by the thought: "If *everyone else* acts like that, it can't be so wrong. If *everyone else* feels that way, it must be right. I'm the one that's crazy, when I see what I see and feel what I feel." Thus the memory of the beginning gradually vanishes, the memory of the time of truth and love.

The false world teaches us to veil and deaden the suffering and pain it brings to our starving hearts by means of various mental subterfuges: barefaced greed and envy are transformed into laudable 'ambition' and meritorious 'achiever mentality'. Fear is called 'reserve', 'tact' and 'prudent caution'. Paralysing lethargy becomes 'the art of living', 'composure', 'leisure'. Irritable impatience is called 'eager expectation', 'creative restlessness', 'euphoria'. People heap applause on confused outbursts of feeling and banal hobbies and call them 'creativity' and 'art'. At the behest of experts, pleasantly befuddled confusions of feeling are mistaken for 'love'. Implacable thirst for revenge is excused by psychotherapists as 'childhood trauma', by priests as 'righteous anger' and by politicians as 'straightforwardness'. And bodily pleasure and sex, the most wonderful medicine that God has given us, arouse fear, hostility and even disgust, because no one is there to give loving instruction in how best to handle them, but especially because repressed sexuality renders human beings exquisitely dependent and susceptible to manipulation.

Finally the veil becomes so thick that it is like a wall surrounding a prison, making one forget freedom at its gates. Its long-serving inmates all help us to make our own cell habitable, and teach us the language of the prison: eventually we call the prison 'the world as it is'.

Every glance outward, every message that points to the freedom beyond its walls, finally becomes a threat to our imagined peace. Formerly it was customary to kill the messengers from outside, those heroes of freedom who bring home our reality to us; nowadays we either ignore them or combat them with the most frightful weapon there is: our thoughts.

And yet occasionally a ray of light penetrates the walls for a few seconds, through the tiny chinks that our instinct opens up. In order to defend ourselves against this we have invented our compulsion to justify and explain. Unceasingly we *justify* ourselves, twenty-four hours a day, in order to keep our inner core, where our infallible instinct sits and watches, in a state of numbness, and to prevent the light that it emits from illuminating the reality – which is that we can escape from the prison any time we want.

We either justify or we fight against violence and declare it to be part of the 'nature' of humanity, instead of recognising it for what it always is: the cry of pain of a soul that wants to be loved unconditionally at last, since this is its only nourishment.

We justify idleness and declare it to be the 'inborn inertia of humanity', instead of recognising it for what it always is: the signal of a soul trying to resist the absurd 'meaning of life' that the world has trumped up for it, but because it lacks a sense of direction and a courageous determination, it remains anxious and helpless.

We justify greed and declare it to be 'healthy ambition', instead of recognising it for what it always is: the attempt of a dried up heart in its fear of death to gild its prison cage.

We justify nuclear power and genetic engineering and declare them to be the expression of the 'inborn human urge to explore', instead of recognising them for what they always are: the expression of a fearful mind that wants to have everything under control, and will not recognise that mankind is already perfect as it is, that nature gives us everything we need, and that we have the key to our prison cells in our own pocket. The expression of a mind that will not acknowledge that from the word go everything that is incomplete springs from its own thinking and feeling.

Endlessly we justify ourselves and many people succeed in forgetting truth, freedom and love to such an extent that for the rest of their lives they are contented with a shadow of true happiness and spend their days gilding the bars of their prison cell or wandering restlessly from one cell to another, in the deluded belief that something is 'changing' or 'improving' as a result.

This is how things have been for a long time.

This sorry story, which each of us has experienced in the most varied forms and shades, and yet which is always essentially the same, could end right here in despair, were it not precisely for this one piece of good news: the key to freedom and to the source of the only nourishment that our hearts long for – every one of us has it within himself.

Neither the key nor the source are hidden anywhere 'out there', in another person, in specific life circumstances, in material things. Possessing it does not have any pre-condition attached to it, any training, any thoughts or feelings. Everything imperfect in the world has its source in our own thinking. A person's thoughts are and remain free, even if we all spent so long growing up in the paralysing force field of the 'phoney game' and the lies that we eventually lost faith in the fact that somewhere on earth or in heaven the genuine, the true and the essential really exists. It is with the power of our thoughts that we create our own prison, and it is with the power of our thoughts that we can tear it down.

The key and the source do exist, here and now, at this very moment, accessible to everyone in the world, to you and to us. We do not even have to learn anything in order to find this door. We merely need to *remember* this door and the fact that we possess the *free will* to step through it at any moment. In other words, it is solely and exclusively the power of your own personal thoughts that can file the key to this door. Other than this thought, nothing else is necessary. No particular 'method', no special meditation is needed, no particular conditions have first to be fulfilled before the door can be opened. Always, at every moment, you have the choice.

A person who is conscious of this freedom of choice gets up every morning and makes a clear decision. He decides for the thought: "What I need for life will come." Every morning he fosters and cherishes the thought for a few minutes and then he leaves it to itself. He does not permit the thought to turn into a desire or even an obsession. No one has ever filed a prison key from desire, pain and suffering. From clear intention, insight and confidence, more likely.

As a rule nowadays and at all times we choose one of three ways to face life in the prison:

Believing the lies, initially against one's better judgement, deadening the pain, accepting, adopting, incorporating, and finally becoming absorbed in the lies – becoming their advocate and salesman. This is the simplest way, the way of the many. The way of gilding the prison cell.

Keeping the memory alive, not accepting, revolting, rebelling, conflict, 'dropping out'. A wearisome, debilitating struggle against hypocrisy, against greed and fear. A hard way that only seldom can be pursued successfully. The way of exchanging one prison cell for another, always with the feeling that 'something is changing'.

Thirdly there is life in the very midst of the lies, surrounded by hypocrisy, plunged into inner and outer chaos, without moving or deviating as much as a hair's breadth from one's own instinct, from the recognition of what is true and essential, uninfluenced and untouched by the 'state of affairs', in the full consciousness that *thoughts are always free*. A way along a razor-sharp knife-edge, which must always be walked alone and by one's own efforts. It is the only way that promises success because it contains the possibility of discovering the prison key that one has been carrying around with one since birth.

In order to go by the third way you must first understand a law of nature:

* What a person does is always only the external expression, the visible consequence of his own thoughts or the thoughts of others.

* The words a person utters are merely the outer audible expression of his own thoughts or the thoughts of others. Their effect is a thousand times more powerful than his deeds.

* The thoughts of a person, whether they be friendly, positive and affectionate, or fearful, angry and greedy are always an invitation to the world that the latter *must* accept. They in their turn have an effect that is a thousand times greater than that of words. They are always transformed somewhere in the near or distant future into perceptible and tangible reality. They are thought, transmitted, travel to their goal and return amplified tenfold to their originator.

In conclusion, here are two stories that will help you to understand this law and always remember it.

Somewhere in the world a long time ago there was once a prison camp whose inmates were totally undernourished because the camp commander and guards always appropriated the rations for themselves or sold them. In all the barracks deaths from malnutrition were a regular occurrence – with one exception: in barrack 27 the prisoners did not seem nearly so exhausted and emaciated as in the rest of the camp; they remained in relatively good health and were able to take part in forced labour regularly and in full strength.

When the guards noticed this they secretly observed the barrack for some time but were unable to detect if the inmates were receiving any kind of extra rations. Finally the camp commander had one of the prisoners from building 27 hauled up to the officers' building for cross-examination in order to extract from him the reason for his physical condition.

"It's hard to say, " said the prisoner. "Maybe it's because we meet together in the morning, at noon and in the evening, sit in a circle and imagine we have the best three-star menu there ever was in front of us. We eat, drink, chew and brandish our spoons until we're all full up."

Somewhere in the world a long time ago there was once another prison camp, whose inmates had to live for years – for the duration of the war – in the worst imaginable circumstances. Many of them did not survive the torture, the rotten food, the bad water, the epidemics. After the camp was liberated a young doctor discovered among the prisoners a man whom everybody knew only by the name of 'Wild Bill' and who was outwardly totally different from all the other miserable specimens: he seemed to be healthy and strong, worked like a horse for eighteen hours a day, assisting the doctor in his work and getting the survivors back on their feet. He was considered by all the prisoners as their 'special friend', sorted out quarrels between the various national groups, spoke seven languages fluently, and was always affectionate towards everyone, cheerful and optimistic. For this reason the young doctor was at first convinced that Wild Bill had only spent a few weeks in the camp.

The doctor's surprise was thus all the greater when he managed to discover from the camp files that Wild Bill had been one of the *first* inmates, and that for years on end he had gone through the same tortures as all the others. At first Wild Bill tried to evade questions as to his origins and the reason for his condition, until finally one night he briefly told his story to the young doctor.

"Doctor, it was night when the militia came and fetched me, my wife and my four children out of our house. Out in the street they shot my wife and children before my eyes, one after the other. I fell on my knees in front of those guys and begged them to shoot me, too. The leader merely said coldly that they were going to need me on account of my knowledge of languages and he had me put in irons. That was the end of my life: everything that up to then had been dear to me had been destroyed by a few shots. I had lost everything: there was no more hope and no future. What I had taken to be my heart was dead.

"At that very moment an inner voice spoke to me and said that it was time to make a decision: either I could use up the rest of my life in hatred and bitterness; or else from now on I would love every human being, without distinction, unconditionally – regardless of what he had done, was doing or was going to do. Believe me, Doctor, I have never had to make an easier decision."

Perhaps these two stories contain a part of the material that you need in order to make your own decisions in life from now on – and in order to have the courage to trust your own instinct, uninfluenced by all the laws and rules in the outside world, unaffected by your positive and negative thoughts and your personal feelings of approval or rejection. We are addressing you quite personally, not the general public or a specific organisation. Try for a little while to forget what friends, neighbours, your partner, children, your boss, your subordinates – 'the world' – would say about this chapter, not to mention what they would say about your personal reaction to it. The choice is always yours how you want to understand and live, what you want to see. It is renewed from one moment to the next and unfettered by any commitment to a particular character or to your past. You are only in the fetters of the past if you yourself *allow* it.

The false world has robbed us of the nourishment that will make us grow and ripen, until only the longing for it remains to condition our behaviour. The substitute nourishment in prison – science, power, money, apparent security – none of that will ever still your hunger. Perhaps we have helped you to recognise the genuine foods of life and to remember them when you come across them.

Remember: nature makes sure that you never have to travel far to obtain what your body needs. What your heart needs is much nearer still – not a hand's breadth away. Do not go seeking for what you already possess... Remember your freedom.

Remember love.

Correspondence to the authors should be addressed to

Johanna Paungger/Thomas Poppe
Post Box 190 723
D – 80607 Munich
Germany

We shall endeavour to answer all enquiries, but ask for your understanding if because of the volume of letters from many countries we are unable to give any guarantee of this. We are sincerely grateful for the confidence in our work that is expressed in such letters and would like to say a few words here in reply that may be of some use to you:

We are only writing from personal experience, and there are limits to that. This is especially true of physical and mental disorders: we are not doctors and we have no right – nor any wish – to presume to make judgements from a distance as to what is beneficial or harmful in a particular case.

Numerous readers have asked us for the addresses of doctors or dowsers or of suppliers of particular products. We are no longer able to do this, either because these people have now become hopelessly overstretched, or because economic success has become more important to them than service to individual customers. The latter reason, however, rules out any close collaboration with us. There is nothing basically wrong with money and economic success: what really matters is the way people handle these things. We take pleasure in success but never make it the goal of our work.

Our entire work, both now and in the future is directed towards awakening in people the courage to make their own decisions and take responsibility for themselves – the courage to get right to the bottom of a problem, look at it from every side and think things through to the end. There is no other person, no 'expert' who can take on this task for you – and that goes for us, too. If our work has been able to awaken in you the courage to do this, then we rejoice with you from the bottom of our heart.

Appendix

Plants and trees mentioned in the text

An asterisk indicates that the name refers to a number of related species.

English	*Latin*
Alder	Rhamnus frangula
Anise	Pimpinella anisum
Apple	Malus*
Arnica	Arnica montana
Baby's Tears	Soleirolia soleirolii
Balm	Melissa officinalis
Barley	Hordeum*
Bedstraw	Galium *
Beetroot	Beta rubra
Bilberry	Vaccinium myrtillus
Birch	Betula*
Blackcurrant	Ribes nigrum
Bloodwort, Bloody Dock	Rumex*
Borage	Borago officinalis
Bramble	Rubus*
Buck-bean	Menyanthes trifoliata
Buckthorn	Rhamnus catharticus
Burdock	Arctium pubens
Burnet Saxifrage	Pimpinella*
Cabbage	Brassica oleracea
Camomile	Anthemis nobilis
Camphor	Cinnamonum camphora
Caraway	Carum carvi
Carline Thistle	Carlina vulgaris
Carrot	Daucus carota
Celery	Apium graveolens
Centaury	Centaurea*
Chickweed	Stellaria media
Chive	Allium schoenoprasum
Coltsfoot	Tussilago farfara
Comfrey	Symphytum officinale

Common Agrimony	Agrimonia eupatoria
Common Clubmoss	Lycopodium clavatum
Common Knotgrass	Polygonum aviculare
Coriander	Coriandrum sativum
Cow Parsley	Anthriscus sylvestris
Cowslip	Primula veris
Crane's Bill	Geranium*
Cress	Lepidum sativum
Cucumber	Cucumis sativus
Daisy	Bellis perennis
Dandelion	Taraxacum officinale
Dog-rose	Rosa canina
Elder	Sambucus nigra
Eyebright	Euphrasia officinalis
Fat Hen	Chenopodium album
Fennel	Foeniculum vulgare
Fenugreek	Trigonella foenum-graecum
Field Horsetail	Equisetum arvense
French Bean	Phaseolus vulgaris
Fumitory	Fumaria officinalis
Gallant Soldier	Galinsoga parviflora
Garlic	Allium sativum
Gentian	Gentiana*
Golden Rod	Solidago virgaurea
Good King Henry	Chenopodium bonus-henricus
Goosefoot	Chenopodium*
Gout-weed	Aegopodium podagraria
Great Burnet	Sanguisorba officinalis
Great Plantain	Plantago major
Greater Celandine	Chelidonium majus
Ground Ivy	Glechoma hederacea
Hairy Willow Herb	Epilobium parviflorum
Heather	Caluna vulgaris
Hemp Agrimony	Eupatorium Cannabinum
Hogweed	Heracleum sphondylium
Hop	Humulus lupulus
Horse Chestnut	Aesculus hippocastanum
Iceland Moss	Cetraria islandica
Juniper	Juniperus communis
Lady's Mantle	Alchemilla*
Lentil	Lens culinaris
Lesser Bindweed	Convolvulus arvensis
Lesser Celandine	Ranunculus ficaria
Lettuce	Lactuca sativa
Lime	Tilia vulgaris
Lovage	Levisticum officinale

Marjoram	Origanum vulgare
Manna Ash	Fraxinus ornus
Marigold	Calendula officinalis
Millet	Panicum miliaceum
Mistletoe	Viscum album
Mugwort	Artemisia vulgaris
Mullein	Verbascum thapsus
Myrrh	Commiphora myrrha
Oat	Avena*
Onion	Allium cepa
Pansy	Viola*
Parsley	Petroselinum crispum
Peppermint	Mentha piperita
Plantain	Plantago*
Pumpkin	Cucurbita pepo
Radish	Raphanus sativus
Rhubarb	Rheum rhabarbarum
Ribwort Plantain	Plantago lanceolata
Rose	Rosa*
Rosemary	Rosmarinus officinalis
Saffron	Crocus sativus
Sage	Salvia officinalis
Savory	Satureia hortensis
Senna	Cassia*
Sesame	Sesamum indicum
Shepherd's Purse	Capsella bursa-pastoris
Silverweed	Potentilla anserina
Snakeweed	Polygonum bistorta
Sorrel	Rumex acetosa
Speedwell	Veronica*
Spinach	Spinacia oleracea
St. John's Wort	Hypericum *
Stinging Nettle	Urtica dioica
Sunflower	Helianthus*
Sweet Woodruff	Asperula odorata
Thyme	Thymus vulgaris
Valerian	Valeriana officinalis
Walnut	Juglans regia
Watercress	Nasturtium officinale
White Dead Nettle	Lamium album
Wild Angelica	Angelica sylvestris
Wild Mallows	Malva*
Willow Herb	Epilobium*
Wood Garlic	Allium ursinum
Wormwood	Artemisia absinthium
Yarrow	Achillea millefolium

Moon Calendar
1995–2005

♈	=	Aries
♉	=	Taurus
♊	=	Gemini
♋	=	Cancer
♌	=	Leo
♍	=	Virgo
♎	=	Libra
♏	=	Scorpio
♐	=	Sagittarius
♑	=	Capricorn
♒	=	Aquarius
♓	=	Pisces
☺	=	Full Moon
☾	=	Waning Moon
●	=	New Moon
☽	=	Waxing Moon
M	=	Monday
T	=	Tuesday
W	=	Wednesday
T	=	Thursday
F	=	Friday
S	=	Saturday
S	=	Sunday

1995

January			February			March			April			May			June		
S 1	♐	●	W 1	♒		W 1	♓	●	S 1	♈		M 1	♊		T 1	♌	
			T 2	♓		T 2	♓		S 2	♈		T 2	♋		F 2	♌	
M 2	♐		F 3	♓		F 3	♈					W 3	♋		S 3	♍	
T 3	♑		S 4	♈		S 4	♈		M 3	♉		T 4	♋		S 4	♍	
W 4	♑		S 5	♈		S 5	♉		T 4	♉		F 5	♌				
T 5	♒								W 5	♊		S 6	♌		M 5	♍	
F 6	♒		M 6	♈		M 6	♉		T 6	♊		S 7	♍	☽	T 6	♎	☽
S 7	♒		T 7	♈	☽	T 7	♉		F 7	♋					W 7	♎	
S 8	♈	☽	W 8	♈		W 8	♊		S 8	♋	☽	M 8	♍		T 8	♏	
			T 9	♉		T 9	♊	☽	S 9	♋		T 9	♎		F 9	♏	
M 9	♈		F 10	♉		F 10	♊					W 10	♎		S 10	♐	
T 10	♉		S 11	♉		S 11	♋		M 10	♌		T 11	♎		S 11	♐	
W 11	♉		S 12	♊		S 12	♋		T 11	♌		F 12	♏				
T 12	♉								W 12	♍		S 13	♏		M 12	♑	
F 13	♊		M 13	♊		M 13	♋		T 13	♍		S 14	♐	☉	T 13	♑	☉
S 14	♊		T 14	♋		T 14	♋		F 14	♎					W 14	♒	
S 15	♋		W 15	♋	☉	W 15	♋		S 15	♎	☉	M 15	♐		T 15	♒	
			T 16	♌		T 16	♌		S 16	♎		T 16	♑		F 16	♓	
M 16	♋	☉	F 17	♌		F 17	♌	☉				W 17	♑		S 17	♓	
T 17	♋		S 18	♍		S 18	♍		M 17	♏		T 18	♐		S 18	♒	
W 18	♌		S 19	♍		S 19	♍		T 18	♏		F 19	♐				
T 19	♌								W 19	♏		S 20	♑		M 19	♒	☾
F 20	♍		M 20	♍		M 20	♎		T 20	♐		S 21	♑	☾	T 20	♒	
S 21	♍		T 21	♎		T 21	♎		F 21	♐					W 21	♓	
S 22	♎		W 22	♎	☾	W 22	♏		S 22	♐	☾	M 22	♒		T 22	♓	
			T 23	♏		T 23	♏	☾	S 23	♑		T 23	♒		F 23	♓	
M 23	♎		F 24	♏		F 24	♐					W 24	♓		S 24	♈	
T 24	♏	☾	S 25	♐		S 25	♐		M 24	♑		T 25	♓		S 25	♈	
W 25	♏		S 26	♐		S 26	♑		T 25	♒		F 26	♈				
T 26	♏								W 26	♒		S 27	♈		M 26	♉	
F 27	♐		M 27	♑		M 27	♑		T 27	♐		S 28	♈		T 27	♉	
S 28	♐		T 28	♑		T 28	♑		F 28	♐					W 28	♊	●
S 29	♐					W 29	♒		S 29	♈	●	M 29	♉	●	T 29	♊	
						T 30	♒		S 30	♈		T 30	♉		F 30	♊	
M 30	♐	●				F 31	♓	●				W 31	♊				
T 31	♑																

1995

July
S 1
S 2
M 3
T 4
W 5 ☽
T 6
F 7
S 8
S 9
M 10
T 11
W 12 ☺
T 13
F 14
S 15
S 16
M 17
T 18
W 19 ☾
T 20
F 21
S 22
S 23
M 24
T 25
W 26
T 27 ●
F 28
S 29
S 30
M 31

August
T 1
W 2
T 3
F 4 ☽
S 5
S 6
M 7
T 8
W 9
T 10 ☺
F 11
S 12
S 13
M 14
T 15
W 16
T 17
F 18 ☾
S 19
S 20
M 21
T 22
W 23
T 24
F 25
S 26 ●
S 27
M 28
T 29
W 30
T 31

September
F 1
S 2
S 3
M 4 ☽
T 5
W 6
T 7
F 8
S 9 ☺
S 10
M 11
T 12
W 13
T 14
F 15
S 16 ☾
S 17
M 18
T 19
W 20
T 21
F 22
S 23
S 24 ●
M 25
T 26
W 27
T 28
F 29
S 30

October
S 1 ☽
M 2
T 3
W 4
T 5
F 6
S 7
S 8 ☺
M 9
T 10
W 11
T 12
F 13
S 14
S 15
M 16 ☾
T 17
W 18
T 19
F 20
S 21
S 22
M 23
T 24 ●
W 25
T 26
F 27
S 28
S 29
M 30 ☽
T 31

November
W 1
T 2
F 3
S 4
S 5
M 6
T 7 ☺
W 8
T 9
F 10
S 11
S 12
M 13
T 14
W 15 ☾
T 16
F 17
S 18
S 19
M 20
T 21
W 22 ●
T 23
F 24
S 25
S 26
M 27
T 28
W 29 ☽
T 30

December
F 1
S 2
S 3
M 4
T 5
W 6
T 7 ☺
F 8
S 9
S 10
M 11
T 12
W 13
T 14
F 15 ☾
S 16
S 17
M 18
T 19
W 20
T 21
F 22 ●
S 23
S 24
M 25
T 26
W 27
T 28 ☽
F 29
S 30
S 31

1996

January	February	March	April	May	June
M 1	T 1	F 1	M 1	W 1	S 1 ☺
T 2	F 2	S 2	T 2	T 2	S 2
W 3	S 3	S 3	W 3	F 3 ☺	
T 4	S 4 ☺		T 4 ☺	S 4	M 3
F 5 ☺		M 4	F 5	S 5	T 4
S 6	M 5	T 5 ☺	S 6		W 5
S 7	T 6	W 6	S 7	M 6	T 6
	W 7	T 7		T 7	F 7
M 8	T 8	F 8	M 8	W 8	S 8 ☾
T 9	F 9	S 9	T 9	T 9	S 9
W 10	S 10	S 10	W 10	F 10 ☾	
T 11	S 11		T 11 ☾	S 11	M 10
F 12		M 11	F 12	S 12	T 11
S 13 ☾	M 12 ☾	T 12 ☾	S 13		W 12
S 14	T 13	W 13	S 14	M 13	T 13
	W 14	T 14		T 14	F 14
M 15	T 15	F 15	M 15	W 15	S 15
T 16	F 16	S 16	T 16	T 16	S 16 ●
W 17	S 17	S 17	W 17 ●	F 17 ●	
T 18	S 18		T 18	S 18	M 17
F 19		M 18	F 19	S 19	T 18
S 20 ●	M 19 ●	T 19 ●	S 20		W 19
S 21	T 20	W 20	S 21	M 20	T 20
	W 21	T 21		T 21	F 21
M 22	T 22	F 22	M 22	W 22	S 22
T 23	F 23	S 23	T 23	T 23	S 23
W 24	S 24	S 24	W 24	F 24	
T 25	S 25		T 25 ☽	S 25 ☽	M 24 ☽
F 26		M 25	F 26	S 26	T 25
S 27 ☽	M 26 ☽	T 26	S 27		W 26
S 28	T 27	W 27 ☽	S 28	M 27	T 27
	W 28	T 28		T 28	F 28
M 29	T 29	F 29	M 29	W 29	S 29
T 30		S 30	T 30	T 30	S 30
W 31		S 31		F 31	

1996

July	August	September	October	November	December
M 1 ☺	T 1	S 1	T 1	F 1	S 1
T 2	F 2		W 2	S 2	
W 3	S 3	M 2	T 3	S 3 ☾	M 2
T 4	S 4	T 3	F 4 ☾		T 3 ☾
F 5		W 4 ☾	S 5	M 4	W 4
S 6	M 5	T 5	S 6	T 5	T 5
S 7 ☾	T 6 ☾	F 6		W 6	F 6
	W 7	S 7	M 7	T 7	S 7
M 8	T 8	S 8	T 8	F 8	S 8
T 9	F 9		W 9	S 9	
W 10	S 10	M 9	T 10	S 10	M 9
T 11	S 11	T 10	F 11		T 10 ●
F 12		W 11	S 12 ●	M 11 ●	W 11
S 13	M 12	T 12	S 13	T 12	T 12
S 14	T 13	F 13 ●		W 13	F 13
	W 14 ●	S 14	M 14	T 14	S 14
M 15 ●	T 15	S 15	T 15	F 15	S 15
T 16	F 16		W 16	S 16	
W 17	S 17	M 16	T 17	S 17	M 16
T 18	S 18	T 17	F 18		T 17 ☽
F 19		W 18	S 19 ☽	M 18 ☽	W 18
S 20	M 19	T 19	S 20	T 19	T 19
S 21	T 20	F 20 ☽		W 20	F 20
	W 21	S 21	M 21	T 21	S 21
M 22	T 22 ☽	S 22	T 22	F 22	S 22
T 23 ☽	F 23		W 23	S 23	
W 24	S 24	M 23	T 24	S 24	M 23
T 25	S 25	T 24	F 25		T 24 ☺
F 26		W 25	S 26 ☺	M 25 ☺	W 25
S 27	M 26	T 26	S 27	T 26	T 26
S 28	T 27	F 27 ☺		W 27	F 27
	W 28 ☺	S 28	M 28	T 28	S 28
M 29	T 29	S 29	T 29	F 29	S 29
T 30 ☺	F 30	M 30	W 30	S 30	M 30
W 31	S 31		T 31		T 31

1997

January	February	March	April	May	June
W 1	S 1	S 1	T 1	T 1	S 1
T 2 ☾	S 2	S 2 ☾	W 2	F 2	
F 3	M 3	M 3	T 3	S 3	M 2
S 4	T 4	T 4	F 4	S 4	T 3
S 5	W 5	W 5	S 5		W 4
M 6	T 6	T 6	S 6	M 5	T 5 ●
T 7	F 7 ●	F 7		T 6 ●	F 6
W 8	S 8	S 8	M 7 ●	W 7	S 7
T 9 ●	S 9	S 9 ●	T 8	T 8	S 8
F 10		M 10	W 9	F 9	
S 11	M 10	T 11	T 10	S 10	M 9
S 12	T 11	W 12	F 11	S 11	T 10
	W 12	T 13	S 12		W 11
M 13	T 13	F 14	S 13	M 12	T 12
T 14	F 14 ☾	S 15		T 13	F 13 ☾
W 15 ☾	S 15	S 16 ☾	M 14 ☾	W 14 ☾	S 14
T 16	S 16		T 15	T 15	S 15
F 17		M 17	W 16	F 16	
S 18	M 17	T 18	T 17	S 17	M 16
S 19	T 18	W 19	F 18	S 18	T 17
	W 19	T 20	S 19		W 18
M 20	T 20	F 21	S 20	M 19	T 19
T 21	F 21	S 22		T 20	F 20 ☺
W 22	S 22 ☺	S 23	M 21	W 21	S 21
T 23 ☺	S 23		T 22 ☺	T 22 ☺	S 22
F 24		M 24 ☺	W 23	F 23	
S 25	M 24	T 25	T 24	S 24	M 23
S 26	T 25	W 26	F 25	S 25	T 24
	W 26	T 27	S 26		W 25
M 27	T 27	F 28	S 27	M 26	T 26
T 28	F 28	S 29		T 27	F 27 ☾
W 29		S 30	M 28	W 28	S 28
T 30		M 31 ☾	T 29	T 29 ☾	S 29
F 31 ☾			W 30 ☾	F 30	M 30
				S 31	

Calendar

1997

July	August	September	October	November	December
T 1	F 1	M 1	W 1 ●	S 1	M 1
W 2	S 2	T 2 ●	T 2	S 2	T 2
T 3	S 3 ●	W 3	F 3		W 3
F 4 ●		T 4	S 4	M 3	T 4
S 5	M 4	F 5	S 5	T 4	F 5
S 6	T 5	S 6		W 5	S 6
	W 6	S 7	M 6	T 6	S 7 ☽
M 7	T 7		T 7	F 7 ☽	
T 8	F 8	M 8	W 8	S 8	M 8
W 9	S 9	T 9	T 9 ☽	S 9	T 9
T 10	S 10	W 10 ☽	F 10		W 10
F 11		T 11	S 11	M 10	T 11
S 12 ☽	M 11 ☽	F 12	S 12	T 11	F 12
S 13	T 12	S 13		W 12	S 13
	W 13	S 14	M 13	T 13	S 14 ☺
M 14	T 14		T 14	F 14 ☺	
T 15	F 15	M 15	W 15	S 15	M 15
W 16	S 16	T 16 ☺	T 16 ☺	S 16	T 16
T 17	S 17	W 17	F 17		W 17
F 18		T 18	S 18	M 17	T 18
S 19	M 18 ☺	F 19	S 19	T 18	F 19
S 20 ☺	T 19	S 20		W 19	S 20
	W 20	S 21	M 20	T 20	S 21 ☾
M 21	T 21		T 21	F 21	
T 22	F 22	M 22	W 22	S 22 ☾	M 22
W 23	S 23	T 23 ☾	T 23 ☾	S 23	T 23
T 24	S 24	W 24	F 24		W 24
F 25		T 25	S 25	M 24	T 25
S 26 ☾	M 25 ☾	F 26	S 26	T 25	F 26
S 27	T 26	S 27		W 26	S 27
	W 27	S 28	M 27	T 27	S 28
M 28	T 28		T 28	F 28	
T 29	F 29	M 29	W 29	S 29	M 29 ●
W 30	S 30	T 30	T 30	S 30 ●	T 30
T 31	S 31		F 31 ●		W 31

359

1998

January	February	March	April	May	June
T 1	S 1	S 1	W 1	F 1	M 1
F 2			T 2	S 2	T 2
S 3	M 2	M 2	F 3	S 3	W 3
S 4	T 3	T 3	S 4		T 4
	W 4	W 4	S 5	M 4	F 5
M 5	T 5	T 5		T 5	S 6
T 6	F 6	F 6	M 6	W 6	S 7
W 7	S 7	S 7	T 7	T 7	
T 8	S 8	S 8	W 8	F 8	M 8
F 9			T 9	S 9	T 9
S 10	M 9	M 9	F 10	S 10	W 10
S 11	T 10	T 10	S 11		T 11
	W 11	W 11	S 12	M 11	F 12
M 12	T 12	T 12		T 12	S 13
T 13	F 13	F 13	M 13	W 13	S 14
W 14	S 14	S 14	T 14	T 14	
T 15	S 15	S 15	W 15	F 15	M 15
F 16			T 16	S 16	T 16
S 17	M 16	M 16	F 17	S 17	W 17
S 18	T 17	T 17	S 18		T 18
	W 18	W 18	S 19	M 18	F 19
M 19	T 19	T 19		T 19	S 20
T 20	F 20	F 20	M 20	W 20	S 21
W 21	S 21	S 21	T 21	T 21	
T 22	S 22	S 22	W 22	F 22	M 22
F 23			T 23	S 23	T 23
S 24	M 23	M 23	F 24	S 24	W 24
S 25	T 24	T 24	S 25		T 25
	W 25	W 25	S 26	M 25	F 26
M 26	T 26	T 26		T 26	S 27
T 27	F 27	F 27	M 27	W 27	S 28
W 28	S 28	S 28	T 28	T 28	
T 29		S 29	W 29	F 29	M 29
F 30			T 30	S 30	T 30
S 31		M 30		S 31	
		T 31			

1998

July	August	September	October	November	December
W 1	S 1	T 1	T 1	S 1	T 1
T 2	S 2	W 2	F 2		W 2
F 3		T 3	S 3	M 2	T 3
S 4	M 3	F 4	S 4	T 3	F 4
S 5	T 4	S 5		W 4	S 5
	W 5	S 6	M 5	T 5	S 6
M 6	T 6		T 6	F 6	
T 7	F 7	M 7	W 7	S 7	M 7
W 8	S 8	T 8	T 8	S 8	T 8
T 9	S 9	W 9	F 9		W 9
F 10		T 10	S 10	M 9	T 10
S 11	M 10	F 11	S 11	T 10	F 11
S 12	T 11	S 12		W 11	S 12
	W 12	S 13	M 12	T 12	S 13
M 13	T 13		T 13	F 13	
T 14	F 14	M 14	W 14	S 14	M 14
W 15	S 15	T 15	T 15	S 15	T 15
T 16	S 16	W 16	F 16		W 16
F 17		T 17	S 17	M 16	T 17
S 18	M 17	F 18	S 18	T 17	F 18
S 19	T 18	S 19		W 18	S 19
	W 19	S 20	M 19	T 19	S 20
M 20	T 20		T 20	F 20	
T 21	F 21	M 21	W 21	S 21	M 21
W 22	S 22	T 22	T 22	S 22	T 22
T 23	S 23	W 23	F 23		W 23
F 24		T 24	S 24	M 23	T 24
S 25	M 24	F 25	S 25	T 24	F 25
S 26	T 25	S 26		W 25	S 26
	W 26	S 27	M 26	T 26	S 27
M 27	T 27		T 27	F 27	
T 28	F 28	M 28	W 28	S 28	M 28
W 29	S 29	T 29	T 29	S 29	T 29
T 30	S 30	W 30	F 30		W 30
F 31	M 31		S 31	M 30	T 31

1999

January			February			March			April			May			June		
F	1	♓	M	1	♐	M	1	♐	T	1	♊	S	1	♋	T	1	♍
S	2	♈ ☺	T	2	♑	T	2	♑ ☺	F	2	♊	S	2	♋	W	2	♎
S	3	♈	W	3	♒	W	3	♒	S	3	♋				T	3	♎
			T	4	♒	T	4	♊	S	4	♋	M	3	♍	F	4	♏
M	4	♉	F	5	♊	F	5	♊				T	4	♍	S	5	♏
T	5	♉	S	6	♊	S	6	♊	M	5	♋	W	5	♐	S	6	♐
W	6	♊	S	7	♋	S	7	♋	T	6	♍	T	6	♐			
T	7	♊							W	7	♍	F	7	♐	M	7	♐ ☾
F	8	♊	M	8	♋ ☾	M	8	♋	T	8	♐	S	8	♏ ☾	T	8	♐
S	9	♊ ☾	T	9	♋	T	9	♍	F	9	♐ ☾	S	9	♏	W	9	♑
S	10	♊	W	10	♍	W	10	♍ ☾	S	10	♐				T	10	♑
			T	11	♍	T	11	♍	S	11	♏	M	10	♐	F	11	♒
M	11	♋	F	12	♐	F	12	♐				T	11	♐	S	12	♒
T	12	♋	S	13	♐	S	13	♐	M	12	♏	W	12	♐	S	13	♓ ●
W	13	♋	S	14	♐	S	14	♏	T	13	♒	T	13	♐			
T	14	♍							W	14	♒	F	14	♐	M	14	♓
F	15	♍	M	15	♏	M	15	♏	T	15	♊	S	15	♐ ●	T	15	♈
S	16	♐	T	16	♏ ●	T	16	♒	F	16	♐ ●	S	16	♓	W	16	♈
S	17	♐ ●	W	17	♒	W	17	♒ ●	S	17	♐				T	17	♉
			T	18	♒	T	18	♒	S	18	♐	M	17	♓	F	18	♉
M	18	♏	F	19	♐	F	19	♐				T	18	♈	S	19	♊
T	19	♏	S	20	♐	S	20	♐	M	19	♓	W	19	♈	S	20	♊ ☽
W	20	♏	S	21	♊	S	21	♊	T	20	♓	T	20	♉			
T	21	♒							W	21	♈	F	21	♉	M	21	♋
F	22	♒	M	22	♐	M	22	♐	T	22	♈ ☽	S	22	♉ ☽	T	22	♋
S	23	♐	T	23	♓ ☽	T	23	♓	F	23	♉	S	23	♊	W	23	♋
S	24	♐ ☽	W	24	♓	W	24	♓ ☽	S	24	♉				T	24	♋
			T	25	♈	T	25	♈	S	25	♊	M	24	♊	F	25	♋
M	25	♐	F	26	♈	F	26	♈				T	25	♋	S	26	♍
T	26	♏	S	27	♈	S	27	♏	M	26	♊	W	26	♋	S	27	♍
W	27	♓	S	28	♐	S	28	♏	T	27	♊	T	27	♋			
T	28	♓							W	28	♊	F	28	♋	M	28	♍ ☺
F	29	♈				M	29	♊	T	29	♊	S	29	♋	T	29	♐
S	30	♈				T	30	♊	F	30	♋ ☺	S	30	♍ ☺	W	30	♐
S	31	♏ ☺				W	31	♊ ☺				M	31	♍			

1999

July	August	September	October	November	December
T 1	S 1	W 1	F 1	M 1	W 1
F 2		T 2	S 2	T 2	T 2
S 3	M 2	F 3	S 3	W 3	F 3
S 4	T 3	S 4		T 4	S 4
	W 4	S 5	M 4	F 5	S 5
M 5	T 5		T 5	S 6	
T 6	F 6	M 6	W 6	S 7	M 6
W 7	S 7	T 7	T 7		T 7
T 8	S 8	W 8	F 8	M 8	W 8
F 9		T 9	S 9	T 9	T 9
S 10	M 9	F 10	S 10	W 10	F 10
S 11	T 10	S 11		T 11	S 11
	W 11	S 12	M 11	F 12	S 12
M 12	T 12		T 12	S 13	
T 13	F 13	M 13	W 13	S 14	M 13
W 14	S 14	T 14	T 14		T 14
T 15	S 15	W 15	F 15	M 15	W 15
F 16		T 16	S 16	T 16	T 16
S 17	M 16	F 17	S 17	W 17	F 17
S 18	T 17	S 18		T 18	S 18
	W 18	S 19	M 18	F 19	S 19
M 19	T 19		T 19	S 20	
T 20	F 20	M 20	W 20	S 21	M 20
W 21	S 21	T 21	T 21		T 21
T 22	S 22	W 22	F 22	M 22	W 22
F 23		T 23	S 23	T 23	T 23
S 24	M 23	F 24	S 24	W 24	F 24
S 25	T 24	S 25		T 25	S 25
	W 25	S 26	M 25	F 26	S 26
M 26	T 26		T 26	S 27	
T 27	F 27	M 27	W 27	S 28	M 27
W 28	S 28	T 28	T 28		T 28
T 29	S 29	W 29	F 29	M 29	W 29
F 30		T 30	S 30	T 30	T 30
S 31	M 30		S 31		F 31
	T 31				

2000

January	February	March	April	May	June
S 1	T 1	W 1	S 1	M 1	T 1
S 2	W 2	T 2	S 2	T 2	F 2
	T 3	F 3		W 3	S 3
M 3	F 4	S 4	M 3	T 4	S 4
T 4	S 5	S 5	T 4	F 5	
W 5	S 6		W 5	S 6	M 5
T 6		M 6	T 6	S 7	T 6
F 7	M 7	T 7	F 7		W 7
S 8	T 8	W 8	S 8	M 8	T 8
S 9	W 9	T 9	S 9	T 9	F 9
	T 10	F 10		W 10	S 10
M 10	F 11	S 11	M 10	T 11	S 11
T 11	S 12	S 12	T 11	F 12	
W 12	S 13		W 12	S 13	M 12
T 13		M 13	T 13	S 14	T 13
F 14	M 14	T 14	F 14		W 14
S 15	T 15	W 15	S 15	M 15	T 15
S 16	W 16	T 16	S 16	T 16	F 16
	T 17	F 17		W 17	S 17
M 17	F 18	S 18	M 17	T 18	S 18
T 18	S 19	S 19	T 18	F 19	
W 19	S 20		W 19	S 20	M 19
T 20		M 20	T 20	S 21	T 20
F 21	M 21	T 21	F 21		W 21
S 22	T 22	W 22	S 22	M 22	T 22
S 23	W 23	T 23	S 23	T 23	F 23
	T 24	F 24		W 24	S 24
M 24	F 25	S 25	M 24	T 25	S 25
T 25	S 26	S 26	T 25	F 26	
W 26	S 27		W 26	S 27	M 26
T 27		M 27	T 27	S 28	T 27
F 28	M 28	T 28	F 28		W 28
S 29	T 29	W 29	S 29	M 29	T 29
S 30		T 30	S 30	T 30	F 30
		F 31		W 31	
M 31					

2000

July	August	September	October	November	December
S 1	T 1	F 1	S 1	W 1	F 1
S 2	W 2	S 2		T 2	S 2
M 3	T 3	S 3	M 2	F 3	S 3
T 4	F 4		T 3	S 4	M 4
W 5	S 5	M 4	W 4	S 5	T 5
T 6	S 6	T 5	T 5		W 6
F 7		W 6	F 6	M 6	T 7
S 8	M 7	T 7	S 7	T 7	F 8
S 9	T 8	F 8	S 8	W 8	S 9
	W 9	S 9		T 9	S 10
M 10	T 10	S 10	M 9	F 10	
T 11	F 11		T 10	S 11	M 11
W 12	S 12	M 11	W 11	S 12	T 12
T 13	S 13	T 12	T 12		W 13
F 14		W 13	F 13	M 13	T 14
S 15	M 14	T 14	S 14	T 14	F 15
S 16	T 15	F 15	S 15	W 15	S 16
	W 16	S 16		T 16	S 17
M 17	T 17	S 17	M 16	F 17	
T 18	F 18		T 17	S 18	M 18
W 19	S 19	M 18	W 18	S 19	T 19
T 20	S 20	T 19	T 19		W 20
F 21		W 20	F 20	M 20	T 21
S 22	M 21	T 21	S 21	T 21	F 22
S 23	T 22	F 22	S 22	W 22	S 23
	W 23	S 23		T 23	S 24
M 24	T 24	S 24	M 23	F 24	
T 25	F 25		T 24	S 25	M 25
W 26	S 26	M 25	W 25	S 26	T 26
T 27	S 27	T 26	T 26		W 27
F 28		W 27	F 27	M 27	T 28
S 29	M 28	T 28	S 28	T 28	F 29
S 30	T 29	F 29	S 29	W 29	S 30
	W 30	S 30		T 30	S 31
M 31	T 31		M 30		
			T 31		

2001

January	February	March	April	May	June
M 1	T 1	T 1	S 1	T 1	F 1
T 2	F 2	F 2		W 2	S 2
W 3	S 3	S 3	M 2	T 3	S 3
T 4	S 4	S 4	T 3	F 4	
F 5			W 4	S 5	M 4
S 6	M 5	M 5	T 5	S 6	T 5
S 7	T 6	T 6	F 6		W 6
	W 7	W 7	S 7	M 7	T 7
M 8	T 8	T 8	S 8	T 8	F 8
T 9	F 9	F 9		W 9	S 9
W 10	S 10	S 10	M 9	T 10	S 10
T 11	S 11	S 11	T 10	F 11	
F 12			W 11	S 12	M 11
S 13	M 12	M 12	T 12	S 13	T 12
S 14	T 13	T 13	F 13		W 13
	W 14	W 14	S 14	M 14	T 14
M 15	T 15	T 15	S 15	T 15	F 15
T 16	F 16	F 16		W 16	S 16
W 17	S 17	S 17	M 16	T 17	S 17
T 18	S 18	S 18	T 17	F 18	
F 19			W 18	S 19	M 18
S 20	M 19	M 19	T 19	S 20	T 19
S 21	T 20	T 20	F 20		W 20
	W 21	W 21	S 21	M 21	T 21
M 22	T 22	T 22	S 22	T 22	F 22
T 23	F 23	F 23		W 23	S 23
W 24	S 24	S 24	M 23	T 24	S 24
T 25	S 25	S 25	T 24	F 25	
F 26			W 25	S 26	M 25
S 27	M 26	M 26	T 26	S 27	T 26
S 28	T 27	T 27	F 27		W 27
	W 28	W 28	S 28	M 28	T 28
M 29		T 29	S 29	T 29	F 29
T 30		F 30		W 30	S 30
W 31		S 31	M 30	T 31	

2001

July	August	September	October	November	December
S 1	W 1	S 1	M 1	T 1 ☺	S 1
	T 2	S 2 ☺	T 2 ☺	F 2	S 2
M 2	F 3		W 3	S 3	
T 3	S 4 ☺	M 3	T 4	S 4	M 3
W 4	S 5	T 4	F 5		T 4
T 5 ☺		W 5	S 6	M 5	W 5
F 6	M 6	T 6	S 7	T 6	T 6
S 7	T 7	F 7		W 7	F 7 ☾
S 8	W 8	S 8	M 8	T 8 ☾	S 8
	T 9	S 9	T 9	F 9	S 9
M 9	F 10		W 10 ☾	S 10	
T 10	S 11	M 10 ☾	T 11	S 11	M 10
W 11	S 12 ☾	T 11	F 12		T 11
T 12		W 12	S 13	M 12	W 12
F 13 ☾	M 13	T 13	S 14	T 13	T 13
S 14	T 14	F 14		W 14	F 14 ●
S 15	W 15	S 15	M 15	T 15 ●	S 15
	T 16	S 16	T 16 ●	F 16	S 16
M 16	F 17		W 17	S 17	
T 17	S 18	M 17 ●	T 18	S 18	M 17
W 18	S 19 ●	T 18	F 19		T 18
T 19		W 19	S 20	M 19	W 19
F 20 ●	M 20	T 20	S 21	T 20	T 20
S 21	T 21	F 21		W 21	F 21
S 22	W 22	S 22	M 22	T 22	S 22 ☽
	T 23	S 23	T 23	F 23 ☽	S 23
M 23	F 24		W 24 ☽	S 24	
T 24	S 25 ☽	M 24 ☽	T 25	S 25	M 24
W 25	S 26	T 25	F 26		T 25
T 26		W 26	S 27	M 26	W 26
F 27 ☽	M 27	T 27	S 28	T 27	T 27
S 28	T 28	F 28		W 28	F 28
S 29	W 29	S 29	M 29	T 29	S 29
	T 30	S 30	T 30 ☺	F 30 ☺	S 30 ☺
M 30	F 31		W 31		
T 31					M 31

2002

January	February	March	April	May	June
T 1	F 1	F 1	M 1	W 1	S 1
W 2	S 2	S 2	T 2	T 2	S 2
T 3	S 3	S 3	W 3	F 3	M 3
F 4	M 4	M 4	T 4	S 4	T 4
S 5	T 5	T 5	F 5	S 5	W 5
S 6	W 6	W 6	S 6	M 6	T 6
M 7	T 7	T 7	S 7	T 7	F 7
T 8	F 8	F 8	M 8	W 8	S 8
W 9	S 9	S 9	T 9	T 9	S 9
T 10	S 10	S 10	W 10	F 10	M 10
F 11	M 11	M 11	T 11	S 11	T 11
S 12	T 12	T 12	F 12	S 12	W 12
S 13	W 13	W 13	S 13	M 13	T 13
M 14	T 14	T 14	S 14	T 14	F 14
T 15	F 15	F 15	M 15	W 15	S 15
W 16	S 16	S 16	T 16	T 16	S 16
T 17	S 17	S 17	W 17	F 17	M 17
F 18	M 18	M 18	T 18	S 18	T 18
S 19	T 19	T 19	F 19	S 19	W 19
S 20	W 20	W 20	S 20	M 20	T 20
M 21	T 21	T 21	S 21	T 21	F 21
T 22	F 22	F 22	M 22	W 22	S 22
W 23	S 23	S 23	T 23	T 23	S 23
T 24	S 24	S 24	W 24	F 24	M 24
F 25	M 25	M 25	T 25	S 25	T 25
S 26	T 26	T 26	F 26	S 26	W 26
S 27	W 27	W 27	S 27	M 27	T 27
M 28	T 28	T 28	S 28	T 28	F 28
T 29		F 29	M 29	W 29	S 29
W 30		S 30	T 30	T 30	S 30
T 31		S 31		F 31	

2002

July	August	September	October	November	December
M 1	T 1	S 1	T 1	F 1	S 1
T 2	F 2		W 2	S 2	
W 3	S 3	M 2	T 3	S 3	M 2
T 4	S 4	T 3	F 4		T 3
F 5		W 4	S 5	M 4	W 4
S 6	M 5	T 5	S 6	T 5	T 5
S 7	T 6	F 6		W 6	F 6
	W 7	S 7	M 7	T 7	S 7
M 8	T 8	S 8	T 8	F 8	S 8
T 9	F 9		W 9	S 9	
W 10	S 10	M 9	T 10	S 10	M 9
T 11	S 11	T 10	F 11		T 10
F 12		W 11	S 12	M 11	W 11
S 13	M 12	T 12	S 13	T 12	T 12
S 14	T 13	F 13		W 13	F 13
	W 14	S 14	M 14	T 14	S 14
M 15	T 15	S 15	T 15	F 15	S 15
T 16	F 16		W 16	S 16	
W 17	S 17	M 16	T 17	S 17	M 16
T 18	S 18	T 17	F 18		T 17
F 19		W 18	S 19	M 18	W 18
S 20	M 19	T 19	S 20	T 19	T 19
S 21	T 20	F 20		W 20	F 20
	W 21	S 21	M 21	T 21	S 21
M 22	T 22	S 22	T 22	F 22	S 22
T 23	F 23		W 23	S 23	
W 24	S 24	M 23	T 24	S 24	M 23
T 25	S 25	T 24	F 25		T 24
F 26		W 25	S 26	M 25	W 25
S 27	M 26	T 26	S 27	T 26	T 26
S 28	T 27	F 27		W 27	F 27
	W 28	S 28	M 28	T 28	S 28
M 29	T 29	S 29	T 29	F 29	S 29
T 30	F 30	M 30	W 30	S 30	M 30
W 31	S 31		T 31		T 31

2003

January	February	March	April	May	June
W 1	S 1	S 1	T 1	T 1	S 1
T 2	S 2	S 2	W 2	F 2	
F 3			T 3	S 3	M 2
S 4	M 3	M 3	F 4	S 4	T 3
S 5	T 4	T 4	S 5		W 4
	W 5	W 5	S 6	M 5	T 5
M 6	T 6	T 6		T 6	F 6
T 7	F 7	F 7	M 7	W 7	S 7
W 8	S 8	S 8	T 8	T 8	S 8
T 9	S 9	S 9	W 9	F 9	
F 10			T 10	S 10	M 9
S 11	M 10	M 10	F 11	S 11	T 10
S 12	T 11	T 11	S 12		W 11
	W 12	W 12	S 13	M 12	T 12
M 13	T 13	T 13		T 13	F 13
T 14	F 14	F 14	M 14	W 14	S 14
W 15	S 15	S 15	T 15	T 15	S 15
T 16	S 16	S 16	W 16	F 16	
F 17			T 17	S 17	M 16
S 18	M 17	M 17	F 18	S 18	T 17
S 19	T 18	T 18	S 19		W 18
	W 19	W 19	S 20	M 19	T 19
M 20	T 20	T 20		T 20	F 20
T 21	F 21	F 21	M 21	W 21	S 21
W 22	S 22	S 22	T 22	T 22	S 22
T 23	S 23	S 23	W 23	F 23	
F 24			T 24	S 24	M 23
S 25	M 24	M 24	F 25	S 25	T 24
S 26	T 25	T 25	S 26		W 25
	W 26	W 26	S 27	M 26	T 26
M 27	T 27	T 27		T 27	F 27
T 28	F 28	F 28	M 28	W 28	S 28
W 29		S 29	T 29	T 29	S 29
T 30		S 30	W 30	F 30	
F 31				S 31	M 30
		M 31			

2003

July	August	September	October	November	December
T 1	F 1	M 1	W 1	S 1 ☾	M 1
W 2	S 2	T 2	T 2 ☾	S 2	T 2
T 3	S 3	W 3 ☾	F 3		W 3
F 4		T 4	S 4	M 3	T 4
S 5	M 4	F 5	S 5	T 4	F 5
S 6	T 5 ☾	S 6		W 5	S 6
	W 6	S 7	M 6	T 6	S 7
M 7 ☾	T 7		T 7	F 7	
T 8	F 8	M 8	W 8	S 8	M 8 ☺
W 9	S 9	T 9	T 9	S 9 ☺	T 9
T 10	S 10	W 10 ☺	F 10 ☺		W 10
F 11		T 11	S 11	M 10	T 11
S 12	M 11	F 12	S 12	T 11	F 12
S 13 ☺	T 12 ☺	S 13		W 12	S 13
	W 13	S 14	M 13	T 13	S 14
M 14	T 14		T 14	F 14	
T 15	F 15	M 15	W 15	S 15	M 15
W 16	S 16	T 16	T 16	S 16	T 16 ☾
T 17	S 17	W 17	F 17		W 17
F 18		T 18 ☾	S 18 ☾	M 17 ☾	T 18
S 19	M 18	F 19	S 19	T 18	F 19
S 20	T 19	S 20		W 19	S 20
	W 20 ☾	S 21	M 20	T 20	S 21
M 21 ☾	T 21		T 21	F 21	
T 22	F 22	M 22	W 22	S 22	M 22
W 23	S 23	T 23	T 23	S 23	T 23 ●
T 24	S 24	W 24	F 24		W 24
F 25		T 25	S 25 ●	M 24 ●	T 25
S 26	M 25	F 26 ●	S 26	T 25	F 26
S 27	T 26	S 27		W 26	S 27
	W 27 ●	S 28	M 27	T 27	S 28
M 28	T 28		T 28	F 28	
T 29 ●	F 29	M 29	W 29	S 29	M 29
W 30	S 30	T 30	T 30	S 30 ☾	T 30 ☾
T 31	S 31		F 31		W 31

2004

January	February	March	April	May	June
T 1	S 1	M 1	T 1	S 1	T 1
F 2		T 2	F 2	S 2	W 2
S 3	M 2	W 3	S 3		T 3 ☺
S 4	T 3	T 4	S 4	M 3	F 4
	W 4	F 5		T 4 ☺	S 5
M 5	T 5	S 6	M 5 ☺	W 5	S 6
T 6	F 6 ☺	S 7 ☺	T 6	T 6	
W 7 ☺	S 7		W 7	F 7	M 7
T 8	S 8	M 8	T 8	S 8	T 8
F 9		T 9	F 9	S 9	W 9 ☾
S 10	M 9	W 10	S 10		T 10
S 11	T 10	T 11	S 11	M 10	F 11
	W 11	F 12		T 11 ☾	S 12
M 12	T 12	S 13 ☾	M 12 ☾	W 12	S 13
T 13	F 13 ☾	S 14	T 13	T 13	
W 14	S 14		W 14	F 14	M 14
T 15 ☾	S 15	M 15	T 15	S 15	T 15
F 16		T 16	F 16	S 16	W 16
S 17	M 16	W 17	S 17		T 17 ●
S 18	T 17	T 18	S 18	M 17	F 18
	W 18	F 19		T 18	S 19
M 19	T 19	S 20 ●	M 19 ●	W 19 ●	S 20
T 20	F 20 ●	S 21	T 20	T 20	
W 21 ●	S 21		W 21	F 21	M 21
T 22	S 22	M 22	T 22	S 22	T 22
F 23		T 23	F 23	S 23	W 23
S 24	M 23	W 24	S 24		T 24
S 25	T 24	T 25	S 25	M 24	F 25 ◗
	W 25	F 26		T 25 ◗	S 26
M 26	T 26	S 27	M 26	W 26	S 27
T 27	F 27	S 28	T 27 ◗	T 27	
W 28	S 28 ◗		W 28	F 28	M 28
T 29 ◗	S 29	M 29 ◗	T 29	S 29	T 29
F 30		T 30	F 30	S 30	W 30
S 31		W 31		M 31	

2004

	July	August	September	October	November	December
1	T	S	W	F	M	W
2	F ☺	T	T	S	T	T
3	S	M	F	S	W	F
4	S	T	S	—	T	S
5	M	W	S	M	F ☾	S ☾
6	T	T	M ☾	W ☾	S	M
7	W	F	T	T	S	T
8	T	S ☾	W	F	M	W
9	F ☾	S	T	S	T	T
10	S	M	F	S	W	F
11	S	T	S	M	T	S
12	M	W	S	T	F ●	S ●
13	T	T	M	W	S	M
14	W	F	T ●	T ●	S	T
15	T	S	W	F	M	W
16	F	S	T	S	T	T
17	S ●	M ●	F	S	W	F
18	S	T	S	—	T	S ☽
19	M	W	S	M	F ☽	S
20	T	F	M	W ☽	S	M
21	W	S	T ☽	T	S	T
22	T	S	W	F	M	W
23	F	M ☽	T	S	T	T
24	S	T	F	S	W	F
25	S ☽	W	S	M	T	S
26	M	T	S	T	F ☺	S ☺
27	T	F	M	W	S	M
28	W	S	T ☺	T ☺	S	T
29	T	S	W	F	M	W
30	F	M ☺	T	S	T	T
31	S ☺	T	—	S	—	F

373

2005

January	February	March	April	May	June
S 1	T 1	T 1	F 1	S 1	W 1
S 2	W 2	W 2	S 2		T 2
	T 3	T 3	S 3	M 2	F 3
M 3	F 4	F 4		T 3	S 4
T 4	S 5	S 5	M 4	W 4	S 5
W 5	S 6	S 6	T 5	T 5	
T 6			W 6	F 6	M 6
F 7	M 7	M 7	T 7	S 7	T 7
S 8	T 8	T 8	F 8	S 8	W 8
S 9	W 9	W 9	S 9		T 9
	T 10	T 10	S 10	M 9	F 10
M 10	F 11	F 11		T 10	S 11
T 11	S 12	S 12	M 11	W 11	S 12
W 12	S 13	S 13	T 12	T 12	
T 13			W 13	F 13	M 13
F 14	M 14	M 14	T 14	S 14	T 14
S 15	T 15	T 15	F 15	S 15	W 15
S 16	W 16	W 16	S 16		T 16
	T 17	T 17	S 17	M 16	F 17
M 17	F 18	F 18		T 17	S 18
T 18	S 19	S 19	M 18	W 18	S 19
W 19	S 20	S 20	T 19	T 19	
T 20			W 20	F 20	M 20
F 21	M 21	M 21	T 21	S 21	T 21
S 22	T 22	T 22	F 22	S 22	W 22
S 23	W 23	W 23	S 23		T 23
	T 24	T 24	S 24	M 23	F 24
M 24	F 25	F 25		T 24	S 25
T 25	S 26	S 26	M 25	W 25	S 26
W 26	S 27	S 27	T 26	T 26	
T 27			W 27	F 27	M 27
F 28	M 28	M 28	T 28	S 28	T 28
S 29		T 29	F 29	S 29	W 29
S 30		W 30	S 30		T 30
M 31		T 31		M 30	
				T 31	

2005

July	August	September	October	November	December
F 1	M 1	T 1	S 1	T 1	T 1
S 2	T 2	F 2	S 2	W 2	F 2
S 3	W 3	S 3		T 3	S 3
	T 4	S 4	M 3	F 4	S 4
M 4	F 5		T 4	S 5	
T 5	S 6	M 5	W 5	S 6	M 5
W 6	S 7	T 6	T 6		T 6
T 7		W 7	F 7	M 7	W 7
F 8	M 8	T 8	S 8	T 8	T 8
S 9	T 9	F 9	S 9	W 9	F 9
S 10	W 10	S 10		T 10	S 10
	T 11	S 11	M 10	F 11	S 11
M 11	F 12		T 11	S 12	
T 12	S 13	M 12	W 12	S 13	M 12
W 13	S 14	T 13	T 13		T 13
T 14		W 14	F 14	M 14	W 14
F 15	M 15	T 15	S 15	T 15	T 15
S 16	T 16	F 16	S 16	W 16	F 16
S 17	W 17	S 17		T 17	S 17
	T 18	S 18	M 17	F 18	S 18
M 18	F 19		T 18	S 19	
T 19	S 20	M 19	W 19	S 20	M 19
W 20	S 21	T 20	T 20		T 20
T 21		W 21	F 21	M 21	W 21
F 22	M 22	T 22	S 22	T 22	T 22
S 23	T 23	F 23	S 23	W 23	F 23
S 24	W 24	S 24		T 24	S 24
	T 25	S 25	M 24	F 25	S 25
M 25	F 26		T 25	S 26	
T 26	S 27	M 26	W 26	S 27	M 26
W 27	S 28	T 27	T 27		T 27
T 28		W 28	F 28	M 28	W 28
F 29	M 29	T 29	S 29	T 29	T 29
S 30	T 30	F 30	S 30	W 30	F 30
S 31	W 31		M 31		S 31